AutoCAD® 2005

FOR

DUMMIES®

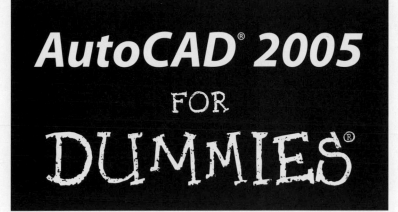

AutoCAD® 2005 FOR DUMMIES®

by Mark Middlebrook

WILEY

Wiley Publishing, Inc.

AutoCAD® 2005 For Dummies®

Published by
Wiley Publishing, Inc.
111 River Street
Hoboken, NJ 07030-5774

About the Author

Mark Middlebrook used to be an engineer but gave it up when he discovered that he couldn't handle a real job. He is now principal of Daedalus Consulting, an independent CAD and computer consulting company in Oakland, California. (In case you wondered, Daedalus was the guy in ancient Greek legend who built the labyrinth on Crete. Mark named his company after Daedalus before he realized that few of his clients would be able to pronounce it and even fewer spell it.) Mark is also a contributing editor for *CADALYST* magazine and Webmaster of `markcad.com`. When he's not busy being a cad, Mark sells and writes about wine for Paul Marcus Wines in Oakland. He also teaches literature and philosophy classes at St. Mary's College of California — hence "Daedalus." *AutoCAD 2005 For Dummies* is his sixth book on AutoCAD.

Dedication

To Puck and Pretzel, two absolute AutoCAD dummies who never cease to inspire and amuse. It was during walks in the woods with them that I originally worked out some of the details of these chapters. I'm pretty sure that Puck could learn AutoCAD, if only he could figure out how to manipulate a mouse. Pretzel, on the other hand, is too interested in squirrels to bother with mice.

Author's Acknowledgments

Thanks first of all to Bud Smith, who initiated this book five editions ago, brought me in on it along the way, and eventually handed it over to me in toto. I hope that I prove as good a steward as he was a midwife (or is the gender-neutral term "midspouse"?). Terri Varveris again shepherded the project through the development process; her enthusiasm and infectious energy have helped make each new edition more than just an obligatory update. It was a genuine pleasure to work once again with Christine Berman, whose combination of patience, persistence, and care make her a model project editor. As always, Dave Byrnes carried out his duties as tech editor with skill and verve; his diligence saved me from a few bloopers, and his thoughtful suggestions helped make the book perceptibly better,

Publisher's Acknowledgments

We're proud of this book; please send us your comments through our online registration form located at www.dummies.com/register/.

Some of the people who helped bring this book to market include the following:

Acquisitions, Editorial, and Media Development

Project Editor: Christine Berman

Acquisitions Editor: Terri Varveris

Copy Editor: Christine Berman

Technical Editor: David Byrnes

Editorial Manager: Carol Sheehan

Media Development Supervisor: Richard Graves

Editorial Assistant: Amanda Foxworth

Cartoons: Rich Tennant (www.the5thwave.com)

Production

Project Coordinator: Courtney MacIntyre

Layout and Graphics: Amanda Carter, Andrea Dahl, Lauren Goddard, Denny Hager, Michael Kruzil, Jacque Schneider, Melanee Wolven

Proofreaders: Laura Albert, Andy Hollandbeck, Carl Pierce, Brian H. Walls, TECHBOOKS Production Services

Indexer: TECHBOOKS Production Services

Publishing and Editorial for Technology Dummies

  Richard Swadley, Vice President and Executive Group Publisher

  Andy Cummings, Vice President and Publisher

  Mary C. Corder, Editorial Director

Publishing for Consumer Dummies

  Diane Graves Steele, Vice President and Publisher

  Joyce Pepple, Acquisitions Director

Composition Services

  Gerry Fahey, Vice President of Production Services

  Debbie Stailey, Director of Composition Services

Contents at a Glance

Table of Contents

Introduction

● ●

*I*t's amazing to think that AutoCAD came into being over two decades ago, at a time when most people thought that personal computers weren't capable of industrial-strength tasks like CAD. (The acronym stands for Computer-Aided Drafting, Computer-Aided Design, or both, depending on whom you talk to). It's almost as amazing that, 20 years after its birth, AutoCAD remains the king of the microcomputer CAD hill by a tall margin. Many competing CAD programs have come to challenge AutoCAD, many have fallen, and a few are still around. One hears rumblings that the long-term future of CAD may belong to special-purpose, 3D-based software such as the Autodesk Inventor and Revit programs. Whether or not those rumblings amplify into a roar remains to be seen, but for the present and the near future anyway, AutoCAD is where the CAD action is.

In its evolution, AutoCAD has grown more complex, in part to keep up with the increasing complexity of the design and drafting processes that AutoCAD is intended to serve. It's not enough just to draw nice-looking lines anymore. If you want to play CAD with the big boys and girls, you need to organize the objects you draw, their properties, and the files in which they reside in appropriate ways. You need to coordinate your CAD work with other people in your office who will be working on or making use of the same drawings. You need to be savvy about shipping drawings around via the Internet.

AutoCAD 2005 provides the tools for doing all these things, but it's not always easy to figure out which hammer to pick up or which nail to bang on first. With this book, you have an excellent chance of creating a presentable, usable, printable, and sharable drawing on your first or second try without putting a T square through your computer screen in frustration.

What's Not in This Book

Unlike many other *For Dummies* books, this one does tell you to consult the official software documentation sometimes. AutoCAD is just too big and complicated for a single book to attempt to describe it completely.

This book focuses on AutoCAD 2005, and also addresses its slightly less-capable, much-lower-cost sibling, AutoCAD LT 2005. (*AutoCAD LT 2005 For Dummies*, a version of this book especially for LT users, comes out several months later than the regular book.) I do occasionally mention differences with previous versions, going back to the highly popular AutoCAD Release 14, so that everyone has some context and upgraders can more readily understand the differences. I also mention the important differences between full AutoCAD and AutoCAD LT, so that you'll know what you — or your LT-using colleagues — are missing. This book does not cover the discipline-specific features in AutoCAD-based products such as AutoCAD Architectural Desktop, except for some general discussion in Chapter 1, but most of the information in this book applies to the general-purpose AutoCAD features in the AutoCAD 2005-based versions of those programs as well.

Who Are — and Aren't — You?

AutoCAD has a large, loyal, and dedicated group of long-time users. This book is not for the sort of people who have been using AutoCAD for a decade, who plan their vacation time around Autodesk University, or who consider 1,000-page-plus technical tomes about AutoCAD as pleasure reading. This book *is* for people who want to get going quickly with AutoCAD, but who also know the importance of developing proper CAD techniques from the beginning.

However, you do need to have some idea of how to use your computer system before tackling AutoCAD — and this book. You need to have a computer system with AutoCAD or AutoCAD LT (preferably the 2004 version). A printer or plotter and a connection to the Internet will be big helps, too.

You also need to know how to use Windows to copy and delete files, create a folder, and find a file. You need to know how to use a mouse to select (highlight) or to choose (activate) commands, how to close a window, and how to minimize and maximize windows. Make sure that you're familiar with the basics of your operating system before you start with AutoCAD.

How This Book Is Organized

If you saw the impressive and apparently random piles of stuff cluttering my desk while I was writing this book, you'd wonder how I could organize a chapter, never mind an entire book. Nevertheless, I hope you'll find that the book reflects some concerted thought about how to present AutoCAD in a way that's both easy-to-dip-into and smoothly-flowing-from-beginning-to-end.

The organization of this book into parts — collections of related chapters — is one of the most important, uh, *parts* of this book. You really can get to know AutoCAD one piece at a time, and each part represents a group of closely related topics. The order of parts also says something about priority; yes, you have my permission to ignore the stuff in later parts until you've mastered most of the stuff in the early ones. This kind of building-block approach can be especially valuable in a program as powerful as AutoCAD.

The following sections describe the parts that the book breaks down into.

Part 1: AutoCAD 101

Need to know your way around the AutoCAD screen? Why does AutoCAD even exist, anyway? What are all the different AutoCAD-based products that Autodesk sells, and should you be using one of them — for example, AutoCAD LT — instead of AutoCAD? Is everything so slooow because it's supposed to be slow, or do I have too wimpy a machine to use this wonder of modern-day computing? And why am I doing this stuff in the first place?

Part I answers all these questions — and more. This part also includes what may seem like a great deal of excruciating detail about setting up a new drawing in AutoCAD. But what's even more excruciating is to do your setup work incorrectly and then feel as though AutoCAD is fighting you every step of the way. With a little drawing setup work done in advance, it won't.

Part II: Let There Be Lines

In this part, it's time for some essential concepts, including object properties and CAD precision techniques. I know that you're raring to make some drawings, but if you don't get a handle on this stuff early on, you'll be terminally (or is that monitor-ally?) confused when you try to draw and edit objects. If you want to make drawings that look good, plot good, and are good, read this stuff!

After the concepts preamble, the bulk of this part covers the trio of activities that you'll probably spend most of your time in AutoCAD doing: drawing objects, editing them, and zooming and panning to see them better on the screen. These are the things that you do in order to create the *geometry* — that is, the CAD representations of the objects in the real world that you're designing. By the end of Part II, you should be pretty good at geometry, even if your ninth-grade math teacher told you otherwise.

Part III: If Drawings Could Talk

CAD drawings do not live on lines alone — most of them require quite a bit of text, dimensioning, and hatching in order to make the design intent clear to the poor chump who has to build your amazing creation. (Whoever said "a picture is worth a thousand words" must not have counted up the number of words on the average architectural drawing!) This part shows you how to add these essential features to your drawings.

After you've gussied up your drawing with text, dimensions, and hatching, you'll probably want to create a snapshot of it to show off to your client, contractor, or grandma. Normal people call this process "printing," but CAD people call it "plotting." Whatever you decide to call it, I'll show you how to do it.

Part IV: Share and Share Alike

A good CAD user, like a good kindergartner, plays well with others. AutoCAD encourages this behavior with a host of drawing- and data-sharing features. Blocks, external reference files, and raster images encourage reuse of parts of drawings, entire drawings, and bitmap image files. The new sheet sets feature in AutoCAD 2005 opens up new possibilities for creating, organizing, and publishing the many drawings that compose a typical CAD project. CAD standards serve as the table manners of the CAD production process — they define and regulate how people create drawings so that sharing can be more productive and predictable. AutoCAD's Internet features enable sharing of drawings well beyond your hard disk and local network.

The drawing and data sharing features in AutoCAD takes you way beyond old-style, pencil-and-paper design and drafting. After you've discovered how to apply the techniques in this part, you'll be well on your way to full CAD-nerd-hood (you may want to warn your family beforehand).

Part V: The Part of Tens

This part contains guidelines that minimize your chances of really messing up drawings (your own or others'), and techniques for swapping drawings with other people and accessing them from other computer programs. There's a lot of meat packed into these two chapters — juicy tidbits from years of drafting, experimentation, and fist-shaking at things that don't work right — not to mention years of compulsive list-making. I hope that you find these lists help you get on the right track quickly and stay there.

Icons Used in This Book

 This icon tells you that herein lies a pointed insight that can save you time and trouble as you use AutoCAD. In many cases, tip paragraphs act as a funnel on AutoCAD's impressive but sometimes overwhelming flexibility: After telling you all the ways that you *can* do something, I tell you the way that you *should* do it in most cases.

 The Technical Stuff icon points out places where delving a little more deeply into AutoCAD's inner workings or pointing out something that most people don't need to know about most of the time. These paragraphs definitely are not required reading the first time through, so if you come to one of them at a time when you've reached your techie detail threshold, feel free to skip over them.

 This icon tells you how to stay out of trouble when living a little close to the edge. Failure to heed its message may have unpleasant consequences for you and your drawing — or maybe for both of you.

 There's a lot to remember when you're using AutoCAD, so I've remembered to remind you about some those things that you should be remembering. These paragraphs usually refer to a crucial point earlier in the chapter or in a previous chapter. So if you're reading sequentially, a remember paragraph serves as a friendly reminder. If you're not reading sequentially, this kind of paragraph may help you realize that you need to review a central concept or technique before proceeding.

 This icon points to new stuff in AutoCAD 2005. It's mostly designed for those of you who are somewhat familiar with a previous version of AutoCAD and want to be alerted to what's new in this version. New AutoCAD users starting out their CAD working lives with AutoCAD 2005 will find this stuff interesting, too — especially when they can show off their new book-learnin' to the grizzled AutoCAD veterans in the office who don't yet know about all the cool, new features.

 This icon highlights differences between AutoCAD LT and AutoCAD. If you're using AutoCAD LT, you'll find out what you're missing compared to "full" AutoCAD. If your friend is using LT, you'll know where to look to find stuff in AutoCAD to brag about.

A Few Conventions — Just in Case

You probably can figure out for yourself all the information in this section, but here are the details just in case.

Text you type into the program at the command line, in a dialog box, in a text box, and so on appears in **boldface type**. Examples of AutoCAD prompts appear in a `special typeface`, as does any other text in the book that echoes a message, a word, or one or more lines of text that actually appear on-screen. Sequences of prompts that appear in the AutoCAD command line area have a shaded background, like so:

```
Specify lower left corner or [ON/OFF] <0.0000,0.0000>:
```

(Many of the figures — especially in Chapters 5 and 6 — also show AutoCAD command line sequences that demonstrate AutoCAD's prompts and example responses.)

Often in this book you see phrases such as "choose File⇨Save As from the menu bar." The funny little arrow (⇨) separates the main menu name from the specific command on that menu. In this example, you open the File menu and choose the Save As command. If you know another way to start the same command (for example, in this example, type **SAVEAS** and press Enter), you're welcome to do it that way instead.

Many AutoCAD commands have shortcut (fewer letter) versions for the benefit of those who like to type commands at the AutoCAD command prompt. In this book, I format command names with the shortcut letters in uppercase and the other letters in lowercase, so that you become familiar with the shortcuts and can use them if you want to. So when you see an instruction like "run the **DimLInear** command to draw a linear dimension," it means "for a linear dimension, type **DIMLINEAR**, or **DLI** for short, at the command line, and then press the Enter key."

Part I

AutoCAD 101

The 5th Wave   By Rich Tennant

GUS & LILY'S DOG GROOMING NOW USING CAD SOFTWARE

In this part . . .

AutoCAD is more than just another application program, it's a complete environment for drafting and design. So if you're new to AutoCAD, you need to know several things to get off to a good start — especially how to use the command line area and set up your drawing properly. These key techniques are described in this part of the book.

If you've used earlier versions of AutoCAD, you'll be most interested in the high points of the new release, including some newer interface components. The lowdown on what's new is here, too.

Chapter 1

Introducing AutoCAD and AutoCAD LT 2005

*W*elcome to the fraternity whose members are the users of one of the weirdest, wackiest, and most wonderful computer programs in the world: AutoCAD. Maybe you're one of the few remaining holdouts who continues to practice the ancient art of manual drafting with pencil and vellum. Or maybe you're completely new to drafting and yearn for the wealth and fame of the drafter's life. Maybe you're an engineer or architect who needs to catch up with the young CAD hotshots in your office. Or maybe you're a full-time drafter whose fingers haven't yet been pried away from your beloved drafting board. Maybe you tried to use AutoCAD a long time ago but gave up in frustration or just got rusty. Or maybe you currently use an older version, such as AutoCAD 2000 or even Release 14.

Whatever your current situation and motivation, I hope that you enjoy the process of becoming proficient with AutoCAD. Drawing with AutoCAD is challenging at first, but it's a challenge worth meeting. CAD rewards those who think creatively about their work and look for ways to do it better. You can always find out more, discover a new trick, or improve the efficiency and quality of your drawing production.

AutoCAD started as an MS-DOS-only program, when real men and women typed commands and didn't need toolbars or dialog boxes. Autodesk flirted briefly with the Macintosh and UNIX operating systems while moving AutoCAD into the GUI (graphical user interface) age, but the company eventually settled on Microsoft Windows as the sole operating system for AutoCAD. (AutoCAD 2005 works with Windows XP — both the Professional and Home versions —

and Windows 2000.) Because of AutoCAD's MS-DOS heritage and its emphasis on efficiency for production drafters, it's not the easiest program to master, but it's gotten easier and more consistent. AutoCAD is pretty well integrated into the Windows environment now, but you still bump into some vestiges of its MS-DOS legacy — especially the command line (that text area lurking at the bottom of the AutoCAD screen — see Chapter 2 for details). This book guides you around the bumps and minimizes the bruises.

Why AutoCAD?

AutoCAD has been around a long time — since 1982. AutoCAD ushered in the transition from *really expensive* mainframe and minicomputer CAD systems costing tens of thousands of dollars to *merely expensive* microcomputer CAD programs costing a few thousand dollars.

AutoCAD is, first and foremost, a program to create *technical drawings;* drawings in which measurements and precision are important, because these kinds of drawings often get used to build something. The drawings you create with AutoCAD must adhere to standards established long ago for hand-drafted drawings. The up-front investment to use AutoCAD is certainly more expensive than the investment needed to use pencil and paper, and the learning curve is much steeper, too. Why bother? The key reasons for using AutoCAD rather than pencil and paper are

- **Precision:** Creating lines, circles, and other shapes of the exactly correct dimensions is easier with AutoCAD than with pencils.

- **Modifiability:** Drawings are much easier to modify on the computer screen than on paper. CAD modifications are a lot cleaner, too.

- **Efficiency:** Creating many kinds of drawings is faster with a CAD program — especially drawings that involve repetition, such as floor plans in a multistory building. But that efficiency takes skill and practice. If you're an accomplished pencil-and-paper drafter, don't expect CAD to be faster at first!

Figure 1-1 shows several kinds of drawings in AutoCAD 2005.

Why choose AutoCAD? AutoCAD is just the starting point of a whole industry of software products designed to work with AutoCAD. Autodesk has helped this process along immensely by designing a series of programming interfaces to AutoCAD that other companies — and Autodesk itself — have used to extend the application. Some of the add-on products have become such winners that Autodesk acquired them and incorporated them into its own products. When you compare all the resources — including the add-ons, extensions, training courses, books, and so on — AutoCAD doesn't have much PC CAD competition.

Figure 1-1:
Tower,
bridge, and
plan —
what do you
want to
draw today?

The Importance of Being DWG

To take full advantage of AutoCAD in your work environment, you need to be aware of the DWG file format, the format in which AutoCAD saves drawings. In some cases an older version of AutoCAD can't open a DWG file that's been saved by a newer version of AutoCAD.

✔ A newer version of AutoCAD *always* can open files saved by an older version.

✔ *Some* previous versions of AutoCAD can open files saved by the subsequent one or two versions. For example, AutoCAD 2004 can open DWG files saved by AutoCAD 2005. That's because Autodesk didn't change the DWG file format between AutoCAD 2004 and AutoCAD 2005.

✔ You can use the "save as" option in newer versions to save the file to some older DWG formats.

Table 1-1 shows which versions (described later in this chapter) use which DWG file formats.

Table 1-1	AutoCAD Versions and DWG File Formats		
AutoCAD Version	*AutoCAD LT Version*	*Release Year*	*DWG File Format*
AutoCAD 2005 ("A2k5")	AutoCAD LT 2005	2004	Acad 2004
AutoCAD 2004 ("A2k4")	AutoCAD LT 2004	2003	Acad 2004
AutoCAD 2002 ("A2k2")	AutoCAD LT 2002	2001	Acad 2000
AutoCAD 2000i ("A2ki")	AutoCAD LT 2000i	2000	Acad 2000
AutoCAD 2000 ("A2k")	AutoCAD LT 2000	1999	Acad 2000
AutoCAD Release 14 ("R14")	AutoCAD LT 98 & 97	1997	Acad R14
AutoCAD Release 13 ("R13")	AutoCAD LT 95	1994	Acad R13
AutoCAD Release 12 ("R12")	AutoCAD LT Release 2	1992	Acad R12

Working with AutoCAD is easier when your co-workers and colleagues in other companies all use the same version of AutoCAD and AutoCAD-related tools. That way, your DWG files, add-on tools, and even the details of your CAD knowledge can be mixed and matched among your workgroup and partners. In the real world, you'll probably work with people — at least in other companies — who use AutoCAD versions as old as Release 14.

Many programs claim to be *DWG-compatible* — that is, capable of converting data to and from AutoCAD's DWG format. But achieving this compatibility is a difficult thing to do well. Even a small error in file conversion can have results ranging in severity from annoying to appalling. If you exchange DWG files with people who use other CAD programs, be prepared to spend time finding and fixing translation problems.

AutoCAD 2005 — like AutoCAD 2004 — does not include an option for saving files to the R14 DWG file format. This omission creates problems if you want to send DWG files to clients or consultants who are still using AutoCAD Release 14. (And there are a surprising number of these folks — R14 was popular, and AutoCAD 2000 through 2004 didn't tempt everyone to upgrade.) To get around this limitation, you can save to the R12 DXF format, which AutoCAD Release 14 will open — see Chapter 18 for instructions.

AutoCAD-based applications

Autodesk has expanded AutoCAD into a whole product line of programs with AutoCAD as a base and specialized, discipline-specific add-ons built on top and included as one complete product. As an AutoCAD 2005 user, you'll be looking for the 2005-compatible versions of these tools, which should appear a few months after AutoCAD 2005 ships. These discipline-specific flavors of AutoCAD include Autodesk Architectural Desktop and Autodesk Building Systems (mechanical, electrical, and plumbing), Autodesk Mechanical Desktop, Autodesk Map, AutoCAD Land Desktop, Autodesk Survey, and Autodesk Civil Design.

To make matters even more confusing, Autodesk now offers Autodesk Revit and Autodesk Inventor, software applications that compete with Architectural Desktop and Mechanical Desktop, respectively. Revit and Inventor are not based on AutoCAD; they sacrifice AutoCAD compatibility in favor of a more fundamentally design- and 3D-oriented approach to CAD. Whether they ultimately will replace the traditional AutoCAD-based applications remains to be seen. Thus far, most companies seem to be sticking with AutoCAD and the AutoCAD-based Desktop applications.

In addition to the products from Autodesk, thousands of AutoCAD add-on products — both discipline-specific and general-purpose — are available from other software developers. These companion products are sometimes called *third-party applications*. Visit `partnerproducts.autodesk.com/` for more information about what's available.

Seeing the LT

AutoCAD LT is one of the best deals around, a shining example of the old 80/20 rule: roughly 80 percent of the capabilities of AutoCAD for roughly 20 percent of the money. Like AutoCAD, AutoCAD LT runs on mainstream Windows computers and doesn't require any additional hardware devices. With AutoCAD LT, you can be a player in the world of AutoCAD, the world's leading CAD program, for a comparatively low starting cost.

AutoCAD LT is a very close cousin to AutoCAD. Autodesk creates AutoCAD LT by starting with the AutoCAD program, taking out a few features to justify charging a lower price, adding a couple of features to enhance ease of use versus full AutoCAD, and testing the result.

As a result, AutoCAD LT looks and works much like AutoCAD. The opening screen and menus of the two programs are nearly identical. (LT is missing a few commands from the AutoCAD menus.)

In fact, the major difference between the programs has nothing to do with the programs themselves. The major difference is that AutoCAD LT lacks support for several customization and programming languages that are used to develop AutoCAD add-ons. So almost none of the add-on programs or utilities offered by Autodesk and others are available to LT users.

AutoCAD LT also has only limited 3D support. You can view and edit 3D objects in AutoCAD LT, so you can work with drawings created in AutoCAD that contain 3D objects. However, you cannot create true 3D objects.

The lack of 3D object creation in LT is not as big a negative for many users as you may think. Despite a lot of hype from the computer press and CAD vendors (including Autodesk), 3D CAD remains a relatively specialized activity. The majority of people use CAD programs to create 2D drawings.

Although you may hear claims that AutoCAD LT is easier to master and use than AutoCAD, the truth is that they're about equally difficult (or easy, depending on your nerd IQ). The LT learning curve doesn't differ significantly from that of AutoCAD. AutoCAD was originally designed for maximum power and then modified somewhat to improve ease of use. AutoCAD LT shares this same heritage.

Fortunately, the minimal differences between LT and AutoCAD mean that after you have climbed that learning curve, you'll have the same great view. You'll have almost the full range of AutoCAD's 2D drafting tools, and you'll be able to exchange DWG files with AutoCAD users without data loss.

This book covers AutoCAD 2005, but almost all the information in it applies to AutoCAD LT 2005 as well. The icon that you see at the left of this paragraph highlights significant differences. If you're an LT user, you may want to look for *AutoCAD LT 2005 For Dummies*, which is aimed squarely at AutoCAD LT and the types of people who use it instead of AutoCAD.

Staying Alive with 2005

You should know this before you upgrade from a previous AutoCAD release:

- **Wash those old Windows:** AutoCAD 2005 does not support older versions of Windows, such as Windows NT, 98, and Me. You must use Windows XP (Professional, Home, or Tablet PC) or Windows 2000.

- **DWG file compatibility:** AutoCAD 2005 uses the same DWG file format as AutoCAD 2004, so you'll be able to exchange files easily with users of

AutoCAD 2004. You can use File⇨Save As to create DWG files for users of AutoCAD 2000, 2000i, and 2002, but not for AutoCAD Release 14 and earlier versions. (To get around this limitation, you can save to the Release 12 DXF format — see Chapter 18 for instructions.)

✔ **Application compatibility:** If you use third-party applications with a previous version of AutoCAD, they may not work with AutoCAD 2005. Most AutoCAD 2004 applications, including those developed with the ARX (AutoCAD Runtime eXtension) and VBA (Visual Basic for Applications) programming interfaces will work with AutoCAD 2005, but older ARX and VBA applications won't work.

Many *LSP (AutoLISP)* programs written for the last several versions of AutoCAD work with AutoCAD 2005.

✔ **Increased computer system requirements:** For AutoCAD 2005, Autodesk recommends an 800 MHz Pentium III or better processor, at least 256MB of RAM, 1024 x 768 or higher display resolution, 300MB of available hard disk space, an Internet connection, and Microsoft Internet Explorer 6.0 with Service Pack 1 or later.

AutoCAD 2005 comes out a mere year after AutoCAD 2004 and thus doesn't sport quite as many new features as did some earlier upgrades, many of which came out at two-year intervals. The new features and feature improvements in AutoCAD 2005, however, are well conceived and worthwhile. My three favorites are:

✔ Sheet sets — a radically new and much more sophisticated way of organizing sets of drawings. (See Chapter 14.)

✔ Text tables, an enormously improved way to place tabular data on drawings quickly and uniformly — including the ability to import the data from Excel spreadsheets. (See Chapter 9.)

✔ An improved plotting interface, including background plotting. (See Chapter 12.)

No Express service?

The AutoCAD 2005 CD-browser screen includes separate links for installing the main AutoCAD 2005 software and the Express Tools — a set of handy utilities for AutoCAD (but not available for AutoCAD LT). If your menu bar doesn't include the Express menu shown in Figure 1-1, you should consider installing the Express Tools from your AutoCAD 2005 CD. Just pop in the CD and, when the CD-browser page appears, click the AutoCAD Express Tools link and follow the installation instructions.

AutoCAD 2005 includes other goodies — look for the icon that you see at the left of this paragraph.

If you're using any version prior to AutoCAD 2004, the new version definitely is worth upgrading to. You'll enjoy a slew of improvements, including a cleaner, more functional interface (Chapter 2), numbered and bulleted text lists (Chapter 9), and many xref enhancements (Chapters 13 and 16).

AutoCAD 2005 is a worthy new version. If you've been putting off upgrading, and especially if you've been hanging out with an old version such as AutoCAD 2000 or Release 14, this probably is a good time to take the plunge.

Chapter 2

Le Tour de AutoCAD 2005

● ●

In This Chapter

▶ Touring the AutoCAD 2005 screen

▶ Going bar-hopping: title bars, the menu bar, toolbars, and the status bar

▶ Commanding the command line

▶ Discovering the drawing area

▶ Making the most of Model and Layout tabs

▶ Dabbling with palettes

▶ Setting system variables and using dialog boxes

▶ Using online help

● ●

AutoCAD 2005 is a full-fledged citizen of the Windows world, with toolbars, dialog boxes, right-click menus, a multiple-document interface, and all the other trappings of a real Windows program. But lurking beneath that pretty face — and literally beneath the drawing area, right at the bottom of the AutoCAD program window — is a weird but essential holdover from the DOS days: the AutoCAD command line area. The command line is one of the few un-Windows-like things in AutoCAD that you'll have to come to terms with, and this chapter shows you how.

Like the rest of the book, this chapter is written for someone who has used other Windows programs but has little or no experience with AutoCAD. If you're experienced with Windows versions of AutoCAD, much of this chapter is old hat for you. Do make sure, though, that you're familiar with the interface features that were added to AutoCAD 2004: palettes and the additional buttons on the right end of the status bar.

AutoCAD Does Windows

Finding your way around AutoCAD 2005 can be an odd experience. You recognize from other Windows applications much of the appearance and workings of the program, such as its toolbars and pull-down menus, which you use for entering commands or changing system settings. But other aspects of the program's appearance — and some of the ways in which you work with it — are quite different from other Windows programs. You can, in many cases, tell the program what to do in at least four ways — pick a toolbar icon, pick from the pull-down menus, type at the command line, or pick from the right-click menus — none of which is necessarily the best method to use for every task. The experience is much like that of having to act as several different characters in a play; you're likely to forget your lines (whichever "you" you are at the time!) every now and then.

As with other Windows programs, the menus at the top of the AutoCAD screen enable you to access most of the program's functions and are the easiest-to-remember method of issuing commands. When you want to get real work done, you'll need to combine the pull-down menus with other methods — especially typing options at the command line or choosing them from the right-click menu. I show you how throughout this book.

Screen test yields high profile

The screen shots and descriptions in this chapter reflect the *default* configuration of AutoCAD — that is, the way the screen looks if you use the standard version of AutoCAD (not a flavored version such as Architectural Desktop) and haven't messed with the display settings. You can change the appearance of the screen with settings on the Display tab of the Options dialog box (choose Tools➪Options➪Display) and by dragging toolbars and other screen components.

The change I've made is to configure the drawing area background to be white instead of black, because the figures in the book show up better that way. On your system, you'll probably want to leave your drawing area background black, because the normal range of colors that appears in most drawings is easier to see against a black background.

If you're using a flavored version of AutoCAD, or if someone has already changed your configuration or added a third-party program to your setup, your screen may look different than the figures in this book. You can restore the default configuration — including display settings — with the Reset button on the Options dialog box's Profiles tab. (AutoCAD LT doesn't include the Profiles feature, so LT users are out of luck here.) But before you click the Reset button, consider whether the modified configuration may be useful to someone in the future — like you! If so, first click the Add to List button to create a new profile. Enter a pithy name for the new profile, such as AutoCAD default. Then select the new profile that you created, click the Set Current button to make it the current profile, and finally click the Reset button. In the future, you can switch between your modified and default configurations with the Set Current button.

AutoCAD's Opening Screen Cuisine

When you launch AutoCAD after first installing it, the opening screen, shown in Figure 2-1, displays an arrangement of menus, toolbars, palettes, and a new, blank drawing. You can close the Sheet Set Manager and Tool Palettes for now — I describe how to turn them back on and how to use them later in this chapter. (If you installed the Express Tools, as I describe at the end of Chapter 1, you'll also see a flock of small toolbars labeled ET. You can safely close all these and use the Express pull-down menu to access all the Express Tools.)

Figure 2-1: The clean AutoCAD 2005 screen.

Labels around the figure:

AutoCAD program's title bar control buttons

Toolbars   Title bar   Menu bar   Current drawing's control buttons

Command line area   Status bar

Drawing area

Standard Windows fare

As you see in Figure 2-1, much of the AutoCAD screen is standard Windows fare — title bars, a menu bar, toolbars, and a status bar.

A hierarchy of title bars

Like most Windows programs, AutoCAD has a *title bar* at the top of its program window that reminds you which program you're in (not that you'd ever
mistake the AutoCAD window for, say, Microsoft Word!).

✔ At the right side of the title bar is the standard set of three Windows
control buttons: Minimize, Maximize/Restore, and Close.

✔ Each drawing window within the AutoCAD program window has its own
title bar. You use the control buttons on a drawing window's title bar to
minimize, maximize/un-maximize, or close that drawing, not the entire
AutoCAD program.

As in other Windows programs, if you maximize a drawing's window, it expands
to fill the entire drawing area. (AutoCAD 2005 starts with the drawing maximized in this way.) As shown in Figure 2-1, the drawing's control buttons move
onto the menu bar, below the control buttons for the AutoCAD program window; the drawing's name appears in the AutoCAD title bar. To un-maximize
the drawing so you can see any other drawings that you have open, click the
lower un-maximize button. The result is as shown in Figure 2-2: a separate
title bar for each drawing with the name and controls for that drawing.

Figure 2-2:
The
AutoCAD
screen
with the
drawing un-
maximized.

Hot-wiring the menu bar

Some standard tips and tricks for Windows are especially useful in AutoCAD. Control-key shortcuts for the most popular functions — Ctrl+S to save, Ctrl+O to open a file, and Ctrl+P to print — work the same way in AutoCAD as in most other Windows programs. Use them!

Also worth exploring are the Alt-key shortcuts, which are available for all menu choices, not just the most popular ones. To fly around the menus, just press and hold the Alt key and then press the letters on your keyboard that correspond to the underlined letters on the menu bar and in the menu choices. To bring up the SAVEAS command, for example, just press and hold the Alt key, press F for File, and then press A for Save As.

Making choices from the menu bar

The *menu bar* contains the names of all the primary menus in your version of AutoCAD. As with any program that's new to you, it's worth spending a few minutes perusing the menus in order to familiarize yourself with the commands and their arrangement. (If your menu bar doesn't include the Express menu, see the end of Chapter 1 for installation instructions.)

Cruising the toolbars

As in other Windows programs, the toolbars in AutoCAD 2005 provide rapid access to the most commonly used AutoCAD commands. AutoCAD ships with toolbars in this default arrangement (as shown in Figure 2-3):

- ✔ **Standard toolbar:** Located on top, just below the menu bar; file management and other common Windows functions, plus some specialized AutoCAD stuff such as zooming and panning.

- ✔ **Styles toolbar:** To the right of the Standard toolbar; analogous to the left part of the Formatting toolbar in Microsoft programs, but formatting of AutoCAD's text, dimension, and table styles. (Table styles are new in AutoCAD 2005.) Chapters 9 and 10 cover these features.

- ✔ **Layers toolbar:** Beneath the Standard toolbar; commands and a drop-down list for manipulating layers, which are AutoCAD's fundamental tools for organizing and formatting objects. Chapter 4 contains the layer lowdown.

- ✔ **Properties toolbar:** To the right of the Layers toolbar; analogous to the right part of the Formatting toolbar in Microsoft programs, but formatting of AutoCAD's properties, such as colors, linetypes, and lineweights. See Chapter 4 when you're ready to play with AutoCAD's object properties.

- ✔ **Draw toolbar:** Vertically down the far-left edge of the screen; the most commonly used commands from the Draw menu. Chapter 5 covers most of the items on this toolbar.

✔ **Modify toolbar:** Vertically down the far-right edge of the screen; the most commonly used commands from the Modify menu. Chapter 8 shows you how to use almost everything on this toolbar.

✔ **Draw Order toolbar:** Beneath the Modify toolbar; commands for controlling which objects appear on top of which other objects. Chapter 13 mentions these features.

You can rearrange, open, and close toolbars as in other Windows programs:

✔ To move a toolbar, point to its border (the double-line control handle at the leading edge of the toolbar is the easiest part to grab), click, and drag.

✔ To open or close toolbars, right-click on any toolbar button and choose from the list of available toolbars, as shown in Figure 2-3.

The AutoCAD screen in Figure 2-3 shows the default toolbar arrangement, which works fine for most people. Feel free to close the Draw Order toolbar; you aren't likely to use its features frequently. You may want to turn on a couple of additional toolbars, such as Object Snap and Dimension, as you discover and make use of additional features. Throughout this book, I point out when a particular toolbar may be useful.

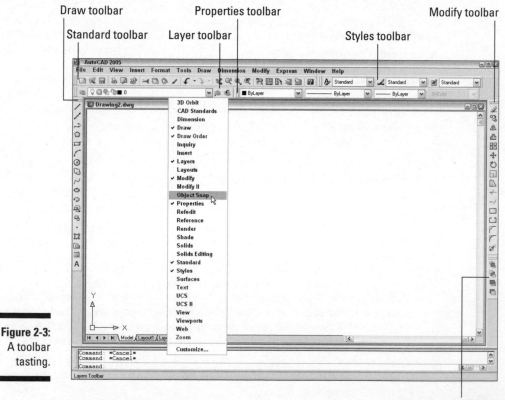

Figure 2-3:
A toolbar
tasting.

The toolbars that ET AutoCAD

If you've installed the Express Tools, you'll also see a flock of Express Tools toolbars, whose labels begin with "ET:", floating over the drawing area. These four small toolbars collect some of the most popular Express Tools. You'll probably want to close most of these or at least dock any favorites along the margin of the AutoCAD window.

The toolbars are extensions to AutoCAD, not part of the core program, so turning them on is a little more complicated than just using the right-click toolbars menu. Right-click on any toolbar, choose Customize, click the Toolbars tab on the Customize dialog box, and choose the EXPRESS Menu Group. Now the Toolbars list displays the names of the four Express Tools toolbars; click the check boxes next to the names in order to toggle each toolbar on or off.

If you're not satisfied with just rearranging the stock AutoCAD toolbars, you can customize their contents or even create new ones. The procedures are beyond the scope of this book; they involve bouncing among the Commands, Toolbars, and Properties tabs on the Customize dialog box in not entirely intuitive ways. Resist slicing and dicing the stock AutoCAD toolbars until you're at least somewhat familiar with them. If you want to get creative thereafter, go to the Contents tab of the AutoCAD 2005 online help and choose Customization Guide⇨Basic Customization⇨Create Custom Toolbars.

AutoCAD toolbar buttons provide *ToolTips,* those short text descriptions that appear in little yellow boxes when you pause the cursor over a toolbar button. A longer description of the icon's function appears in the status bar at the bottom of the screen.

Looking for Mr. Status Bar

The *status bar* appears at the bottom of the AutoCAD screen, as shown in Figure 2-4. The status bar displays and allows you to change several important settings that affect how you draw and edit in the current drawing. Some of these settings won't make complete sense until you've used the AutoCAD commands that they influence, but here's a brief description, with pointers to detailed descriptions of how to use each setting elsewhere in this book:

✔ **Coordinates of the cursor:** The *cursor coordinates* readout displays the current X,Y,Z location of the cursor in the drawing area, with respect to the origin point (whose coordinates are 0,0,0). It's a bit like having a GPS (Global Positioning System) device in your drawing. Chapter 4 describes AutoCAD's coordinate conventions and how to use this area of the status bar.

Running object on/off Status bar menu

Cursor coordinates Ortho on/off Lineweight display on/off Manage Xrefs

Figure 2-4:
Status (bar)
check.

16.3117, 14.2006, 0.0000 SNAP GRID ORTHO POLAR OSNAP OTRACK LWT MODEL

Snap on/off Communication center

Polar tracking on/off Cursor in model space or paper space

Object snap tracking on/off

If the coordinates in the lower-left corner of the screen are grayed out, then coordinate tracking is turned off. Click the coordinates so that they appear in dark lettering that changes when you move the cursor in the drawing area.

✔ **SNAP, GRID, and ORTHO mode buttons:** These three buttons control three of AutoCAD's tools for ensuring precision drawing and editing:

• **Snap** constrains the cursor to regularly spaced hot spots, enabling you to draw objects a fixed distance apart more easily.

• **Grid** displays a series of regularly spaced dots, which serve as a distance reference.

• **Ortho** constrains the cursor to horizontal and vertical relative movement, which makes drawing orthogonal (straight horizontal and vertical) lines easy.

See Chapter 3 for instructions on how to configure these modes and Chapter 4 for information about why, when, and how to use them in actual drawing operations.

✔ **POLAR tracking mode button:** Polar tracking causes the cursor to prefer certain angles when you draw and edit objects. By default, the preferred angles are multiples of 90 degrees, but you can specify other angle increments, such as 45 or 30 degrees. See Chapter 4 for instructions to specify the polar tracking angles that you prefer. Clicking the POLAR button toggles polar tracking on or off. Ortho and polar tracking are mutually exclusive — turning on one mode disables the other.

✔ **Running Object Snap (OSNAP) and Object Snap Tracking (OTRACK) buttons:** *Object snap* is another AutoCAD tool for ensuring precision drawing and editing. You use object snaps to grab points on existing objects — for example, the endpoint of a line or the center of a circle.

• When you turn on *running object snap,* AutoCAD continues to hunt for object snap points. Chapter 4 contains detailed instructions on how to use this feature.

• When you turn on *object snap tracking,* AutoCAD hunts in a more sophisticated way for points that are derived from object snap points. Chapter 4 briefly describes this advanced feature.

AutoCAD LT doesn't include the object snap tracking feature, so you won't see an OTRACK button on its status bar.

✔ **Lineweight (LWT) display mode button:** One of the properties that you can assign to objects in AutoCAD is *lineweight* — the thickness that lines appear when you plot the drawing. This button controls whether you see the lineweights on the screen. (This button doesn't control whether lineweights appear on plots; that's a separate setting in the Plot dialog box.) Chapter 4 gives you the skinny (and the wide) on lineweights.

✔ **MODEL/PAPER space button:** As I describe in the section "Main course: The drawing area" later in this chapter, the drawing area is composed of overlapping tabbed areas labeled Model, Layout1, and Layout2 by default. The Model tab displays a part of the drawing called *model space,* where you create most of your drawing. Each of the remaining tabs displays a *paper space layout,* where you can compose a plotable view with a title block. A completed layout will include one or more *viewports*, which reveal some or all the objects in model space at a particular scale.

The MODEL/PAPER status bar button (not to be confused with the Model *tab*) comes into play after you click one of the paper space layout tabs. The MODEL/PAPER button provides a means for moving the cursor between model and paper space while remaining in the particular layout.

 • When the MODEL/PAPER button says MODEL, drawing and editing operations take place in model space, inside a viewport.

 • When the button says PAPER, drawing and editing operations take place in paper space on the current layout.

Don't worry if you find model space and paper space a little disorienting at first. The paper space layout setup information in Chapter 3 and plotting instructions in Chapter 12 will help you get your bearings and navigate with confidence.

✔ **Maximize/Minimize Viewport button** (paper space layouts only): When you're looking at one of the Layout tabs instead of the Model tab, the status bar displays an additional Maximize Viewport button. Click this button to expand the current paper space viewport so that it fills the entire drawing area. Click the button — now called Minimize Viewport — again to restore the viewport to its normal size. (Chapter 3 describes viewports.)

✔ **Communication Center:** This button opens a dialog box containing recent AutoCAD-related headlines that Autodesk thinks you may find useful. The headlines are grouped into categories called *channels*: Live Update Maintenance Patches, Articles and Tips, Product Support Information, and so on. Each headline is a link to a Web page with more information, such as how to download a software update or fix a problem. Click the Settings button to select channels you see in the Communication Center window.

✔ **Manage Xrefs:** You won't see this combination button and notification symbol until you open a drawing that contains xrefs (external DWG files that are incorporated into the current drawing). Chapter 13 tells you how to use xrefs and what the Manage Xrefs button does.

✔ **Status Bar Menu:** When you click the easy-to-miss downward-pointing arrow near the right edge of the status bar, you open a menu with options for toggling off or on each status bar button. Now you can decorate your status bar to your taste.

You can open dialog boxes for configuring many of the status bar button functions by right-clicking the status bar button and choosing Settings. Chapters 3 and 4 give you specific guidance about when and how to change these settings.

A button's appearance shows whether the setting is turned on or off. Depressed, or down, means on; raised, or up, means off. If you're unclear whether a setting is on or off, click its button; its mode will change and the new setting will be reflected on the command line — <Osnap off>, for example. Click again to restore the previous setting.

Take an order: The command line area

If the title bars, menu bar, and status bar are the Windows equivalent of comfort food — familiar, nourishing, and unthreatening — then the command line area, shown in Figure 2-5, must be the steak tartare or blood sausage of the AutoCAD screen feast. It looks weird, turns the stomachs of newcomers, and delights AutoCAD aficionados. The hard truth is that you have to come to like — or at least tolerate — the command line if you want to become at all comfortable using AutoCAD.

Figure 2-5:
Obey the command line.

```
Command: *Cancel*
Command: *Cancel*
Command:
```

You need to get up close and personal with the command line for four reasons:

✔ **The command line area is AutoCAD's primary communications conduit with you.** This is the most important reason to pay attention to the command line. AutoCAD frequently displays prompts, warnings, and error messages in the command line area. If you don't keep an eye on this area, you'll miss a lot of vital information. You'll continually be frustrated, because you won't "hear" what AutoCAD is trying to tell you.

✔ **The command line is an efficient way to run some commands and the only way to run a few others.** Instead of clicking a toolbar button or a menu choice, you can start a command by typing its command name and then pressing the Enter key. Even better, you can type the keyboard short-cut for a command name and press Enter. Most of the keyboard shortcuts for command names are just one or two letters — for example, L for the LINE command and CP for the COPY command. Most people who dis-cover how to use the shortcuts for the commands that they run most fre-quently find that their AutoCAD productivity improves noticeably. Even if you're not worried about increasing your productivity with this technique, there are some commands that aren't on the toolbars or pull-down menus. If you want to run those commands, you have to type them!

✔ **After you've started a command — whether from a toolbar, from a menu, or by typing — the command line is where AutoCAD prompts you with options for that command.**

You activate one of these options by typing the uppercase letter(s) in the option and pressing Enter.

In many cases, you can activate a command's options by right-clicking in the drawing area and choosing the desired option from the right-click menu, instead of by typing the letter(s) for the option and pressing Enter. But if you don't watch the command line, you probably won't real-ize that there *are* any options!

✔ **You sometimes need to type coordinates at the command line to specify precise points or distances.** Chapter 4 describes this technique in detail.

You don't have to click in the command line area to type command names, keyboard shortcuts, or command options there. AutoCAD knows that your typing is supposed to go to the command line. The only exception is when you're within a text command (you're adding a text note to the drawing itself); in that case, the text appears in the drawing, not in the command line area.

The following sequence demonstrates how you use the command line area to run commands, view and select options, and pay attention to messages from AutoCAD:

1. **Type** L **and press Enter.**

   AutoCAD starts the LINE command and displays the following prompt in the command line area:

   ```
   LINE Specify first point:
   ```

2. **Click a point anywhere in the drawing area.**

   The command line prompt changes to:

   ```
   Specify next point or [Undo]:
   ```

   AutoCAD always displays command options in brackets. In this case, the Undo option appears in brackets. To activate the option, type the letter(s) shown in uppercase and press Enter. (You can type the option letter(s) in lowercase or uppercase.)

3. **Click another point anywhere in the drawing area.**

   AutoCAD draws the first line segment.

4. **Click a third point anywhere in the drawing area.**

   AutoCAD draws the second line segment. The command line prompt changes to:

   ```
   Specify next point or [Close/Undo]:
   ```

   AutoCAD now displays two options, Close and Undo, separated by a slash.

5. **Type** U **and press Enter.**

   AutoCAD undoes the second line segment.

6. **Type** 3,2 **(without any spaces) and press Enter.**

   AutoCAD draws a new line segment to the point whose the X coordinate is 3 and the Y coordinate is 2.

7. **Click several more points anywhere in the drawing area.**

   AutoCAD draws additional line segments.

8. **Type** X **and press Enter.**

   AutoCAD displays an error message (because X isn't a valid option of the LINE command) and reprompts for another point:

   ```
   Point or option keyword required.
   Specify next point or [Close/Undo]:
   ```

   Option keyword is programmer jargon for the letter(s) shown in upper-case that you type to activate a command option. This error message is AutoCAD's way of saying "I don't understand what you mean by typing 'X.' Either specify a point or type a letter that I do understand."

9. **Type** C **and press Enter.**

   AutoCAD draws a final line segment, which creates a closed figure, and ends the LINE command. The naked command prompt returns, indicating that AutoCAD is ready for the next command:

   ```
   Command:
   ```

10. **Press the F2 key.**

    AutoCAD displays the AutoCAD Text Window, which is simply an enlarged, scrollable version of the command line area, as shown in Figure 2-6.

    The normal three-line command line area usually shows you what you need to see, but occasionally you'll want to review a larger chunk of command line history ("what was AutoCAD trying to tell me a minute ago?!").

11. **Press the F2 key again.**

    AutoCAD closes the AutoCAD Text Window.

Here are a few other tips and tricks for using the command line effectively:

✔ **Use the Esc key to bail out of the current operation.** There will be times when you get confused about what you're doing in AutoCAD and/or what you're seeing in the command line area. If you need to bail out of the current operation, just press the Esc key one or more times until you see the naked command prompt — Command: at the bottom of the command line area, with nothing after it. As in most other Windows programs, Esc is the cancel key. Unlike many other Windows programs, AutoCAD keeps you well informed of whether an operation is in progress. The naked command prompt indicates that AutoCAD is in a quiescent state, waiting for your next command.

✔ **Press Enter to accept the default action.** Some command prompts include a default action in angled brackets. For example, the first prompt of the POLygon command is

```
Enter number of sides <4>:
```

The default here is four sides, and you can accept it simply by pressing the Enter key. (That is, you don't have to type **4** first.)

AutoCAD uses two kinds of brackets in command line prompts.

• Command options appear in regular brackets: [Close/Undo].

To activate a command option, type the letter(s) that appear in uppercase and then press Enter.

- A Default value or option appears in angled brackets: <>.

  To choose the default value or option, simply press Enter.

✔ **Observe the command line.** You'll discover a lot about how to use the command line simply by watching it after each action that you take. When you click a toolbar button or menu choice, AutoCAD types the name of the command automatically, so if you're watching the command line, you'll absorb the command names more-or-less naturally.

When AutoCAD types commands automatically in response to your toolbar and menu clicks, it usually adds one or two extra characters to the front of the command name.

- AutoCAD usually puts an underscore in front of the command name (for example, _LINE instead of LINE). The underscore is an Autodesk programmers' trick that enables non-English versions of AutoCAD to understand the English command names that are embedded in the menus.

- AutoCAD sometimes puts an apostrophe in front of the command name and any underscore (for example, '_ZOOM instead of ZOOM). The apostrophe indicates a *transparent* command; you can run the command in the middle of another command without canceling the first command. For example, you can start the LINE command, run the ZOOM command transparently, and then pick up where you left off with the LINE command.

✔ **Leave the command line in the default configuration initially.** The command line area, like most other parts of the AutoCAD screen, is resizable and relocateable. The default location (docked at the bottom of the AutoCAD screen) and size (three lines deep) work well for most people. Resist the temptation to mess with the command line area's appearance — at least until you're comfortable with how to use the command line.

✔ **Right-click in the command line area for options.** If you right-click in the command line area, you'll see a menu with some useful choices, including Recent Commands — the last six commands that you ran.

✔ **Press the up- and down-arrow keys to cycle through the stack of commands that you've typed recently.** This is another handy way to recall and rerun a command. Press the left- and right-arrow keys to edit the command line text that you've typed or recalled.

Main course: The drawing area

After all these screen hors d'oeuvres, you're probably getting hungry for the main course — the AutoCAD drawing area. This is where you do your drawing, of course. In the course of creating drawings, you click points to specify locations and distances, click objects to select them for editing, and zoom and pan to get a better view of what you're working on.

AutoCAD is no *vin ordinaire*

The back and forth needed to get AutoCAD to draw and complete a line is a great example of AutoCAD's power — and its power to confuse new users. It's kind of like a wine that tastes a bit harsh initially, but that ages better than something more immediately drinkable.

In other programs, if you want to draw a line, you just draw it. In AutoCAD, you have to press Enter one extra time when you're done just to tell AutoCAD you really are finished drawing.

But the fact that the Line command remains active after you draw the first line segment makes it much faster to draw complicated, multisegment lines, which is a common activity in a complex drawing.

This is just one example of how AutoCAD favors ease of use for power users doing complex drawings over ease of mastery for beginners, who frequently forget to hit Enter that extra time to close out a command.

Most of this book shows you how to interact with the drawing area, but you should know a few things up front.

The Model and Layout tabs (Model and Paper Space)

One of the initially disorienting things about AutoCAD is that finished drawings can be composed of objects drawn in different *spaces*, which AutoCAD indicates with the tabs along the bottom of the drawing area (Model, Layout1, and Layout2 by default).

✔ *Model space* is where you create and modify the objects that represent things in the real world — walls, widgets, waterways, or whatever.

✔ *Paper space* is where you create particular views of these objects for plotting, usually with a title block around them. Paper space comprises one or more *layouts*, each of which can contain a different arrangement of model space views and different title block information.

When you click the Model tab in the drawing area, you see pure, unadulterated model space, as shown in Figure 2-7. When you click one of the paper space layout tabs (Layout1 or Layout2, unless someone has renamed or added to them), you see a paper space layout, as shown in Figure 2-8. A completed layout usually includes one or more *viewports*, which are windows that display all or part of model space at a particular scale. A layout also usually includes a title block or other objects that exist only in the layout and don't appear when you click the Model tab. (Think of the viewport as a window looking into model space and the title block as a frame around the window.) Thus, a layout displays model space and paper space objects together, and AutoCAD lets you draw and edit objects in either space. See Chapter 3 for information about creating paper space layouts and Chapter 12 for the lowdown on plotting them.

As I describe in the "Looking for Mr. Status Bar" section in this chapter, after you've clicked one of the layout tabs, the status bar's MODEL/PAPER button moves the cursor between model and paper space while remaining in the particular layout. (As shown in Figures 2-7 and 2-8, the orientation icon at the lower-left corner of the AutoCAD drawing area changes between an X-Y axis for model space and a drafting triangle for paper space as an additional reminder of which space the cursor currently resides in.) Chapter 3 describes the consequences of changing the MODEL/PAPER setting and advises you on how to use it.

This back-and-forth with the MODEL/PAPER button or double-clicking is necessary only when you're drawing things while viewing one of the paper space layouts. In practice, you probably won't encounter that situation very often. Instead, you'll do most of your drawing on the Model tab and, after you've set up a paper space layout, click its layout tab only when you want to plot.

Drawing on the drawing area

Here a few other things to know about the AutoCAD drawing area:

✔ Efficient, confident use of AutoCAD requires that you continually glance from the drawing area to the command line area (to see those all-important prompts!) and then back up to the drawing area. This sequence is not a natural reflex for most people. Get in the habit of looking at the command line after each action that you take, whether picking something on a toolbar, on a menu, or in the drawing area.

Figure 2-7: Our model lounging around in model space.

Figure 2-8:
Freshly laid
out in paper
space.

✔ Clicking at random in the drawing area is not quite as harmless in
   AutoCAD as it is in many other Windows programs. When you click in
   the AutoCAD drawing area, you're almost always performing some
   action — usually specifying a point or selecting objects for editing. Feel
   free to experiment, but look at the command line after each click. If you
   get confused, press the Esc key a couple of times to clear the current
   operation and return to the naked command prompt.

✔ In most cases, you can right-click in the drawing area to display a menu
   with some options for the current situation.

A Palette-Cleanser

In AutoCAD 2005, two features called Properties and DesignCenter, a toolbar-
like interface called Tool Palettes, and the new Sheet Set Manager appear in
spiffy modeless dialog boxes, or *palettes*.

✔ **Properties and DesignCenter:** Used to control object properties and
   named objects (layers, blocks, and so on), respectively. Chapter 4 shows
   you how.

✔ **Tool Palettes:** Resembles a stack of painter's palettes, except that each palette holds *content* (drawing symbols and hatch patterns) and/or *commands* (toolbar-like macros — a new feature in AutoCAD 2005) instead of paints. Chapters 11, 13, and 15 help you unlock your inner Tool Palette artistry.

✔ **Sheet Set Manager:** Provides tools for managing all of a project's drawings as a *sheet set.* Chapter 14 gives you the lowdown on why you might want to and how to do so.

You toggle these palettes on and off by clicking three buttons near the end of the Standard toolbar or by pressing Ctrl+1 (Properties), Ctrl+2 DesignCenter), Ctrl+3 (Tool Palettes), or Ctrl+4 (Sheet Set Manager). Figure 2-9 shows all four toggled on.

Modeless is just a fancy way of saying that these dialog boxes don't take over AutoCAD in the way that *modal* dialog boxes do. Modal dialog boxes demand your undivided attention. You enter values, click buttons, or whatever, and then click the OK or Cancel button to close the dialog box. While the modal dialog box is open, you can't do anything else in AutoCAD. A modeless dialog box, on the other hand, can remain open while you execute other commands that have nothing to do with the dialog box. You return to the modeless dialog box when or if you need its features.

Manipulating AutoCAD modeless dialog boxes — or *palettes* — is similar to manipulating a regular Windows dialog box, except that the title bar is along the side instead of at the top. In other words, you click and drag the title strip along the side to move the palette. If you experiment with the control buttons at the bottom of this strip (or right-click anywhere on the strip), you'll quickly get the hang of what you can do with these palettes. In particular, turning on the auto-hide feature causes the dialog box to "roll up" into the strip so that it's not taking up much screen space. When you point the cursor at the strip, the palette unfurls again.

Another cool feature — for the Tool Palettes but not the Properties and DesignCenter palettes — is *transparency*. Right-click the Tool Palettes' title strip and choose Transparency to control this feature. With transparency turned on, you can see your drawing objects behind a faded version of the Tool Palettes. (According to my dictionary, that would make the palettes *translucent*, not transparent, but whatever.) If you combine transparency with auto-hide, you end up with Tool Palettes that have a low impact on your drawing area. And if you're bothered by the amount of screen space taken by the command line area, you can make it transparent, too: Undock it, right-click the title bar and turn off Allow Docking, and then right-click again and choose Transparency. After you've set the transparency to your taste, click and drag the command line area to where you want it.

Properties palette   DesignCenter palette   Tool palettes

Figure 2-9:
A modeless
menagerie.

What Really Makes AutoCAD Cook?

Knowing how to use the command line, as described in the section, "Take an order: The command line area," is one of the secrets of becoming a competent AutoCAD user. In reading about and using AutoCAD, you encounter two additional topics frequently: *system variables,* which are AutoCAD's basic control levers, and *dialog boxes,* many of which put a friendlier face on the system variables.

Sizzling system variables

System variables are settings that AutoCAD checks before it decides how to do something. If you set the system variable SAVETIME to 10, AutoCAD automatically saves your drawing file every ten minutes; if you set SAVETIME to 60, the time between saves is one hour. Hundreds of system variables control AutoCAD's operations.

Of these hundreds of system variables in AutoCAD, 70 system variables control dimensioning alone. (*Dimensioning* is the process of labeling objects with their lengths, angles, or special notes. Different professions have different standards for presenting dimensions on their drawings. Using dimensions is described in detail in Chapter 10.)

To change the value of a system variable, just type its name at the AutoCAD command prompt and press Enter. AutoCAD will display the current value of the system variable setting and prompt you for a new value. Press Enter alone to keep the existing setting, or type a value and press Enter to change the setting.

The procedure for entering a system variable is exactly the same as for entering a command name — type the name and press Enter. The only difference is what happens afterward:

✔ A system variable changes a setting.

✔ A command usually adds objects to the drawing, modifies objects, or changes your view of the drawing.

Being able to change system variables by typing their names at the command line is a boon to power users and occasionally a necessity for everybody else. The only problem is finding or remembering what the names are. In most cases, you'll be told what system variable name you need to type — by me in this book or by the local AutoCAD guru in your office.

To see a listing of all the system variables in AutoCAD and their current settings, use the following steps:

1. **Type SETvar at the AutoCAD command prompt and press Enter.**

   AutoCAD prompts you to type the name of a system variable (if you want to view or change just one) or question mark (if you want to see the names and current settings of more than one):

   ```
   Enter variable name or [?]
   ```

2. **Type ? (question mark) and press Enter.**

   AutoCAD asks which system variables to list:

   ```
   Enter variable(s) to list <*>:
   ```

3. **Press Enter to accept the default asterisk (which means "list all system variables").**

   AutoCAD displays the first 16 system variables and their settings:

   ```
   ACADLSPASDOC        0
   ACADPREFIX          "C:\Documents and..." (read only)
   ACADVER             "16.1"                (read only)
   ACISOUTVER          70
   ```

```
AFLAGS              0
ANGBASE             0
ANGDIR              0
APBOX               0
APERTURE            10
AREA                0.0000          (read only)
ATTDIA              0
ATTMODE             1
ATTREQ              1
AUDITCTL            0
AUNITS              0
AUPREC              0
AUTOSNAP            63
BACKGROUNDPLOT      2
BACKZ               0.0000          (read only)
BINDTYPE            0
BLIPMODE            0
Press ENTER to continue:
```

4. **Press Enter repeatedly to scroll through the entire list, or press Esc to bail out.**

   AutoCAD returns to the command prompt:

   ```
   Command:
   ```

If you want to find out more about what a particular system variable controls, see the System Variables chapter in the Command Reference in the AutoCAD online help.

Three kinds of system variables exist:

✔ Those saved in the Windows Registry. If you change this kind of system variable, it affects all drawings when you open them with AutoCAD on your system.

✔ Those saved in the drawing. If you change this kind, the change affects only the current drawing.

✔ Those that aren't saved anywhere. If you change this kind, the change lasts only for the current drawing session.

The System Variables chapter in the online Command Reference tells you which kind of system variable each one is.

Delicious dialog boxes

Fortunately, you don't usually have to remember the system variable names. AutoCAD exposes most of the system variable settings in dialog boxes so that you can change their values simply by clicking check boxes or typing values in edit boxes. This approach is a lot more user-friendly than remembering an obscure name like "ACADLSPASDOC."

For example, many of the settings on the tabs in the Options dialog box, shown in Figure 2-10, are in fact system variables. If you use the dialog box quick help (click the question mark in the Options dialog box's title bar, and then click an option in the dialog box), the pop-up description not only describes the setting, but also tells which system variable it corresponds to.

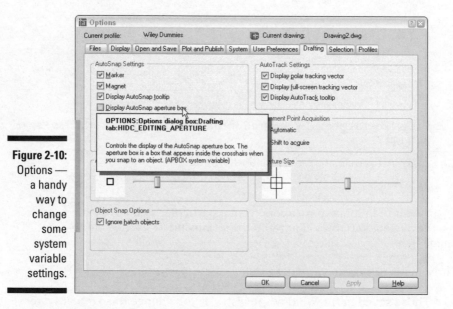

Figure 2-10:
Options —
a handy
way to
change
some
system
variable
settings.

Fun with F1

The AutoCAD 2005 Help menu, shown in Figure 2-11, offers a slew of online help options. I describe most of them here:

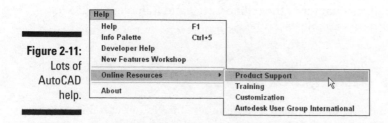

Figure 2-11:
Lots of
AutoCAD
help.

✔ **Help:** The main AutoCAD 2005 online help system, shown in Figure 2-12, uses the same help engine as the Microsoft Office programs, Internet Explorer, and other modern Windows applications. Click the Contents tab to browse through the various online reference manuals, the Index tab to look up commands and concepts, and the Search tab to look for specific words. In this book, I sometimes direct you to the AutoCAD online help system for information about advanced topics.

✔ **Info Palette:** This option opens a Quick Help Info Palette, which is the Autodesk version of the Microsoft paper clip guy who tries to tell you what to do in Word or Excel at each step along the way. Like paper-clip guy, Info Palette *seems* helpful — for 30 seconds. Then you get tired of the distraction and the wasted screen space.

✔ **New Features Workshop:** This describes the new and enhanced features in AutoCAD 2005. It's especially useful for people who are upgrading from a previous AutoCAD version.

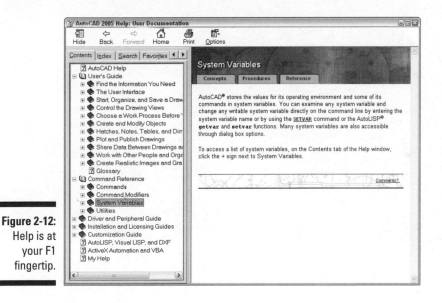

Figure 2-12:
Help is at
your F1
fingertip.

✔ **Online Resources:** Most of the choices in the Online Resources sub-menu connect you to various parts of Autodesk's Web site. The most useful is Product Support. From the support Web page, you can search the Autodesk Knowledge Base, download software updates, and get help from Web- and newsgroup-based discussion groups.

AutoCAD is one program with which you really need to take advantage of the online help resources. AutoCAD contains many commands, options, and quirks, and everyone from the greenest beginner to the most seasoned expert can find out something by using the AutoCAD online help. Take a moment to peruse the Contents tab of the main help system so that you know what's available. Throughout this book, I direct you to pages in the help system that I think are particularly useful, but don't be afraid to explore on your own when you get stuck or feel curious.

Chapter 3

Setup for Success

Surprisingly, drawing setup is one of the trickier aspects of using AutoCAD. It's an easy thing to do incompletely or wrong, and AutoCAD 2004 doesn't provide a dialog box or other simple, all-in-one-fell-swoop tool to help you do all of it right. And yet, drawing setup is a crucial thing to get right. Setup steps that you omit or don't do right will come back to bite you — or at least gnaw on your leg — later.

Sloppy setup really becomes apparent when you try to plot your drawing. Things that seemed more or less okay as you zoomed around on the screen suddenly are completely the wrong size or scale on paper. And nothing brands someone as a naive AutoCAD wannabe as quickly as the inability to plot a drawing at the right size and scale. Chapter 12 covers plotting procedures, but the information in this chapter is a necessary prerequisite to successful plotting. If you don't get this stuff right, there's a good chance you'll find that . . . the plot sickens.

This chapter describes the decisions you need to make before you set up a new drawing, shows the steps for doing a complete and correct setup, and demonstrates how to save setup settings for reuse.

Don't assume that you can just create a new blank DWG file and start drawing things. In other words, *do* read this chapter before you get too deep into the later chapters in this book. Many AutoCAD drawing commands and concepts depend on proper drawing setup, so you'll have a much easier time of drawing and editing things if you've done your setup homework. A few minutes invested in setting up a drawing well can save hours of thrashing around later on.

After you've digested the detailed drawing setup procedures described in this chapter, use the Drawing Setup Roadmap on the Cheat Sheet at the front of this book to guide you through the process.

An Appetizing Setup Strategy

You need to set up AutoCAD correctly, partly because AutoCAD is so flexible and partly because, well, you're doing *CAD* — computer-aided drafting (or design). The computer can't aid your drafting (or design) if you don't clue it in on things like drawing scale, paper size, and units. In this context, the following reasons help explain why AutoCAD drawing setup is important:

- **Electronic paper:** The most important thing you can do to make using AutoCAD fun is to work on a correctly set up drawing so that your screen acts like paper, only smarter. When drawing on real paper, you constantly have to translate between units on the paper and the real-life units of the object you're drawing. But when drawing in AutoCAD, you can draw directly in real-life units — feet and inches, millimeters, or whatever you typically use on your projects. AutoCAD can then calculate distances and dimensions for you and add them to the drawing. You can make the mouse pointer jump directly to hot spots on-screen, and a visible, resizable grid gives you a better sense of the scale of your drawing. However, this smart paper function works well only if you tell AutoCAD some crucial parameters for your specific drawing. AutoCAD can't really do its job until you tell it how to work.

- **Dead-trees paper:** Creating a great drawing on-screen that doesn't fit well on paper is all too easy. After you finish creating your drawing on the smart paper AutoCAD provides on-screen, you usually must then plot it on the good, old-fashioned paper that people have used for thousands of years. At that point, you must deal with the fact that people like to use certain standard paper sizes and drawing scales. (Most people also like everything to fit neatly on one sheet of paper.) If you set up AutoCAD correctly, good plotting results automatically; if not, plotting time can become one colossal hassle.

- **It ain't easy:** AutoCAD provides templates and Setup Wizards for you, but the templates don't work well unless you understand them, and some of the wizards don't work well even if you do understand them. This deficiency is one of the major weaknesses in AutoCAD. You must figure out on your own how to make the program work right. If you just plunge in without carefully setting it up, your drawing and printing efforts are likely to wind up a real mess.

Fortunately, setting up AutoCAD correctly is a bit like cooking a soufflé: Although the steps for performing your setup are complex, you can master them with attention and practice. Even more fortunately, this chapter provides a detailed and field-tested recipe.

AutoCAD and paper

In other Windows programs, you can use any scaling factor you want to squeeze content onto paper. You've probably printed an Excel spreadsheet or Web page at some odd scaling factor, such as 82.5 percent of full size, because that's what it took to squeeze the content onto a single sheet of paper while keeping the text as large as possible.

In drafting, your printout needs to use a specific, widely accepted scaling factor, such as ¼" = 1'–0", to be useful and understandable to others. But the AutoCAD screen does not automatically enforce any one scaling factor or paper size. If you just start drawing stuff on the AutoCAD screen to fit your immediate needs, it's unlikely that the final result will fit neatly on a piece of paper at a desirable scale.

This chapter tells you how to start your drawing in such a way that you'll like how it ends up. With practice, this kind of approach will become second nature.

While you're working in AutoCAD, always keep in mind what your final output should look like on real paper. Even your first printed drawings should look just like hand-drawn ones — only without all those eraser smudges.

Before you start the drawing setup process, you need to make decisions about your new drawing. These three questions are absolutely critical. If you don't answer them, or you answer them wrong, you'll probably need to do lots of reworking of the drawing later:

- ✔ What drawing units will you use?
- ✔ At what scale — or scales — will you plot it?
- ✔ On what size paper does it need to fit?

In some cases, you can defer answering one additional question, but it's usually better to deal with it up front: What kind of border or title block does your drawing require?

If you're in a hurry, it's tempting to find an existing drawing that was set up for the drawing scale and paper size that you want to use, make a copy of that DWG file, erase the objects, and start drawing. Use this approach with care, though. When you start from another drawing, you inherit any setup mistakes in that drawing. Also, drawings that were created in much older versions of AutoCAD may not take advantage of current program features and CAD practices. If you can find a suitable drawing that was set up in a recent version of AutoCAD by an experienced person who is conscientious about doing setup right, consider using it. Otherwise, you're better off setting up a new drawing from scratch.

Choosing your units

AutoCAD is extremely flexible about drawing units; it lets you have them *your* way. Usually, you choose the type of units that you normally use to talk about whatever you're drawing: feet and inches for a building in the United States, millimeters for a metric screw, and so on.

During drawing setup, you choose two units characteristics: a *type* of unit — Scientific, Decimal, Engineering, Architectural, and Fractional — and a *precision* of measurement in the Drawing Units dialog box, shown in Figure 3-1. (I show you how later in this chapter.) Engineering and Architectural units are in feet and inches; Engineering units use *decimals* to represent partial inches, and Architectural units use *fractions* to represent them. AutoCAD's other unit types — Decimal, Fractional, and Scientific — are *unitless* because AutoCAD doesn't know or care what the base unit is. If you configure a drawing to use Decimal units, for example, each drawing unit could represent a micron, millimeter, inch, foot, meter, kilometer, mile, parsec, the length of the king's forearm, or any other unit of measurement that you deem convenient. It's up to you to decide.

After you specify a type of unit, you draw things on-screen full size in those units just as though you were laying them out on the construction site or in the machine shop. You draw an 8-foot-high line, for example, to indicate the height of a wall and an 8-inch-high line to indicate the cutout for a doggie door (for a Dachshund, naturally). The on-screen line may actually be only 2 inches long at a particular zoom resolution, but AutoCAD stores the length as 8 feet. This way of working is easy and natural for most people for whom CAD is their first drafting experience, but it seems weird to people who've done a lot of manual drafting. If you're in the latter category, don't worry; you'll soon get the hang of it.

Figure 3-1:
The
Drawing
Units dialog
box.

Drawing scale versus the drawing scale factor

CAD users employ two different ways of talking about a drawing's intended plot scale: drawing scale and drawing scale factor.

Drawing scale is the traditional way of describing a scale — traditional in that it existed long before CAD came to be. Drawing scales are expressed with an equal sign or colon; for example ⅛" = 1'–0", 1 = 20, or 2:1. Translate the equal sign or colon as "corresponds to." In all cases, the measurement to the left of the equal sign or colon indicates a paper measurement, and the number to the right indicates a CAD drawing and real-world measurement. In other words, the architectural scale ⅛" = 1'–0" means "⅛" on the plotted drawing corresponds to 1'–0" in the CAD drawing and in the real world," assuming that the plot was made at the proper scale.

Drawing scale factor is a single number that represents a multiplier, such as 96, 20, or 0.5. The drawing scale factor for a drawing is the conversion factor between a measurement on the plot and a measurement in a CAD drawing and the real world.

Those of you who did your math homework in junior high will realize that drawing scale and drawing scale factor are two interchangeable ways of describing the same relationship. The drawing scale factor is the multiplier that converts the first number in the drawing scale into the second number.

When you use dash-dot linetypes (Chapter 4) and hatching (Chapter 11) in a drawing, AutoCAD imposes one additional units consideration — whether the drawing uses an imperial (inches, feet, miles, and so on) or metric (millimeters, meters, kilometers, and so on) system of units. The MEASUREMENT system variable controls whether the linetype and hatch patterns that AutoCAD lists for you to choose from are scaled with inches or millimeters in mind as the plotting units. MEASUREMENT=0 means inches (that is, an imperial units drawing), whereas MEASUREMENT=1 means millimeters (that is, a metric units drawing). If you start from an appropriate template drawing, as described later in this chapter, the MEASUREMENT system variable will be set correctly and you won't ever have to think about it.

Weighing your scales

The next decision you should make before setting up a new drawing is choosing the scale at which you'll eventually plot the drawing. This decision gives you the *drawing scale* and *drawing scale factor* — two ways of expressing the same relationship between the objects in the real world and the objects plotted on paper.

You shouldn't just invent some arbitrary scale based on your CD-ROM speed or camera's zoom lens resolution. Most industries work with a fairly small set of approved drawing scales that are related to one another by factors of 2 or 10. If you use other scales, you'll at best be branded a clueless newbie — and at worst have to redo all your drawings at an approved scale.

Table 3-1 lists some common architectural drawing scales, using both English and metric units. (Ratios such as 1:200 are unitless. Building plan and detail measurements often are expressed in millimeters, so you can think of 1:200 as meaning "1 millimeter on the plotted drawing equals 200 millimeters in actual building.") The table also lists the drawing scale factor corresponding to each drawing scale and the common uses for each scale. If you work in other industries than those listed here, ask drafters or coworkers what the common drawing scales are and for what kinds of drawings they're used.

Table 3-1	Common Architectural Drawing Scales	
Drawing Scale	*Drawing Scale Factor*	*Common Uses*
¹⁄₁₆″ = 1′–0″	192	Large building plans
⅛″ = 1′–0″	96	Building plans
¼″ = 1′–0″	48	House plans
½″ = 1′–0″	24	Plan details
1″ = 1′–0″	12	Details
1:200	200	Large building plans
1:100	100	Building plans
1:50	50	House plans
1:20	20	Plan details
1:10	10	Details

After you choose a drawing scale, engrave the corresponding drawing scale factor on your desk, write it on your hand, and put it on a sticky note on your monitor. You need to know the drawing scale factor for many drawing tasks, as well as for some plotting. You should be able to recite the drawing scale factor of any drawing you're working on in AutoCAD without even thinking about it.

Even if you will use the Plot dialog box's Fit to Paper option, rather than a specific scale factor, to plot the drawing, you need to choose an artificial scale to make text, dimensions, and other annotations appear at a useful size. Choose a scale that's in the neighborhood of the Fit to Paper plotting factor, which AutoCAD displays in the Plot Scale area of the Plot dialog box. For example, if you determine that you need to squeeze your drawing down about 90 times to fit on the desired sheet size, choose a drawing scale of ⅛ inch = 1 foot – 0 inches (drawing scale factor = 96) if you're using architectural units or 1 = 100 (drawing scale factor = 100) for other kinds of units.

Thinking about paper

With knowledge of your industry's common drawing scales, you can choose a provisional scale based on what you're depicting. But you won't know for sure whether that scale works until you compare it with the size of the paper that you want to use for plotting your drawing. Here again, most industries use a small range of standard sheet sizes. Three common sets of sizes exist, as shown in Figure 3-2 and Table 3-2:

✔ ANSI (American National Standards Institute)

✔ Architectural

✔ ISO (International Standard Organization)

Figure 3-2: Relationships among standard paper sizes.

Table 3-2	Common Plot Sheet Sizes	
Sheet Size	*Dimensions*	*Comment*
ANSI *E*	34 x 44"	
ANSI *D*	22 x 34"	*E* sheet folded in half
ANSI *C*	17 x 22"	*D* sheet folded in half
ANSI *B*	11 x 17"	*C* sheet folded in half
ANSI *A*	8½ x 11"	*B* sheet folded in half
Architectural Large *E*	36 x 48"	
Architectural *E*	30 x 42"	
Architectural *D*	24 x 36"	

(continued)

Table 3-2 *(continued)*

Sheet Size	Dimensions	Comment
Architectural *C*	18 x 24″	
Architectural *B*	12 x 18″	
Architectural *A*	9 x 12″	
ISO *A0*	841 x 1189 mm	
ISO *A1*	594 x 841 mm	*A0* sheet folded in half
ISO *A2*	420 x 594 mm	*A1* sheet folded in half
ISO *A3*	297 x 420 mm	*A2* sheet folded in half
ISO *A4*	210 x 297 mm	*A3* sheet folded in half

You select a particular set of sheet sizes based on the common practices in your industry. You then narrow down your choice based on the area required by what you're going to draw. For example, most architectural plans are plotted on Architectural D or E size sheets.

If you know the desired sheet size and drawing scale factor, you can calculate the available drawing area easily. Simply multiply each of the sheet's dimensions (X and Y) by the drawing scale factor. For example, if you choose an 11-x-17-inch sheet and a drawing scale factor of 96 (corresponding to a plot scale of ⅛″ = 1'–0″), you multiply 17 times 96 and 11 times 96 to get an available drawing area of 1,632 inches x 1,056 inches (or 136 feet x 88 feet). If your sheet size is in inches but your drawing scale is in millimeters, you need to multiply by an additional 25.4 to convert from inches to millimeters. For example, with an 11-x-17-inch sheet and a scale of 1:200 (drawing scale factor = 200), you multiply 17 times 200 times 25.4 and 11 times 200 times 25.4 to get 86,360 x 55,880 mm or 86.36 x 55.88 m — not quite big enough for a football field (United States *or* European football).

Conversely, if you know the sheet size that you're going to use and the real-world size of what you're going to draw, and you want to find out the largest plot scale you can use, you have to divide, not multiply. Divide the needed real-world drawing area dimensions (X and Y) by the sheet's dimensions (X and Y). Take the larger number — either X or Y — and round up to the nearest real drawing scale factor (that is, one that's commonly used in your industry). For example, suppose you want to draw a 60-x-40-foot or, 720-x-480-inch, floor plan and print it on 11-x-17-inch paper. You divide 720 by 17 and 480 by 11 to get 42.35 and 43.64, respectively. The larger number, 43.64, corresponds in this example to the short dimension of the house and the paper. The nearest larger common architectural drawing scale factor is 48 (corresponding to ¼″ = 1'–0″), which leaves a little room for the plotting margin and title block.

The Cheat Sheet at the front of this book includes two tables that list the available drawing areas for a range of sheet sizes and drawing scales. Use those tables to help you decide on an appropriate paper size and drawing scale, and revert to the calculation method for situations that the tables don't cover. (If you don't keep a favorite old calculator on your physical desktop, this may be a good time to put a shortcut to the Windows Calculator on your virtual one.)

When you select a sheet size and drawing scale, always leave some extra room for the following two reasons:

✔ Most plotters and printers can't print all the way to the edge of the sheet — they require a small margin. For example, my trusty old Hewlett-Packard LaserJet III has a printable area of about 7.9 x 10.5 inches on an 8.5-x-11-inch ANSI A size (letter size) sheet. (You'll find this information in the Plot dialog box, as described in Chapter 12.) If you're a stickler for precision, you can use the printable area instead of the physical sheet area in the calculations described earlier in this section.

✔ Most drawings require some annotations — text, grid bubbles, and so on — outside the objects you're drawing, plus a title block surrounding the objects and annotations. If you don't leave some room for the annotations and title block, you'll end up having to cram things together too much or to change to a different sheet size. Either way, you'll be slowed down later in the project when you can least afford it. Figure 3-3 shows an extreme example of selecting a sheet size that's too small or, conversely, a drawing scale that's too large. In this example, the building is too long for the sheet, and it overlaps the title block on both the right and left sides.

Some industries deal with the "sheet-is-too-small/drawing-scale-is-too-large" problem by breaking drawings up onto multiple plotted sheets.

Don't be afraid to *start* with paper. Experienced drafters often make a quick, throwaway pencil and paper sketch called a *cartoon*. A drawing cartoon usually includes a rectangle indicating the sheet of paper you intend to plot on, a sketch of the title block, and a very rough, schematic sketch of the thing you're going to draw. It helps to scribble down the dimensions of the sheet, the main title block areas, and the major objects to be drawn. By sketching out a cartoon, you'll often catch scale or paper size problems before you set up a drawing, when repairs only take a few minutes, not after you've created the drawing, when fixing the problem can take hours.

Figure 3-3:
"This sheet
size is too
small," said
Goldilocks.

Defending your border

The next decision to make is what kind of border your drawing deserves. The options include a full-blown title block, a simple rectangle, or nothing at all around your drawing. If you need a title block, do you have one, can you borrow an existing one, or will you need to draw one from scratch? Although you can draw title block geometry in an individual drawing, you'll save time by reusing the same title block for multiple drawings. Your company may already have a standard title block drawing ready to use, or someone else who's working on your project may have created one for the project.

The right way to draw a title block is in a separate DWG file at its normal plotted size (for example, 36 inches long by 24 inches high for an architectural D size title block). You then insert or xref the title block drawing into each sheet drawing. Chapter 13 describes how to insert and xref separate DWG files.

All system variables go

As Chapter 2 describes, AutoCAD includes a slew of *system variables* that control the way your drawing and the AutoCAD program work. Much of the drawing setup process involves setting system variables based on the drawing scale, sheet size, and other desired properties of the drawing. You can set some system variables in AutoCAD dialog boxes, but a few require that you type at the command line. Table 3-3 shows the settings that you most commonly need to change — or at least check — during drawing setup, along with the names of the corresponding system variables. Later in the chapter, in the section "The Main Course: Model Space," I show you the procedure for changing these settings.

Table 3-3	System Variables for Drawing Setup	
Setting	*Dialog Box*	*System Variables*
Linear units and precision	Drawing Units	LUNITS, LUPREC
Angular units and precision	Drawing Units	AUNITS, AUPREC
Grid spacing and visibility	Drafting Settings	GRIDUNIT, GRIDMODE
Snap spacing and on/off	Drafting Settings	SNAPUNIT, SNAPMODE
Drawing limits	None (use command line)	LIMMIN, LIMMAX
Linetype scale	Linetype Manager	LTSCALE, PSLTSCALE
Dimension scale	Dimension Style Manager	DIMSCALE

Getting Creative with Templates

When you start AutoCAD 2004 with its desktop shortcut or from the Windows Start menu, AutoCAD creates a new, blank drawing based on the default template drawing (Acad.dwt). When you explicitly create a new drawing from within AutoCAD, the Select Template dialog box, shown in Figure 3-4, appears by default so that you can choose a template on which to base your new drawing.

A *template* is simply a drawing whose name ends in the letters DWT, which you use as the starting point for another drawing. When you create a new drawing from a template, AutoCAD makes a copy of the template file and opens the copy in a new drawing editor window. The first time you save the file, you're prompted for a new filename to save to; the original template file stays unchanged.

You may be familiar with the Microsoft Word or Excel template documents, and AutoCAD template drawings work pretty much the same way — because Autodesk stole the idea from them! (Encouraged, of course, by Microsoft.)

Figure 3-4:
A plateful of
templates to
contemplate.

Using a suitable template can save you time and worry because many of the setup options are already set correctly for you. You know the drawing will print correctly; you just have to worry about getting the geometry and text right. Of course, all this optimism assumes that the person who set up the template knew what he or she was doing.

The stock templates that come with AutoCAD are okay as a starting point, but you'll need to modify them to suit your purposes, or create your own from scratch. In particular, the stock AutoCAD templates aren't set up for the scales that you'll want to use. The instructions in the rest of this chapter tell you how to specify scale-dependent setup information.

So the only problems with templates are creating good ones and then later finding the right one to use when you need it. Later in this chapter, in the section "Cooking Up Terrific Templates," I show you how to create templates from your own setup drawings. Here I show you how to use an already created template, such as one of the templates that comes with AutoCAD 2004 or from one of your CAD-savvy colleagues. If you're lucky, someone in your office will have created suitable templates that you can use to get going quickly.

Follow these steps to create a new drawing from a template drawing:

1. **Run the NEW command by pressing Ctrl+N or choosing File⇨New.**

   The Select Template dialog box appears.

   The first button on the Standard toolbar runs the QNEW ("Quick NEW") command instead of the ordinary NEW command. Unless you or someone else has changed the Drawing Template Settings in the Options dialog box, QNEW does the same thing as NEW. See "Cooking Up Terrific Templates," later in this chapter, for information about how to take advantage of QNEW.

2. **Click the name of the template that you want to use as the starting point for your new drawing.**

3. **Click the Open button.**

   A new drawing window with a temporary name, such as `Drawing2.dwg`, appears. (The template you opened remains unchanged on your hard disk.)

   Depending on which template you choose, your new drawing may open with a paper space layout tab, not the Model tab, selected. If that's the case, click the Model tab before changing the settings described in "The Main Course: Model Space." The section "Plot Layouts for Any Palate," later in this chapter, describes how to set up and take advantage of paper space layouts.

4. **Press Ctrl+S and save the file under a new name.**

   Take the time to save the drawing to the appropriate name and location now.

5. **Make needed changes.**

   For most of the templates that come with AutoCAD, you need to consider changing the units, limits, grid and snap settings, linetype scale, and dimension scale. See the section, "The Main Course: Model Space," for instructions.

6. **Consider saving the file as a template.**

   If you'll need other drawings in the future similar to the current one, consider saving your modified template as a template in its own right. See the section "Cooking Up Terrific Templates" later in this chapter.

   The simplest, no-frills templates are `Acad.dwt` (for people who customarily work with sheet sizes expressed in inches) and `Acadiso.dwt` (for people who customarily work with sheet sizes expressed in millimeters). Most of the remaining templates that come with AutoCAD include title blocks for various sizes of sheets. In addition, most templates come in two versions — one for people who use color-dependent plot styles and one for people who use named plot styles. You probably want the color-dependent versions. (Chapter 12 describes the two kinds of plot styles and why you probably want the color-dependent variety.) I warned you that this drawing setup stuff would be complicated!

   If you dig around in the Options dialog box, you may discover a setting that turns on the old Startup dialog box, which offers several options other than starting with a template. Among these options are the enticingly named *Setup Wizards.* These so-called wizards were lame when they first appeared; they're no better now. Autodesk acknowledges as much by making them almost impossible to find in AutoCAD 2005.

The Main Course: Model Space

Most drawings require a two-part setup:

1. First, set up the model space tab, where you'll create most of your drawing.

2. Next, create one or more paper space layout tabs for plotting.

After you've decided on drawing scale and sheet size, you can perform model space setup as described in this section.

Setting your units

First, you should set the linear and angular units that you want to use in your new drawing. The following procedure describes how:

1. **Choose Format⇨Units from the menu bar.**

   The Drawing Units dialog box appears, as shown in Figure 3-5.

Figure 3-5:
The default
unit-less
units.

2. **Choose a linear unit type from the Length Type drop-down list.**

   Choose the type of unit representation that's appropriate for your work. Engineering and Architectural units are displayed in feet and inches; the other types of units aren't tied to any particular unit of measurement. You decide whether each unit represents a millimeter, centimeter, meter, inch, foot, or something else. Decimal units usually are a good choice for metric drawings.

AutoCAD can think in inches! If you're using Engineering or Architectural units (feet and inches), AutoCAD understands any coordinate you enter as a number of inches. You use the ' (apostrophe) character on your keyboard to indicate a number in feet instead of inches.

3. **From the Length Precision drop-down list, choose the degree of precision you want when AutoCAD displays coordinates and linear measurements.**

The precision setting controls how precisely AutoCAD displays coordinates, distances, and prompts in some dialog boxes. In particular, the Coordinates box on the status bar displays the current cursor coordinates using the current precision. A *grosser* — that is, less precise — precision setting makes the numbers displayed in the status bar more readable and less jumpy. So be gross for now; you can always act a little less gross later.

The linear and angular precision settings only affect AutoCAD's *display* of coordinates, distances, and angles on the status bar, in dialog boxes, and in the command line area. For drawings stored as DWG files, AutoCAD always uses maximum precision to store the locations and sizes of all objects that you draw. In addition, AutoCAD provides separate settings for controlling the precision of dimension text — see Chapter 10 for details.

4. **Choose an angular unit type from the Angle Type drop-down list.**

   Decimal Degrees and Deg/Min/Sec are the most common choices.

   The Clockwise check box and the Direction button provide additional angle measurement options, but you'll rarely need to change the default settings: Measure angles counterclockwise and use east as the 0 degree direction.

5. **From the Angle Precision drop-down list, choose the degree of precision you want when AutoCAD displays angular measurements.**

6. **In the Drag-and-Drop Scale area, choose the units of measurement for this drawing.**

   Choose your base unit for this drawing — that is, the real-world distance represented by one AutoCAD unit.

7. **Click OK to exit the dialog box and save your settings.**

Telling your drawing its limits

The next model space setup task is to set your drawing's *limits*. You wouldn't want it staying out all night and hanging out with just anybody, would you? The limits represent the rectangular working area that you'll draw on, which usually corresponds to the paper size. Setting limits correctly gives you the following advantages:

✔ When you turn on the grid (described in the section, "Making the drawing snap-py (and grid-dy)," later in this chapter), the grid displays in the rectangular limits area. With the grid on and the limits set correctly, you always see the working area that corresponds to what you'll eventually be plotting, so you won't accidentally color outside the lines.

✔ The ZOOM command's All option zooms to the greater of the limits or the drawing extents. (The extents of a drawing consist of a rectangular area just large enough to include all the objects in the drawing.) When you set limits properly and color within the lines, ZOOM All gives you a quick way to zoom to your working area.

✔ If you plot from model space, you can choose to plot the limits area. This option gives you a quick, reliable way to plot your drawing, but only if you've set limits correctly!

Many CAD drafters don't set limits properly in their drawings. After you read this section, you can smugly tell them why they should and how.

You can start the LIMITS command from a menu choice, but all subsequent action takes place on the command line; despite the importance of the topic, AutoCAD has no dialog box for setting limits.

The following procedure shows you how to set your drawing limits:

1. **Choose Format⇨Drawing Limits from the menu bar to start the LIMITS command; or type** LIMITS **on the command line and press Enter.**

   The LIMITS command appears on the command line, and the command line displays the following prompt at the bottom of the screen:

   ```
   Command: limits
   Reset Model space limits:
   Specify lower left corner or [ON/OFF] <0.000,0.0000>:
   ```

   The value at the end of the last line of the prompt is the default value for the lower-left corner of the drawing limits. It appears according to the units and precision that you selected in the Drawing Units dialog box — for example, 0'-0" if you selected Architectural units with precision to the nearest inch.

2. **Type the lower-left corner of the limits you want to use and press Enter.**

   The usual value to enter at this point is **0,0**. (Type a zero, a comma, and then another zero, with no spaces.) You can just press Enter to accept the default value.

   AutoCAD now prompts you for the upper-right corner of the limits:

   ```
   Specify upper right corner <12.0000,9.0000>:
   ```

The initial units offered by AutoCAD correspond to an architectural A size sheet of paper in landscape orientation. (Almost no one uses Architectural A size paper; here's a classic example of a programmer choosing a silly default that no one has bothered to change in 22 years!)

3. **Type the upper-right corner of the limits you want to use and press Enter.**

You calculate the usual setting for the limits upper-right corner by multiplying the paper dimensions by the drawing scale factor. For example, if you're setting up a ⅛" = 1'–0" drawing (drawing scale factor = 96) to be plotted on a 24-x-36-inch sheet in landscape orientation, the upper-right corner of the limits should be 36 inches times 96, 24 inches times 96. Okay, pencils down. The correct answer is 3456,2304 (or 288 feet,192 feet).

Alternatively, you can cheat when specifying limits and read the limits from the tables on the Cheat Sheet.

If you have the grid turned on, AutoCAD redisplays it in the new limits area after you press Enter.

If you're using Architectural or Engineering units and you want to enter measurements in feet and not inches, you must add the foot designator after the number, such as **6'**; otherwise, AutoCAD assumes that you mean inches.

4. **Choose View⇨Zoom⇨All.**

AutoCAD zooms to the new limits.

Making the drawing area snap-py (and grid-dy)

AutoCAD's *grid* is a set of evenly spaced, visible dots that serve as a visual distance reference. (As I describe in "Telling your drawing its limits," earlier in this section, the grid also indicates how far the drawing limits extend.) AutoCAD's *snap* feature creates a set of evenly spaced, invisible hot spots, which makes the cursor move in nice, even increments. Both grid and snap are like the intersection points of the lines on a piece of grid paper, but grid is simply a visual reference, whereas snap constrains the points that you can pick with the mouse. You can — and usually will — set the grid and snap spacing to different distances.

Set the grid and the snap intervals in the Drafting Settings dialog box with these steps:

1. **Right-click the Snap or Grid button in the status bar and choose Settings.**

The Drafting Settings dialog box appears with the Snap and Grid tab selected, as shown in Figure 3-6.

Drafting Settings

Snap and Grid | Polar Tracking | Object Snap

☑ Snap On (F9)   ☑ Grid On (F7)

┌ Snap ─────────────────┐   ┌ Grid ─────────────────┐
Snap X spacing: 0.5000   Grid X spacing: 10.0000
Snap Y spacing: 0.5000   Grid Y spacing: 10.0000
Angle: 0
X base: 0.0000   ┌ Snap type & style ───────┐
Y base: 0.0000   ⦿ Grid snap
                                  ⦿ Rectangular snap
┌ Polar spacing ────────┐   ○ Isometric snap
Polar distance: 0.0000   ○ PolarSnap

[Options...]   [OK] [Cancel] [Help]

Figure 3-6:
Get your
Drafting
Settings
here!

The Snap and Grid tab has four parts, but the Snap and Grid sections are all you need to worry about for most drafting work.

2. **Select the Snap On check box to turn on snap.**

   This action creates default snaps half a unit apart.

3. **Enter the Snap X Spacing for the snap interval in the accompanying text box.**

   Use the information in the sections preceding this procedure to decide on a reasonable snap spacing.

   The Y spacing automatically changes to equal the X spacing, which is almost always what you want.

4. **Select the Grid On check box to turn on the grid.**

5. **Enter the Grid X Spacing for the grid in the accompanying text box.**

   Use the information in the sections preceding this procedure to decide on a reasonable grid spacing.

   The Y spacing automatically changes to equal the X spacing. As with the snap spacing, you usually want to leave it that way.

   X measures horizontal distance; Y measures vertical distance. The AutoCAD drawing area normally shows an X and Y icon in case you forget.

6. **Click OK to close the Drafting Settings dialog box.**

You can also click the SNAP button on the status bar to toggle snap on and off; the same goes for the GRID button and the grid setting.

Making snap (and grid) decisions

You can set your grid spacing to work in one of two ways: to help with your drawing or to help you remain aware of how objects will relate to your plot. For *a grid that helps with your drawing,* set the grid points a logical number of measurement units apart. For example, you might set the grid to 30 feet (10 yards) on a drawing of a (U.S.) football field. This kind of setting makes your work easier as you draw.

Another approach is to choose *a grid spacing that represents a specific distance,* such as 1 inch or 25 millimeters, on your final plot. If you want the grid to represent 1 inch on the plot and your drawing units are inches, enter the drawing scale factor. For example, in a ¼" = 1'-0" drawing, you'd enter the drawing scale factor of 48. A 48-inch grid interval in your drawing corresponds to a 1-inch interval on the plot when you plot to scale. If your drawing units are millimeters and you want the grid to represent 25 millimeters on the plot, enter the drawing scale factor times 25. For example, in a 1:50 drawing, you'd enter 25 x 50, or 1250.

In most cases, you'll want to set the snap interval considerably smaller than the grid spacing. A good rule is to start with a snap spacing in the range of the size of the smallest objects that you'll be drawing — 6 inches or 100 millimeters for a building plan, 0.5 inches or 5 millimeters for an architectural detail, ¹⁄₁₆ inch or 1 millimeter for a small mechanical component, and so on.

Leaving the grid on in your drawing all the time is worthwhile because it provides a visual reminder of how far apart things are. This visual reference is especially useful as you zoom in and out.

You don't always want to leave snap turned on, however. Some drawings, such as contour maps, are made up mostly of objects with weird, uneven measurements. Even drawings with many objects that fall on convenient spacings will have some unruly objects that don't. In addition, you sometimes need to turn off snap temporarily to select objects. Despite these caveats, snap is a useful tool in most drawings.

Setting the snap spacing to a reasonable value when you set up a new drawing is a good idea. Toggle snap off (by clicking the SNAP button on the status bar or pressing the F9 key) when you don't need it or find that it's getting in the way. Toggle snap on before drawing objects that align with specific spacings, including text and dimension strings that you want to align neatly.

To use snap effectively, you need to make the snap setting smaller as you zoom in and work on more detailed areas, and larger as you zoom back out. You are likely to find yourself changing the snap setting fairly frequently. The grid setting, on the other hand, can usually remain constant even as you work at different zoom settings; that keeps you oriented as to how far zoomed in you are in the drawing.

Setting linetype and dimension scales

Even though you've engraved the drawing scale factor on your desk and written it on your hand — not vice versa — AutoCAD doesn't know the drawing scale until you enter it. Keeping AutoCAD in the dark is fine as long as you're just drawing continuous lines and curves representing real-world geometry, because you draw these objects at their real-world size, without worrying about plot scale.

As soon as you start adding dimensions (measurements that show the size of the things you're drawing) and using dash-dot linetypes (line patterns that contain gaps in them), you need to tell AutoCAD how to scale the parts of the dimensions and the gaps in the linetypes based on the plot scale. If you forget this, the dimension text and arrowheads can come out very tiny or very large when you plot the drawing, and dash-dot linetype patterns can look waaaay too big or too small. Figure 3-7 shows what I mean.

Figure 3-7:
The dimension and linetype scales need to be just right.

The scale factor that controls dash-dot linetypes is found in a system variable called *LTSCALE* (as in LineType SCALE). The scaling factor that controls dimensions is found in a system variable called *DIMSCALE*. You can change either of these settings at any time, but it's best to set them correctly when you're setting up the drawing.

The following sequence includes directions for typing system variable and command names. When the names are mixed case (for example, LTScale), you can type the full name (**LTSCALE**) or just the letters shown in uppercase (**LTS**) before pressing Enter.

To set the linetype scale from the command line, follow these steps:

1. **Type** LTScale **on the command line and press Enter.**

   AutoCAD responds with a prompt, asking you for the scale factor. The value at the end of the prompt is the current linetype scale setting, as in the following example:

   ```
   Enter new linetype scale factor <1.0000>:
   ```

2. **Type the value you want for the linetype scale on the command line and press Enter.**

   The easiest choice is to set the linetype scale to the drawing scale factor. Some people (myself included) find that the dashes and gaps in dash-dot linetypes get a bit too long when they use the drawing scale factor. If you're one of those people, set LTSCALE to one-half of the drawing scale factor.

Alternatively, you can set LTSCALE in the Linetype Manager dialog box: Choose Format⇨Linetype, click the Show Details button, and type your desired linetype scale in the Global Scale Factor edit box.

To change the dimension scale, use the Dimension Style Manager dialog box. I describe dimensions in detail in Chapter 10, but you should get in the habit of setting the dimension scale during drawing setup. To do so, follow these steps:

1. **Choose Format⇨Dimension Style from the menu bar, or enter** Dimstyle **at the command line.**

   The Dimension Style Manager dialog box appears. New drawings contain the default dimension style named Standard (for English units drawings) or ISO25 (for metric drawings).

2. **Click the Modify button.**

   The Modify Dimension Style dialog box appears.

3. **Click the Fit tab.**

   The Fit tab options appear, including an area called *Scale for Dimension Features.*

4. **In the Scale for Dimension Features area, make sure that the radio button next to the Use Overall Scale Of setting is selected.**

5. **In the text box next to Use Overall Scale Of, type the drawing scale factor for the current drawing.**

   I told you that you'd be using that drawing scale factor a lot!

6. **Click OK to close the Modify Dimension Style dialog box.**

   The Dimension Style Manager dialog box reappears.

7. **Click Close.**

   The Dimension Style Manager dialog box closes. Now when you draw dimensions (see Chapter 10), AutoCAD will scale the dimension text and arrowheads correctly.

Before you start creating dimensions, create your own dimension style(s) for the settings that you want to use. Chapter 10 explains why and how.

Entering drawing properties

You need to do one last bit of bookkeeping before you're finished with model space drawing setup: Enter summary information in the Drawing Properties dialog box, as shown in Figure 3-8. Choose File⇨Drawing Properties to open the Drawing Properties dialog box and then click the Summary tab. Enter the drawing scale you're using and the drawing scale factor, plus any other information you think useful.

Floor plan.dwg Properties

General | Summary | Statistics | Custom

Title: Sheet S3: First floor plan

Subject: Project 024: Kelvin Throop home renovation

Author: Mark Middlebrook

Keywords: Chez Kelvin Casa Kelvino Kelvin's House

Comments: Last updated 22-Feb-2004

Drawing scale factor = 48 (1/4"=1'-0")
LTScale = 24

Hyperlink base:

OK | Cancel | Help

Figure 3-8:
Surveying
your
drawing's
properties.

Plot Layouts for Any Palate

As I describe in Chapter 2, *paper space* is a separate space in each drawing for composing a printed version of that drawing. You create the drawing itself, called the *model,* in *model space.* You then can create one or more plottable views, complete with title block. Each of these plottable views is called a *layout.* AutoCAD saves separate plot settings with each layout — and with the Model tab — so that you can plot each tab differently. In practice, you'll need to use only one of the paper space layout tabs, especially when you're getting started with AutoCAD.

A screen image is worth a thousand paper space explanations. If you haven't yet seen an example out in the wild, refer to Figures 2-7 and 2-8 in Chapter 2. You also may want to open a few of the AutoCAD 2004 sample drawings and click the Model and layout tabs to witness the variety of ways in which paper space is used. A good place to start is `\Program Files\AutoCAD 2005\ Sample\Wilhome.dwg`.

After you complete model space setup, you should create a layout for plotting. You don't need to create the plotting layout right after you create the drawing and do model space setup; you can wait until after you've drawn some geometry. You should set up a layout sooner, not later, however. If any scale or sheet size problems exist, it's better to discover them early.

In AutoCAD 2005, it's still possible to ignore paper space layouts entirely and do all your drawing *and* plotting in model space. But you owe it to yourself to give layouts a try. You'll probably find that they make plotting more consistent and predictable. They'll certainly give you more plotting flexibility when you need it. And you'll certainly encounter drawings from other people that make extensive use of paper space, so you need to understand it if you plan to exchange drawings with anyone else.

Creating a layout

Creating a simple paper space layout is straightforward, thanks to the AutoCAD 2005 Create Layout Wizard, shown in Figure 3-9. (Yes! Finally, a useful AutoCAD wizard.) The command name is LAYOUTWIZARD, which is not to be confused with the WAYOUTLIZARD command for drawing geckos and iguanas! In any event, you can avoid a lot of typing by choosing Tools➪ Wizards➪Create Layout.

Figure 3-9:
The Create
Layout
Wizard.

Although the Create Layout Wizard guides you step by step through the process of creating a paper space layout from scratch, it doesn't eliminate the necessity of coming up with a sensible set of layout parameters. The sheet size and plot scale that you choose provide a certain amount of space for showing your model (see the information earlier in this chapter), and wizards aren't allowed to bend the laws of arithmetic to escape that fact. For example, a map of Texas at a scale of 1 inch = 1 foot won't fit on an -x-11-inch sheet, no way, no how. In other words, garbage in, garbage (lay)out. Fortunately the Create Layout Wizard lends itself to experimentation, and you can easily delete layouts that don't work.

Follow these steps to create a layout:

1. **Choose Tools➪Wizards➪Create Layout, or type** LAYOUTWIZARD **and press Enter.**

2. **Give the new layout a name and then click Next.**

In place of the default name, Layout3, I recommend something more descriptive — for example, *D Size Sheet*.

3. **Choose a printer or plotter to use when plotting this layout, and then click Next.**

   Think of your choice as the *default* plotter for this layout. You can change to a different plotter later, or create page setups that plot the same layout on different plotters.

   Many of the names in the configured plotter list should look familiar because they're your Windows printers (*system printers* in AutoCAD lingo). Names with a PC3 extension represent nonsystem printer drivers. See Chapter 12 for details.

4. **Choose a paper size and specify whether to use inches or millimeters to represent paper units, and then click Next.**

   The available paper sizes depend on the printer or plotter that you selected in Step 3.

5. **Specify the orientation of the drawing on the paper, and then click Next.**

   The icon showing the letter *A* on the piece of paper shows you which orientation is which.

6. **Select a title block, or None (see Figure 3-10).**

   If you choose a title block, specify whether AutoCAD should insert it as a Block — which is preferable in this case — or attach it as an xref. Then click Next.

Figure 3-10: Title block options in the Create Layout Wizard.

Attaching a title block as an xref is a good practice if your title block DWG file is in the same folder as the drawing that you're working on. The Create Layout Wizard's title blocks live in the Template folder that's stored with the AutoCAD Application Data files under your Windows user profile, which isn't — or shouldn't be — where you keep your project files. Thus, in this case Block is a safer choice.

Choose a title block that fits your paper size. If the title block is larger than the paper, the Create Layout Wizard simply lets it run off the paper.

If you don't like any of the supplied title blocks, choose None. You can always draw, insert, or xref a title block later. See Chapter 13 for information about inserting or xrefing a title block.

The list of available title blocks comes from all the DWG files in your AutoCAD Template folder. You can add custom title block drawings to this directory (and delete ones that you never use). If you want to know where to put them, see "Cooking Up Terrific Templates," later in this chapter.

7. Define the arrangement of viewports that AutoCAD should create, and the paper space to model space scale for all viewports. Then click Next.

A paper space layout viewport is a window into model space. You must create at least one viewport to display the model in your new layout. For most 2D drawings, a single viewport is all you need. 3D models often benefit from multiple viewports, each showing the 3D model from a different perspective.

The default Viewport scale, Scaled to Fit, ensures that all of your model drawing displays in the viewport but results in an arbitrary scale factor. Most technical drawings require a specific scale, such as 1 = 10 or ⅛" = 1'–0".

8. Specify the location of the viewport(s) on the paper by picking its corners. Then click Next.

After you click the Select Location button, the Create Layout Wizard displays the preliminary layout with any title block that you've chosen. Pick two points to define a rectangle that falls within the drawing area of your title block (or within the plottable area of the sheet, if you chose no title block in Step 6).

AutoCAD represents the plottable area of the sheet with a dashed rectangle near the edge of the sheet. If you don't select a location for the viewport(s), the Create Layout Wizard creates a viewport that fills the plottable area of the sheet.

9. Click Finish.

AutoCAD creates the new layout.

If your projects require lots of drawings, you can parlay layouts into *sheet sets* — a new feature in AutoCAD 2005 that makes for more sophisticated creation, management, plotting, and electronic transfer of multi-sheet drawing sets. See Chapter 14 for details.

Copying and changing layouts

After you create a layout, you can delete, copy, rename, and otherwise manipulate it by right-clicking its tab. Figure 3-11 shows the right-click menu options.

Figure 3-11:
The right-click menu for a layout tab.

The From Template option refers to layout templates. After you create layouts in a template (DWT) or drawing (DWG) file, you use the From Template option to import these layouts into the current drawing. For details, see the LAYOUT command's Template option in the Command Reference section of online help.

Many drawings require only one paper space layout. If you always plot the same view of the model and always plot to the same device and on the same size paper, a single paper space layout should suffice. If you want to plot your model in different ways (for example, at different scales, with different layers visible, with different areas visible, or with different plotted line characteristics), you may want to create additional paper space layouts.

Some different ways of plotting the same model can be handled in a single paper space layout with different page setups. See Chapter 12 for more details.

If you want to add another viewport to an existing layout, you need to become familiar with the MVIEW command and the ZOOM command's mysterious XP option. See the MVIEW and ZOOM commands in the Command Reference section of AutoCAD online help. After you have the concepts down, using the Viewports dialog box (choose View⇨Viewports⇨New Viewports) and Viewports toolbar can help you create and manage viewports more efficiently.

Lost in paper space

After you create a paper space layout, you suddenly have two views of the same drawing geometry: the view on your original Model tab and the new layout tab view (perhaps decorated with a handsome title block and other accoutrements of plotting nobility). It's important to realize that both views are of the *same* geometry. If you change the model geometry on one tab, you're changing it on all tabs, because all tabs display the same model space objects. It's like seeing double after downing a few too many drinks — the duplication is in your head, not in the real world (or in this case, in the CAD world).

When you make a paper space layout current by clicking its tab, you can move the cursor between paper space (that is, drawing and zooming on the sheet of paper) and model space (drawing and zooming on the model, inside the viewport) in several ways, including:

✓ Clicking the PAPER/MODEL button on the status bar

✓ In the drawing area, double-clicking over a viewport to move the cursor into model space in that viewport, or double-clicking outside all viewports (for example, in the gray area outside the sheet) to move the cursor into paper space

✓ Entering **MSpace** or **PSpace** at the command prompt

When the cursor is in model space, anything you draw or edit changes the model (and thus appears on the Model tab and on all paper space layout tabs, assuming that the given paper space layout displays that part of the underlying model). When the cursor is in paper space, anything you draw appears only on that one paper space layout tab. It's as though you were drawing on an acetate sheet over the top of that sheet of plotter paper — the model beneath remains unaffected.

This distinction can be disorienting at first — even if you haven't had a few too many drinks. To avoid confusion, stick with the following approach (at least until you're more familiar with paper space):

✓ If you want to edit the model, switch to the Model tab first. (Don't try to edit the model in a paper space viewport.)

✔ If you want to edit a particular plot layout without affecting the model, switch to that layout's tab and make sure that the cursor is in paper space.

Cooking Up Terrific Templates

You can create a template from any DWG file by using the Save As dialog box. Follow these steps to save your drawing as a template:

1. **Choose File➪Save As from the menu bar.**

   The Save Drawing As dialog box appears, as shown in Figure 3-12.

Figure 3-12:
Saving a
drawing as
a template.

2. **From the Save As Type pull-down menu, choose AutoCAD Drawing Template (*.dwt).**

3. **Navigate to the folder where you want to store the drawing.**

   AutoCAD 2005's default folder for template drawings is called Template and is buried deep in the bowels of your Windows user profile. Save your templates there if you want them to appear in the AutoCAD's Select Template list. You can save your templates in another folder, but if you want to use them later, you'll have to navigate to that folder each time to use them. See the Technical Stuff paragraph after this procedure for additional suggestions.

4. **Enter a name for the drawing template in the File Name text box.**

5. **Click the Save button to save your drawing template.**

The drawing is saved as a template. A dialog box for the template description and units appears.

6. **Enter the template's measurement units (English or Metric).**

   Enter the key info now; you can't do it later unless you save the template to a different name. Don't bother filling in the Description field. AutoCAD doesn't display it later in the Select Template dialog box.

7. **Click OK to save the file.**

8. **To save your drawing as a regular drawing, choose File⇨Save As from the menu bar.**

   The Save Drawing As dialog box appears again.

9. **From the Save As Type pull-down menu, choose AutoCAD 2004 Drawing (*.dwg).**

   AutoCAD 2005 uses the same DWG file format as AutoCAD 2004, so the file type is listed that way.

10. **Navigate to the folder where you want to store the drawing.**

    Use a different folder from the one with your template drawings.

11. **Enter the name of the drawing in the File Name text box.**

12. **Click the Save button to save your drawing.**

    The file is saved. Now, when you save it in the future, the regular file, not the template file, gets updated.

AutoCAD 2005 includes a new command called QNEW ("Quick NEW"), which, when properly configured, can bypass the Select Template dialog box and create a new drawing from your favorite template. The first button on the Standard toolbar — the one with the plain white sheet of paper — runs the new QNEW command instead of the old NEW command.

To put the Quick into QNEW, though, you have to tell AutoCAD which default template to use: Choose Tools⇨Options⇨Files⇨Drawing Template Settings⇨ Default Template File for QNEW. AutoCAD 2005's default setting for Default Template File for QNEW is None, which causes QNEW to act just like NEW (that is, QNEW opens the Select Template dialog box).

AutoCAD 2005, unlike AutoCAD 2002 and earlier versions, stores template drawings and many other support files under your Windows user folder. If you want to discover where your Template folder is, choose Tools⇨Options⇨ Files⇨Drawing Template Settings⇨Drawing Template File Location. In all likelihood, your Template folder lives under a hidden folder, so you won't at first be able to see it in Windows Explorer. If you want to find the template folder, choose Tools⇨Folder Options⇨View in Windows Explorer. Set the Hidden Files and Folders setting to Show Hidden Files and Folders, click the OK button, and then choose View⇨Refresh. (After you snoop around, you'll probably want to switch back to Do Not Show Hidden Files and Folders.)

If you want to avoid this nonsense, create a folder where you can find it easily (for example, C:\Acad-templates or F:\Acad-custom\templates on a network drive). Put the templates that you actually use there and change the Drawing Template File Location so that it points to your new template folder.

As this chapter demonstrates, there's quite a bit to drawing setup in AutoCAD. As with any other initially forbidding task, take it step by step and soon the sequence will seem natural. The Drawing Setup Roadmap on the Cheat Sheet will help you stay on track and avoid missing a step.

Part II
Let There Be Lines

The 5th Wave   By Rich Tennant

LARRY, THE BALLOON MAN, EMPLOYS A CAD/CAM SOFTWARE PACKAGE INTO HIS BALLOON ANIMAL ACT.

LARRY the BALLOON MAN

In this part . . .

*L*ines, circles, and other elements of geometry make up the heart of your drawing. AutoCAD offers many different drawing commands, many ways to use them to draw objects precisely, and many properties for controlling the objects' display and plot appearance. After you draw your geometry, you'll probably spend at least as much time editing it as your design and drawings evolve. And in the process, you need to zoom in and out and pan all around to see how the entire drawing is coming together. Drawing geometry, editing it, and changing the displayed view are the foundation of the drawing process; this part shows you how to make that foundation solid. And for those who want to build a little higher, this section ends with an introduction to 3D modeling and presentation.

Chapter 4

Get Ready to Draw

CAD programs are different from other drawing programs. You need to pay attention to little details like object properties and the precision of the points that you specify when you draw and edit objects. If you just start drawing objects without taking heed of these details, you'll end up with an unruly mess of imprecise geometry that's hard to edit, view, and plot.

This chapter introduces you to the AutoCAD tools and techniques that help you prevent making CAD messes. This information is essential before you start drawing objects and editing them, which I describe in Chapters 5 and 6.

Drawing and Editing with AutoCAD

When you first start using AutoCAD, its most daunting requirement is the number of property settings and precision controls that you need to pay attention to — even when you draw a simple line. Unlike in many other programs, it's not enough to draw a line in a more-or-less adequate location and then slap some color on it. All those settings and controls can inspire the feeling that you have to find out how to pilot an airliner to make a trip down the street. (The advantage is that, after you *are* comfortable in the cockpit, AutoCAD will take you on the long-haul trips and get you there faster.)

These are the three keys to good CAD drawing practice:

- Pay attention to and manage the *properties* of every object that you draw — especially the layer that each object is on.

- Pay attention to and manage the *named objects* in every drawing — the layers, text styles, block definitions, and other nongraphical objects that serve to define the look of all the graphical objects in the drawing.

- Pay attention to and control the *precision* of every point and distance that you use to draw and edit each object.

These can seem like daunting tasks at first, but the following three sections help you cut them down to size.

Managing Your Properties

All the objects that you draw in AutoCAD are like good Monopoly players: They own *properties*. In AutoCAD, these properties aren't physical things; they're an object's characteristics such as layer, color, linetype, and lineweight. You use properties to communicate information about the characteristics of the objects you draw, such as the kinds of real-world objects they represent, their materials, their relative location in space, or their relative importance. In CAD, you also use the properties to organize objects for editing and plotting purposes.

You can view — and change — all of an object's properties in the Properties palette. In Figure 4-1, the Properties palette shows properties for a line object.

Figure 4-1:
A line
rich in
properties.

TIP

To toggle the Properties palette on and off, click the Properties button on the Standard toolbar. Before you select an object, the Properties palette displays the *current properties* — properties that AutoCAD applies to new objects when you draw them. After you select an object, AutoCAD displays the properties for that object. If you select more than one object, AutoCAD displays the properties that they have in common.

Putting it on a layer

Every object has a *layer* as one of its properties. You may be familiar with layers — independent drawing spaces that stack on top of each other to create an overall image — from using drawing programs. AutoCAD, like most CAD programs, uses layers as the primary organizing principle for all the objects that you draw. Layers organize objects into logical groups of things that belong together; for example, walls, furniture, and text notes usually belong on three separate layers, for a couple of reasons:

- ✔ They give you a way to turn groups of objects on and off — both on the screen and on the plot.
- ✔ They provide the best way of controlling object color, linetype, and lineweight.

Looking at layers

If you spent any time "on the boards," as grizzled old-timers like to call paper-and-pencil drafting, you may be familiar with the manual drafting equivalent of layers. In *pin-bar drafting*, you stack a series of transparent Mylar sheets, each of which contains a part of the overall drawing — walls on one sheet, the plumbing system on another, the electrical system on another, and so on. You can get different views of the drawing set by including or excluding various sheets.

If you're too young to remember pin-bar drafting — or old enough to prefer not to — you may remember something similar from a textbook about human anatomy. There's the skeleton on one sheet, the muscles on the next sheet that you laid over the skeleton, and so on until you built up a complete picture of the human body — that is, if your parents didn't remove some of the more grown-up sections.

CAD layers serve a similar purpose; they enable you to turn on or off groups of related objects. But layers do a lot more. You use them in AutoCAD to control other object display and plot properties, such as color, linetype, and lineweight. You also can use them to make some editing tasks more efficient and reduce the time that it takes AutoCAD to load some drawings. Take the time to give each of your drawings a suitably layered look.

You create layers, assign them names, assign them properties such as color and linetype, and then put objects on them. When you draw an object, AutoCAD automatically puts it on the *current* layer, which appears in the drop-down list on the Layers toolbar.

Before you draw any object in AutoCAD, you should set an appropriate layer current — creating it first, if necessary, using the procedure described later in this section. If the layer already exists in your drawing, you can make it the current layer by choosing it in the Layers toolbar, as shown in Figure 4-2.

Make sure that no objects are selected before you use the Layer drop-down list to change the current layer. (Press the Esc key twice to be sure.) If objects are selected, the Layer drop-down list displays — and lets you change — those objects' layer. When no objects are selected, the Layer drop-down list displays — and lets you change — the current layer.

If you forget to set an appropriate layer before you draw an object, you can select the object and then change its layer by using either the Properties palette or the Layer drop-down list.

Figure 4-2:
Set a current layer before you draw.

Stacking up your layers

How do you decide what to call your layers and which objects to put on them? Some industries have developed layer guidelines, and many offices have created documented layer standards. Some projects even impose specific layer requirements. (But be careful; if someone says, "You need a brick layer for this project," that can mean a couple of different things.) Ask experienced CAD drafters in your office or industry how they use layers in AutoCAD. If you can't find any definitive answer, create a chart of layers for yourself. Each row in the chart should list the layer name, default color, default linetype, default lineweight, and what kinds of objects belong on that layer. Chapter 15 includes an example.

Accumulating properties

Besides layers, the remaining object properties that you're likely to want to use often are color, linetype, lineweight, and possibly plot style. Table 4-1 summarizes these four properties.

Table 4-1	Useful Object Properties
Property	*Controls*
Color	Displayed color and plotted color or lineweight
Linetype	Displayed and plotted dash-dot line pattern
Lineweight	Displayed and plotted line width
Plot style	Plotted characteristics (see Chapter 12)

In Release 14 and older versions of AutoCAD, color also controlled the plotted lineweight of each object — strange, but now very common in the AutoCAD world. You may find yourself working this way even in AutoCAD 2005, for compatibility with drawings (and co-workers) that use the old way, as described in the "About colors and lineweights" sidebar.

AutoCAD gives you two different ways of controlling object properties:

✔ **By layer:** Each layer has a default color, linetype, lineweight, and plot style property. Unless you tell AutoCAD otherwise, objects inherit the properties of the layers on which they're created. AutoCAD calls this approach controlling properties *by layer*.

✔ **By object:** AutoCAD also enables you to override an object's layer's property setting and give the object a specific color, linetype, lineweight, or plot style that differs from the layer's. AutoCAD calls this approach controlling properties *by object*.

If you've worked with other graphics programs, you may be used to assigning properties such as color to specific objects. If so, you'll be tempted to use the by object approach to assigning properties in AutoCAD. Resist the temptation. In almost all cases, it's better to create layers, assign properties to each layer, and let the objects on each layer inherit that layer's properties. Here are some benefits of using the by layer approach:

✔ You can easily change the properties of a group of related objects that you put on one layer. You simply change the property for the layer, not for a bunch of separate objects.

✔ Experienced drafters use the by layer approach, so if you work with drawings from other people, you'll be much more compatible with them if you do it the same way. You'll also avoid getting yelled at by irate CAD managers, whose jobs include haranguing any hapless newbies who assign properties by object.

About colors and lineweights

AutoCAD drafters traditionally have achieved different printed lineweights by mapping various on-screen display colors of drawing objects to different plotted lineweights. An AutoCAD-using company may decide that red lines are to be plotted thin, green lines are to be plotted thicker, and so on. This indirect approach sounds strange, but until AutoCAD 2000, it was the only practical way to plot from AutoCAD with a variety of lineweights. Also, not many people plotted in color until recently, so few folks minded the fact that color was used to serve a different master.

AutoCAD 2000 added lineweight as an inherent property of objects and the layers that they live on. Thus, object display color can revert to being used for — surprise! — color. You can use display colors to control plot colors, of course. But even if you make monochrome plots, you can use color to help you distinguish different kinds of objects when you view them on-screen or to make jazzy on-screen presentations of drawings for others.

Lineweights are handy, but they have quirks. Watch for these problems as you work with them:

✔ Although lineweights may have been assigned to objects in a drawing that you open, you won't necessarily see them on the screen. You must turn on the Show/Hide Lineweight button on the AutoCAD status bar (the button labeled LWT).

✔ On a slow computer or a complex drawing, showing lineweights may cause AutoCAD to redraw the screen more slowly when you zoom and pan.

✔ You may need to zoom in on a portion of the drawing before the differing lineweights become apparent.

If you take my advice and assign properties by layer, all you have to do is set layer properties in the Layer Properties Manager dialog box, as shown in Figure 4-3. Before you draw any objects, make sure the Color Control, Linetype Control, Lineweight Control, and Plotstyle Control drop-down lists on the Properties toolbar are set to ByLayer, as shown in Figure 4-4.

Figure 4-3:
Use layer properties to control object properties.

Figure 4-4:
ByLayer all the way.

If the drawing is set to use color-based plot styles instead of named plot styles (see Chapter 12), the Plotstyle Control drop-down list will be inactive and will display `ByColor`.

If you don't like doing things the wrong way and getting yelled at by CAD managers, don't assign properties to objects in either of these ways:

✔ Don't choose a specific color, linetype, lineweight, or plot style from the appropriate drop-down list on the Object Properties toolbar, and then draw the objects.

✔ Don't draw the objects, select them, and then choose a property from the same drop-down lists.

If you prefer to do things the right way, assign these properties by layer, as I describe in this section.

Creating new layers

If a suitable layer doesn't exist, you need to create one by using the Layer Properties Manager dialog box. Follow these steps:

1. **Click the Layer Properties Manager button on the Layers toolbar; or type** LAyer **at the command line and press Enter.**

   The Layer Properties Manager dialog box appears. A new drawing has only one layer, Layer 0. You need to add the layers you need for your drawing.

2. **Click the New Layer button (the little yellow explosion just above the Status column) to create a new layer.**

   A new layer appears. AutoCAD names it Layer1, but you can type a new name to replace it easily, as shown in Figure 4-5.

Figure 4-5:
Adding a new layer in the Layer Properties Manager dialog box.

3. **Type a name for the new layer.**

   For the following reasons, type the layer name with *initial caps* (only the first letter of words in uppercase) if you can:

   • Layer names written completely in uppercase are much wider, which means that they often get *truncated* in the Layers toolbar's Layer drop-down list.

   • Uppercase layer names look like they're *SHOUTING*, which is not very polite.

4. **On the same line as the new layer, click the color block or color name (White) of the new layer.**

   The Select Color dialog box appears, as shown in Figure 4-6.

Figure 4-6:
The Select
Color dialog
box.
Magenta is
selected
from the
Standard
Colors list.

The normal AutoCAD color scheme — AutoCAD Color Index (ACI) — provides 255 colors. So many choices are nice for rendering work but overkill for ordinary drafting.

For now, stick with the first nine colors — the ones that appear in a single, separate row to the left of the ByLayer and ByBlock buttons on the Index Color tab of the Select Color dialog box.

- These colors are easy to distinguish from one another.

- Using a small number of colors makes configuring your plot parameters easier. (I describe the procedure in Chapter 12.)

AutoCAD (but not AutoCAD LT) provides an even more extravagant set of color choices than the 255 shown on the ACI tab. In the Select Color dialog box, the True Color tab offers a choice of more than 16 million colors, which you can specify by using HSL (Hue Saturation Luminance) or RGB (Red Green Blue) numbers. The Color Book tab enables you to use PANTONE and RAL color schemes, which are popular in publishing. If your work requires tons of colors or close color matching between the computer screen and printed output, you're probably familiar with the relevant color palette and how to use it. If you're using AutoCAD for ordinary drafting or design, stick with the AutoCAD Color Index palette.

5. Click a color to select it as the color for this layer; then click OK.

The Layer Properties Manager dialog box reappears. In the Name list, the color for the new layer changes to either the name or the number of the color that you selected.

AutoCAD's first seven colors have both assigned numbers and standard names: 1 = red, 2 = yellow, 3 = green, 4 = cyan, 5 = blue, 6 = magenta, and 7 = white (but it appears black when displayed on a white background). The remaining 248 colors have numbers only. You can play fashion designer and make up your own names for these colors. How about Overly Oxidized Ocher for color number 16?

6. On the same line as the new layer, click the Linetype name of the new layer.

The default AutoCAD linetype is Continuous, which means no gaps in the line.

The Select Linetype dialog box appears, as shown in Figure 4-7.

Figure 4-7:
The Select
Linetype
dialog box.

Linetype	Appearance	Description
CENTER	———— – ————	Center
Continuous	————————	Solid line
HIDDEN	————————	Hidden

(Select Linetype dialog box — Loaded linetypes, with OK, Cancel, Load..., Help buttons)

If you already loaded the linetypes you need for your drawing, the Select Linetype dialog box displays them in the Loaded Linetypes list. If not, click the Load button to open the Load or Reload Linetypes dialog box. By default, AutoCAD displays linetypes from the standard AutoCAD 2004 linetype definition file — `Acad.lin` for imperial units drawings or `Acadiso.lin` for metric units drawings. Load the desired linetype by selecting its name and clicking the OK button.

The linetypes whose names begin with ACAD_ISO are for people who use ISO (International Organization for Standardization) linetype patterns. If you don't follow ISO standards, you'll probably find it easier to use the linetypes with the more descriptive names: CENTER, DASHED, and so on.

7. Click the desired linetype in the Loaded Linetypes list to select it as the linetype for the layer; then click OK.

The Select Linetype dialog box disappears, returning you to the Layer Properties Manager dialog box. In the Name list, the linetype for the selected layer changes to the linetype you just chose.

8. On the same line as the new layer, click the new layer's lineweight.

The Lineweight dialog box appears, as shown in Figure 4-8.

9. Select the lineweight you want from the scrolling list, then click OK.

The lineweight 0.00 mm tells AutoCAD to use the thinnest possible lineweight on the screen and on the plot. I recommend that, for now, you leave lineweight set to Default and instead map screen color to plotted lineweight, as described briefly in the "About colors and lineweights" sidebar earlier in this chapter and in greater detail in Chapter 12.

Figure 4-8:
The
Lineweight
dialog box.

The default lineweight for the current drawing is defined in the Lineweight Settings dialog box. After you close the Layer Properties Manager dialog box, choose Format⇨Lineweight or enter **LWeight** at the command line to change the default lineweight.

You use the plot style property to assign a named plot style to the layer, but only if you're using named plot styles in the drawing (Chapter 12 explains why you probably don't want to). The final property, Plot, controls whether the layer's objects appear on plots. Toggle this setting off for any layer whose objects you want to see on the screen but hide on plots.

10. **If you want to add a description to the layer, scroll the layer list to the right to see the Description column, click twice in the Description box corresponding to your new layer, and type a description.**

   Layer descriptions are a new feature of AutoCAD 2005. If you choose to use them, stretch the Layer Properties Manager dialog box to the right so that you can see the descriptions without having to scroll the layer list.

11. **Repeat Steps 2 through 10 to create any other layers that you want.**

12. **Select the new layer that you want to make current and click the Set Current button (the green check mark).**

   The current layer is the one on which AutoCAD places new objects that you draw.

13. **Click OK to accept the new layer settings.**

   The Layer drop-down list on the Layers toolbar now displays your new layer as the current layer.

After you create layers, you can set any one of them to be the current layer. Make sure that no objects are selected; then choose the layer name from the Layer drop-down list on the Layers toolbar.

After you create layers and drawn objects on them, you use the Layer Properties Manager dialog box to change layer properties. For example, you can turn a layer off or on to hide or show the objects on that layer.

If you find yourself using lots of layers, you can create *layer filters* to make viewing and managing the layer list easier. AutoCAD 2005 provides two kinds of layer filters: group and property. A *group filter* is simply a subset of layers that you choose (by dragging layer names into the group filter name or by selecting objects in the drawing). A *property filter* is a subset of layers that AutoCAD creates and updates automatically based on layer property criteria that you define (for example, all layer names whose names contain the text **Wall** or whose color is green). To find out more, click the Help button on the Layer Properties Manager dialog box and read about the New Property Filter and New Group Filter buttons.

A load of linetypes

My layer creation procedure demonstrates how to load a single linetype, but AutoCAD comes with a whole lot of linetypes, and there are other ways of working with them. You don't have to go through the Layer Properties Manager dialog box to load linetypes. You can perform the full range of linetype management tasks by choosing Format⇨Linetype, which displays the Linetype Manager dialog box. This dialog box is similar to the Select Linetype dialog box described in the layer creation procedure, but it includes some additional options.

After you click the Load button to display the Load or Reload Linetypes dialog box, you can load multiple linetypes in one fell swoop by holding down the Shift or Ctrl key while you click linetype names. As in most Windows dialog boxes, Shift+click selects all objects between the first and second clicks, and Ctrl+click enables you to select multiple objects, even if they aren't next to each other.

When you load a linetype, AutoCAD copies its *linetype definition* — a recipe for how to create the dashes, dots, and gaps in that particular linetype — from the Acad.lin (imperial units) or Acadiso.lin (metric units) file into the drawing. The recipe doesn't automatically

appear in other drawings; you have to load each linetype that you want to use into each drawing in which you want to use it. If you find yourself loading the same linetypes repeatedly into different drawings, consider adding them to your template drawings instead. (See Chapter 3 for information about templates and how to create them.) After you add linetypes to a template drawing, all new drawings that you create from that template will start with those linetypes loaded automatically.

Don't go overboard on loading linetypes. For example, you don't need to load all the linetypes in the Acad.lin file on the off chance that you might use them all someday. The resulting linetype list would be long and unwieldy. Most drawings require only a few linetypes, and most industries and companies settle on a half dozen or so linetypes for common use. Your industry, office, or project may have guidelines about which linetypes to use for which purposes.

If you're the creative type and don't mind editing a text file that contains linetype definitions, you can define your own linetypes. Choose Contents⇨Customization Guide⇨Custom Linetypes in the AutoCAD 2005 online help system.

Using AutoCAD DesignCenter

DesignCenter is a dumb name for a useful, if somewhat busy, palette. (Chapter 2 describes how to turn on and work with palettes.) The DesignCenter palette is handy for mining data from all kinds of drawings. Whereas the Properties palette, described earlier in this chapter, is concerned with object properties, the DesignCenter palette deals primarily with named objects: layers, linetypes, block (that is, symbol) definitions, text styles, and other organizational objects in your drawings.

Named objects

Every drawing includes a set of *symbol tables,* which contain *named objects.* For example, the *layer table* contains a list of the layers in the current drawing, along with the settings for each layer (color, linetype, on/off setting, and so on). Each of these table objects, be it a layer or some other type, has a name, so Autodesk decided to call them *named objects* (duh!).

Neither the symbol tables nor the named objects appear as graphical objects in your drawing. They're like hardworking stagehands who keep the show running smoothly behind the scenes. The named objects include

- Layers (this chapter)
- Linetypes (this chapter)
- Text styles (Chapter 9)
- Dimension styles (Chapter 10)
- Block definitions and xrefs (Chapter 13)
- Layouts (Chapter 3)

When you use commands such as LAyer, LineType, and Dimstyle, you are creating and editing named objects. After you've created named objects in a drawing, DesignCenter gives you the tools to copy them to other drawings.

Getting (Design) Centered

The DesignCenter palette (shown in Figure 4-9) consists of a toolbar at the top, a set of tabs below that, a navigation pane on the left, and a content pane on the right. The navigation pane displays a tree view with drawing files and the symbol tables contained in each drawing. The content pane usually displays the contents of the drawing or symbol table.

Navigation pane

Toolbar   Tabs   Content pane

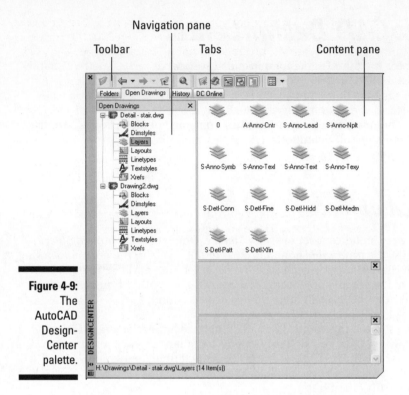

Figure 4-9:
The
AutoCAD
Design-
Center
palette.

The four tabs just below the DesignCenter toolbar control what you see in the navigation and content panes:

✔ **Folders** shows the folders on your local and network disks, just like the Windows Explorer Folders pane does. Use this tab to copy named objects from drawings that you don't currently have open in AutoCAD.

✔ **Open Drawings** shows the drawings that are open in AutoCAD. Use this tab to copy named objects between open drawings.

✔ **History** shows drawings that you've recently browsed in DesignCenter. Use this tab to jump quickly to drawings that you've used recently on the Folders tab.

✔ **DC Online** shows parts libraries that are available on Autodesk's and other companies' Web sites. This tab is essentially an advertising vehicle for software companies offering to sell you symbol libraries and manufacturers encouraging you to specify their products. Browse the offerings on this tab to see whether any of the online libraries can be useful in your work.

The toolbar buttons further refine what you see in the navigation and content panes. A few of these buttons toggle off and on different parts of the panes. If your DesignCenter palette is missing an area that appears in Figure 4-9, click each of the buttons until the missing part reappears.

Follow these steps to use DesignCenter:

1. **Load the drawing(s) whose content you want to view or use into the navigation pane on the left.**

    If a drawing doesn't appear on the Open Drawings tab, click the Load button — the first one on the DesignCenter toolbar — to load it into the navigation pane.

2. **Navigate the symbol tables (such as blocks and layers), viewing their individual named objects in the content pane on the right.**

3. **If you need them, drag or copy and paste individual named objects from the content pane into other open AutoCAD drawings.**

Copying layers between drawings

The following steps copy layers from one drawing to another using Design-Center. You can use the same technique to copy dimension styles, layouts, linetypes, and text styles.

1. **Toggle the DesignCenter palette on by choosing the DesignCenter button on the Standard toolbar or pressing Ctrl+2.**

2. **Open or create a drawing containing named objects you want to copy.**

    You can also use the Folders tab, the Open button, or the Search button to load a drawing into DesignCenter without opening it in AutoCAD.

3. **Open or create a second drawing to which you want to copy the named objects.**

4. **Click the Open Drawings tab to display your two currently opened drawings in DesignCenter's navigation pane on the left.**

    If you used the Folders tab, the Open button, or the Search button in Step 2, skip this step; DesignCenter already displays the drawing you selected on the Folders tab.

5. **If DesignCenter doesn't display the symbol tables indented underneath the source drawing (the one you opened in Step 2), as shown in Figure 4-9, click the plus sign next to the drawing's name to display them.**

6. **Click the Layers table to display the source drawing's layers in the content pane.**

7. **Choose one or more layers in the content pane.**

8. **Right-click in the content pane and choose Copy from the cursor menu to copy the layer(s) to the Windows Clipboard.**

9. **Click in the AutoCAD destination drawing's window (the drawing that you opened in Step 3).**

10. **Right-click and choose Paste from the cursor menu.**

    AutoCAD copies the layers into the current drawing, using the colors, linetypes, and other settings from the source drawing.

Two other ways exist to copy layers from DesignCenter. You can drag layers from the content pane to a drawing window. You also can right-click in the content pane and choose Add Layer(s) from the cursor menu, which adds layers to the current drawing. The copy-and-paste method in my example requires the least amount of manual dexterity and less guesswork about which drawing the layers get added to.

If the current drawing contains a layer whose name matches the name of one of the layers you're copying, AutoCAD doesn't change that layer's definition. For example, if you drag a layer named Doors whose color is red into a drawing that already includes a layer called Doors whose color is green, the target drawing's Doors layer remains green. Named objects from DesignCenter never overwrite objects with the same name in the destination drawing. AutoCAD always displays the message "Duplicate definitions will be ignored" even if there aren't any duplicates.

If you're repeatedly copying named objects from the same drawings or folders, add them to your DesignCenter favorites list. On the Folders tab, right-click the drawing or folder and choose Add to Favorites from the cursor menu. This procedure adds another shortcut to your list of favorites.

  ✔ To see your favorites, click the DesignCenter toolbar's Favorites button.
  ✔ To return to a favorite, double-click its shortcut in the content pane.

Precise-liness Is Next to CAD-liness

Drawing precision is vital to good CAD drafting practice, even more than for manual drafting. If you think CAD managers get testy when you assign properties by object instead of by layer, wait until they berate someone who doesn't use precision techniques when creating drawings in AutoCAD.

CAD precision versus accuracy

We often use the words *precision* and *accuracy* interchangeably, but I think it's useful to maintain a distinction. When I use the word *precision*, I mean controlling the placement of objects so they lie exactly where you want them to lie in the drawing. For example, lines whose endpoints meet must meet exactly, and a circle that's supposed to be centered on the coordinates 0,0 must be drawn with its center exactly at 0,0. I use *accuracy* to refer to the degree to which your drawing matches its real-world counterpart. An accurate floor plan is one in which the dimensions of the CAD objects equal the dimensions of the as-built house.

CAD precision usually helps produce accurate drawings, but that's not always the case. You can produce a precise CAD drawing that's inaccurate because you started from inaccurate information (for example, the contractor gave you a wrong field measurement). Or you might deliberately exaggerate certain distances to convey the relationship between objects more clearly on the plotted drawing. Even where you must sacrifice accuracy, aim for precision.

In CAD, lack of precision makes later editing, hatching, and dimensioning tasks much more difficult and time consuming:

- Small errors in precision in the early stages of creating or editing a drawing often have a big effect on productivity and precision later.

- Drawings may guide manufacturing and construction projects; drawing data may drive automatic manufacturing machinery. Huge amounts of money, even lives, can ride on a drawing's precision.

In recognition of this, a passion for precision permeates the profession. Permanently. Precision is one of the characteristics that separates CAD from ordinary illustration-type drawing work. The sooner you get fussy about precision in AutoCAD, the happier everyone is.

In the context of drawing objects, *precision* means specifying points and distances precisely, and AutoCAD provides a range of tools for doing so. Table 4-2 lists the more important AutoCAD precision techniques, plus the status bar buttons that you click to toggle some of the features off and on.

Precision is especially important when you're drawing or editing *geometry* — the lines, arcs, and so on that make up whatever you're representing in the CAD drawing. Precision placement usually is less important with notes, leaders, and other *annotations* that describe, not show.

Table 4-2	Precision Techniques	
Technique	**Status Bar Button**	**Description**
Coordinate entry	—	Type exact X,Y coordinates.
Single-point object snaps	—	Pick points on existing objects (lasts for one point pick).
Running object snaps	OSNAP	Pick points on existing objects (lasts for multiple point picks).
Snap	SNAP	Pick points on an imaginary grid of equally spaced "hot spots."
Ortho	ORTHO	Constrain the cursor to move at an angle of 0, 90, 180, or 270 degrees from the previous point.
Direct distance entry	—	Point the cursor in a direction and type a distance.
Object snap tracking	OTRACK	Helps the cursor locate points based on multiple object snap points.
Polar tracking	POLAR	Makes the cursor prefer certain angles.
Polar snap	—	Causes the cursor to prefer certain distances along polar tracking angles.

Before you draw objects, always check the status bar's SNAP, ORTHO, POLAR, OSNAP, and OTRACK buttons and set the buttons according to your precision needs.

✔ A button that looks *pushed in* indicates that the feature is *on*.

✔ A button that looks *popped up* indicates that the feature is *off*.

Keyboard capers: Coordinate entry

The most direct way to enter points precisely is to type numbers at the command line. AutoCAD uses these keyboard coordinate entry formats:

✔ Absolute rectangular coordinates in the form *X,Y* (for example: 7,4)

✔ Relative rectangular coordinates in the form *@X,Y* (for example: @3,2)

✔ Relative polar coordinates in the form *@distance<angle* (for example: @6<45)

AutoCAD locates *absolute rectangular coordinates* with respect to the 0,0 point of the drawing — usually its lower-left corner. AutoCAD locates *relative rectangular coordinates* and *relative polar coordinates* with respect to the previous point that you picked or typed. Figure 4-10 demonstrates how to use all three coordinate formats to draw a pair of line segments that start at absolute coordinates 2,1; go 3 units to the right and 2 units up; then go 4 units at an angle of 60 degrees.

AutoCAD also understands *absolute polar coordinates* in the form *distance<angle*, but this format is almost never useful.

Relative rectangular coordinates

Absolute rectangular coordinates   Relative polar coordinates

Figure 4-10:
Coordinating
from the
keyboard.

You can view coordinate locations by moving the cursor around in the drawing area and reading the Coordinates area at the left of the status bar. The X,Y coordinates should change as you move the cursor. If the coordinates don't change, click the Coordinates area until the command line says <Coords on>. Although it's not apparent at first, there are in fact two <Coords on> display modes: absolute coordinates and polar coordinates. If you start a command such as LINE, pick a point, and then click the Coordinates area a few times, the display changes from coordinates off to live absolute coordinates (X,Y position) to live polar coordinates (distance and angle from the previous point). The live polar coordinates display mode is the most informative most of the time.

When you type coordinates at the command line, do *not* add any spaces, because AutoCAD interprets them as though you've pressed Enter. This "Spacebar = Enter" weirdness is a productivity feature that's been in AutoCAD forever. It's easier to find the spacebar than the Enter key when you're entering lots of commands and coordinates in a hurry.

If you're working in architectural or engineering units, the default unit of entry is *inches,* not feet.

✔ To specify feet, you must enter the symbol for feet after the number, for example:

> **6'** for 6 feet

✔ You can enter a dash to separate feet from inches, as architects often do:

> **6'–6"** is 6 feet, 6 inches.

✔ Both the dash and the inch mark are optional when you're entering coordinates and distances:

> AutoCAD understands **6'6"** and **6'6** as the same as **6'–6"**.

✔ If you're typing a coordinate or distance that contains fractional inches, you *must* enter a dash — not a space — between the whole number of inches and the fraction:

> **6'6–1/2** (or **6'–6–1/2**) represents 6 feet, 6½ inches.

✔ If all this dashing about confuses you, enter partial inches by using decimals instead:

> **6'6.5** is the same as **6'6–1/2** to AutoCAD, whether you're working in architectural or engineering units.

Grab an object and make it snappy

After you've drawn a few objects precisely in a new drawing, the most efficient way to draw more objects with equal precision is to grab *points,* such as endpoints, midpoints, or quadrants, on the existing objects. AutoCAD calls this *object snapping*, because the program pulls, or *snaps*, the cursor to a point on an existing *object*. The object snapping feature in general and object snap points in particular often are called *osnaps*.

I'd like to make just one point

AutoCAD provides two kinds of object snapping modes:

✔ *Single point* (or *override*) object snaps

A single point object snap lasts just while you pick one point.

✔ *Running* object snaps

A running object snap stays in effect until you turn it off.

Here's how you draw precise lines by using single point object snaps:

1. **Open a drawing containing some geometry.**

2. **Turn off running osnap mode by clicking the OSNAP button on the status bar until the button appears to be pushed out and the words** `<Osnap off>` **appear on the command line.**

Although you can use single point object snaps while running object snap mode is turned on, you should turn off running osnap mode while you're getting familiar with single point object snaps. After you've gotten the hang of each feature separately, you can use them together.

3. **Start the LINE command by clicking the Line button on the Draw toolbar.**

The command line prompts you to select the first endpoint of the line:

```
Specify first point:
```

4. **Hold down the Shift key, right-click anywhere in the drawing area, and release the Shift key.**

If you find the Shift+right-click sequence awkward, you can avoid it by using the Object Snap toolbar instead. To turn the toolbar on, point to any toolbar button, right-click, and choose Object Snap. Now you can activate a single point object snap by clicking its toolbar button.

The object snap cursor menu appears, as shown in Figure 4-11.

5. **Choose an object snap mode, such as Endpoint, from the object snap cursor menu.**

The object snap cursor menu disappears, and the command line displays an additional prompt indicating that you've directed AutoCAD to seek out, for example, endpoints of existing objects:

```
_endp of:
```

Figure 4-11:
The object
snap cursor
menu.

6. **Move the cursor slowly around the drawing, pausing over various lines and other objects without clicking yet.**

   When you move the cursor near an object with an endpoint, a colored square icon appears at the endpoint, indicating that AutoCAD can snap to that point. If you stop moving the cursor for a moment, a yellow ToolTip displaying the object snap mode (for example, Endpoint) appears to reinforce the idea.

7. **When the endpoint object snap square appears on the point you want to snap to, click.**

   AutoCAD snaps to the endpoint, which becomes the first point of the new line segment that you're about to draw. The command line prompts you to select the other endpoint of the new line segment:

   ```
   Specify next point or [Undo]:
   ```

   When you move the cursor around the drawing, AutoCAD no longer seeks out endpoints because single point object snaps last only for a single pick. Use the object snap cursor menu again to snap the other end of your new line segment to another point on an existing object.

8. **Use the "press Shift, right-click, release Shift" sequence described in Step 4 to display the object snap cursor menu, and then choose another object snap mode, such as Midpoint, from the object snap cursor menu.**

   The command line displays an additional prompt indicating that you've directed AutoCAD to seek, for example, midpoints of existing objects:

   ```
   _mid of:
   ```

When you move the cursor near the midpoint of an object, a colored triangle appears at the snap point. Each object snap type (endpoint, midpoint,
intersection, and so on) displays a different symbol. If you stop moving
the cursor, the ToolTip text reminds you what the symbol means. Figure
4-12 shows what the screen looks like during this step.

9. **Draw additional line segments by picking additional points. Use the
   object snap cursor menu to specify a single object snap type before
   you pick each point.**

   Try the Intersection, Perpendicular, and Nearest object snaps. If your
   drawing contains arcs or circles, try Center and Quadrant.

10. **When you're finished experimenting with single point object snaps,
    right-click anywhere in the drawing area and choose Enter from the
    cursor menu.**

New line segment

Already object-snapped to endpoint   About to object-snap to midpoint

Figure 4-12:
A snappy
line.

There's a difference between right-clicking and Shift+right-clicking in the drawing area:

- Right-clicking displays menu options for the current command (or common commands and settings when no command is active).
- Shift+right-clicking always displays the same object snap cursor menu.

AutoCAD 2005 includes a new Mid Between 2 Points (**M2P**) object snap mode, which finds the point lying exactly halfway between two other points. You should use precision techniques, such as other object snaps, to select the two points.

Run with object snaps

Often, you use an object snap mode (such as endpoint) repeatedly. Running object snaps address this need. These steps set a running object snap:

1. **Right-click the OSNAP button on the status bar.**

2. **Choose the Settings option.**

   The Object Snap tab on the Drafting Settings dialog box appears, as shown in Figure 4-13.

3. **Select one or more object snap modes by checking the appropriate boxes.**

4. **Click OK to close the dialog box.**

Figure 4-13: Grabbing multiple object features is an osnap.

You click the OSNAP button on the status bar to toggle running object snap mode off and on. After you turn on running object snap, AutoCAD hunts for points that correspond to the object snap modes you checked in the Drafting Settings dialog box. As with single-point object snaps, AutoCAD displays a special symbol — such as a square for an endpoint object snap — to indicate that it has found an object snap point. If you keep the cursor still, AutoCAD also displays a ToolTip that lists the kind of object snap point.

Use single point or running object snaps to enforce precision by making sure that new points you pick coincide *exactly* with points on existing objects. In CAD, it's not good enough for points to almost coincide or to look like they coincide. AutoCAD knows the difference between "looks the same" and "*is* the same," and will cause you untold amounts of grief if you try to make do with "looks the same." You lose points, both figuratively and literally, if you don't use object snaps or one of the other precision techniques covered in this chapter to enforce precision.

Other precision practices

The following are some other AutoCAD precision techniques (refer to Table 4-2, earlier in this chapter):

✔ **Snap:** If you turn on snap mode, AutoCAD constrains the cursor to an imaginary rectangular grid of points at the spacing that you've specified. Follow these steps to turn on snap mode:

  1. Right-click the SNAP button on the status bar.

  2. Choose the Settings option.

  The Snap and Grid tab on the Drafting Settings dialog box appears.

  3. Enter a snap spacing in the Snap X Spacing field and then click OK.

  Click the SNAP button on the status bar or Press F9 to toggle snap mode off and on. To use snap effectively, change the snap spacing frequently — changing to a smaller spacing as you zoom in and work on smaller areas. You often need to toggle snap off and on, because selecting objects and some editing tasks are easier with snap off.

✔ **Ortho:** Ortho mode constrains the cursor to move at right angles (orthogonally) to the previous point. Click the ORTHO button on the status bar or Press F8 to toggle ortho mode off and on. Because technical drawings often include lots of orthogonal lines, you'll use ortho mode a lot.

✔ **Direct distance entry:** This "point and type" technique is an easy and efficient way to draw with precision. You simply point the cursor in a particular direction, type a distance at the command line, and press Enter. AutoCAD calls it "direct distance entry" because it avoids the indirect command line method of specifying a distance by typing relative or polar coordinates. (I describe this older method earlier in this chapter.) You can use direct distance entry any time the crosshair cursor is anchored to a point and the command line prompts you for another point or a distance. You'll usually use direct distance entry with ortho mode turned on, to specify a distance in an orthogonal direction (0, 90, 180, or 270 degrees). You also can combine direct distance entry with polar tracking to specify distances in non-orthogonal directions (for example, in angle increments of 45 degrees).

✔ **Object snap tracking:** This feature extends running object snaps so that you can locate points based on more than one object snap point. For example, you can pick a point at the center of a square by tracking to the midpoints of two perpendicular sides. (AutoCAD LT lacks the object snap tracking feature.)

✔ **Polar tracking:** When you turn on polar tracking, the cursor jumps to increments of the angle you selected. When the cursor jumps, a ToolTip label starting with `Polar:` appears. Right-click the POLAR button on the status bar and choose the Settings option to display the Polar Tracking tab on the Drafting Settings dialog box. Select an angle from the Increment Angle drop-down list and then click OK. Click the POLAR button on the status bar or press F10 to toggle polar tracking mode off and on.

✔ **Polar snap:** You can force polar tracking to jump to specific incremental distances along the tracking angles by changing the snap type from Grid snap to Polar snap. For example, if you turn on polar tracking and set it to 45 degrees and turn on polar snap and set it to 2 units, polar tracking jumps to points that are at angle increments of 45 degrees and distance increments of 2 units from the previous point. Polar snap has a similar effect on object snap tracking.

To activate polar snap, follow these steps:

1. **Right-click the SNAP button on the status bar.**

2. **Choose the Settings option.**

   The Snap and Grid tab on the Drafting Settings dialog box appears.

3. **Click the Polar Snap radio button, type a distance in the Polar Distance edit box, and then click OK.**

When you want to return to ordinary rectangular snap, as described at the beginning of this list, select the Grid Snap radio button in the Drafting Settings dialog box.

If you're new to AutoCAD, its wide range of precision tools probably seems overwhelming at this point. Rest assured that there's more than one way to skin a cat precisely, and not everyone needs to understand all the ways. You can make perfectly precise drawings with a subset of AutoCAD's precision tools. I recommend these steps:

1. Get comfortable with typing coordinates, ortho mode, direct distance entry, and single point object snaps.

2. Become familiar with running object snaps and try snap.

3. After you have all these precision features under your belt, feel free to experiment with polar tracking, polar snap, and object snap tracking.

It's easy to confuse the names of the snap and object snap (osnap) features. Remember that snap limits the cursor to locations whose coordinates are multiples of the current snap spacing. Object snap (osnap) enables you to grab points on existing objects, whether those points happen to correspond with the snap spacing or not.

Chapter 5

Where to Draw the Line

As you probably remember from your crayon and coloring book days, drawing stuff is *fun*. CAD imposes a little more discipline, but drawing AutoCAD objects is still fun. In computer-aided drafting, you usually start by drawing *geometry* — shapes such as lines, circles, rectangles, and so on that represent the real-world object that you're documenting. This chapter shows you how to draw geometry.

After you've created some geometry, you'll probably need to add some dimensions, text, and hatching, but those elements come later (in Part III of this book). Your first task is to get the geometry right; then you can worry about labeling things.

Drawing geometry properly in AutoCAD depends on paying attention to object properties and the precision of the points that you specify to create the objects. I cover these matters in Chapter 4, so if you eagerly jumped to this chapter to get right to the fun stuff, take a moment to review that chapter first.

Introducing the AutoCAD Drawing Commands

For descriptive purposes, this chapter divides the drawing commands into three groups:

- ✔ Straight lines and objects composed of straight lines
- ✔ Curves
- ✔ Points

AutoCAD-based application-specific programs such as Architectural Desktop add extra drawing tools to the mix — for example, commands for drawing walls and doors. See the documentation that comes with the application-specific program for information on such tools.

Table 5-1 offers an overview of most of the drawing commands in AutoCAD, without the 3D-related commands. It describes the commands' major options and shows you how to access them from the command line, the Draw menu, and the Draw toolbar. (Don't worry if not all the terms in the table are familiar to you; they become clear as you read through the chapter and use the commands.)

Table 5-1		AutoCAD Drawing Commands		
Button	**Command**	**Major Options**	**Toolbar Button**	**Draw Menu**
	Line	Start, end points	Line	Line
	RAY	Start point, point through which ray passes	None	Ray
	XLine	Two points on line	Construction line	Construction line
	PLine	Vertices	Polyline	Polyline
	POLygon	Number of sides,	Polygon	Polygon inscribed/ circumscribed

Button	Command	Major Options	Toolbar Button	Draw Menu
	RECtang	Two corners	Rectangle	Rectangle
	Arc	Various methods of definition	Arc	Arc; submenu for definition methods
	Circle	Three points, two points, tangent	Circle	Circle; submenu for definition methods
	REVCLOUD	Arc length	Revcloud	Revision Cloud
	DOnut	Inside, outside diameters	None	Donut
	SPLine	Convert polyline or create new	Spline	Spline
	ELlipse	Arc, center, axis	Ellipse	Ellipse; submenu for definition methods
	POint	Point style	Point	Point; submenu for definition methods

Many of the choices on the AutoCAD Draw menu open submenus containing several variations on each drawing command.

The AutoCAD drawing commands depend heavily on your reading the command line area and sometimes typing things there. Don't worry; I remind you to do so. (If "command line area" sounds to you like a place to order cafeteria food, not an AutoCAD essential concept, see Chapter 2.) Many of the command options that you see in command line prompts are available as well by right-clicking in the drawing area.

So what's the best course: to enter drawing commands from the command line or to choose them from the menus or toolbars? I suggest that you start a drawing command the first few times — until you remember its command name — by clicking its button on the Draw toolbar. After you click the button, fasten your eyes on the command line area so that you see the name of the command and its command line options. Use the keyboard or the right-click menus to select options, depending on whether your hand is on the keyboard or the mouse at that moment. After you're acquainted with a drawing command and decide that you like it enough to use it often, find out how to type its keyboard shortcut (the uppercase letters in the command names in Table 5-1).

A few drawing commands, such as DOnut, aren't on the Draw toolbar; you have to type those or choose them on the Draw menu.

The Straight and Narrow: Lines, Polylines, and Polygons

As I harp on a bunch of times elsewhere in this book, CAD programs are for precision drawing, so you'll spend a lot of your AutoCAD time drawing objects composed of straight-line segments. This section covers these commands:

- ✔ **Line:** Draws a series of straight line segments; each segment is a separate object
- ✔ **PLine:** Draws a *polyline* — a series of straight and/or curved line segments; all the segments remain connected to each other as a single object
- ✔ **RECtang:** Draws a polyline in the shape of a rectangle
- ✔ **POLygon:** Draws a polyline in the shape of a regular polygon (that is, a closed shape with all sides equal and all angles equal)

The following additional straight-line drawing commands also are available in AutoCAD:

- ✔ **RAY:** Draws a *semi-infinite line* (a line that extends infinitely in one direction)
- ✔ **XLine:** Draws an *infinite line* (a line that extends infinitely in both directions)

The RAY and XLine commands are used to draw *construction lines* that guide the construction of additional geometry. Drawing construction lines is less common in AutoCAD than in some other CAD programs. AutoCAD's many precision techniques often provide more efficient methods than construction lines of creating new geometry.

Toe the line

The Line command in AutoCAD draws a series of one or more connected line segments. Well, it *appears* to draw a series of connected segments. In fact, each *segment,* or piece of a line with endpoints, is a separate object. This construction doesn't seem like a big deal until you try to move or otherwise edit a series of segments that you drew with the Line command; you must select every piece separately. To avoid such a hassle, use polylines, described later in this chapter, not lines and arcs when you want the connected segments to be a single object.

If you're used to drawing lines in other programs, you may find it confusing at first that AutoCAD's Line command doesn't stop after you draw a single segment. AutoCAD keeps prompting you to specify additional points so that you can draw a series of (apparently) connected segments. When you're finished drawing segments, just press the Enter key to finish the Line command and return to the `Command` prompt.

Unlike a lot of AutoCAD drawing commands, Line doesn't offer a bunch of potentially confusing options. There's a Close option to create a closed polygon and an Undo option to remove the most recent segment that you drew.

Like all drawing commands, Line puts the line segment objects that it draws on the current layer, and uses the current color, linetype, lineweight, and plot style properties.

 ✔ Make sure that you've set these properties correctly before you start drawing. (I recommend that you set color, linetype. lineweight, and plot style to ByLayer.) See Chapter 4 for information on setting the current properties with the Object Properties toolbar.

 ✔ When you're doing real drafting as opposed to just experimenting, make sure that you use one of AutoCAD's precision tools, such as object snaps, typed coordinates, or tracking to ensure that you specify each object point precisely. Chapter 4 describes these tools.

Follow these steps to draw a series of line segments by using the Line command:

1. **Set object properties to the layer and other properties that you want applied to the line segments that you'll draw.**

2. **Click the Line button on the Draw toolbar.**

 AutoCAD starts the Line command and prompts you at the command line:

 ```
 Specify first point:
 ```

3. **Specify the starting point by clicking a point or typing coordinates.**

 Remember to use one of the precision techniques described in Chapter 4 if you're doing real drafting. For the first point, object snap, snap, tracking, and typing coordinates all work well.

AutoCAD prompts you at the command line to specify the other end-point of the first line segment:

```
Specify next point or [Undo]:
```

4. **Specify additional points by clicking or typing.**

   Again, use one of the AutoCAD precision techniques if you're doing real drafting. For the second and subsequent points, all the techniques mentioned in the previous step work well, plus ortho and direct distance entry.

   After you specify the third point, AutoCAD adds the Close option to the command line prompt:

```
Specify next point or [Close/Undo]:
```

5. **When you're finished drawing segments, end with one of these steps:**

   • Press Enter, or right-click anywhere in the drawing area and choose Enter (as shown in Figure 5-1), to leave the figure open.

   • Type C and press Enter, or right-click anywhere in the drawing area and choose Close from the cursor menu, to close the figure.

   AutoCAD draws the final segment and returns to the Command prompt, indicating that the Line command is finished:

```
Command:
```

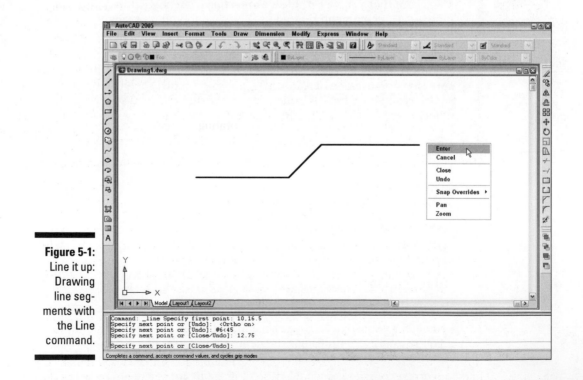

Figure 5-1:
Line it up: Drawing line segments with the Line command.

Connect the lines with polyline

The Line command is fine for some drawing tasks, but the PLine command is a better, more flexible choice in many situations. The PLine command draws a special kind of object called a *polyline*. You may hear CAD drafters refer to a polyline as a *pline* because of the command name. (By the way, PLine is pronounced to rhyme with "beeline" — in other words, it sounds like the place you stand when you've drunk a lot of beer at the ball game.)

The most important differences between the Line and PLine commands are these:

- ✔ The Line command draws a series of single line segment objects. Even though they appear on the screen to be linked, each segment is a separate object. If you move one line segment, the other segments that you drew at the same time don't move with it. The PLine command, on the other hand, draws a single, connected, multisegment object. If you select any segment for editing, your changes affect the entire polyline. Figure 5-2 shows how the same sketch drawn with the Line and the PLine commands responds when you select one of the objects.

  Use the PLine command instead of Line in most cases where you need to draw a series of connected line segments. If you're drawing a series of end-to-end segments, there's a good chance that those segments are logically connected — for example, they might represent the outline of a single object or a continuous pathway. If the segments are connected logically, it makes sense to keep them connected in AutoCAD. The most obvious practical benefit of grouping segments together into a polyline is that many editing operations are more efficient when you use polylines. If you move a single, disconnected line segment, the other segments that you drew at the same time don't move with it — likewise for other common editing operations, such as copying, erasing, rotating, and mirroring. When you select any segment in a polyline for editing, the entire polyline is affected.

- ✔ The PLine command can draw curved segments as well as straight ones.

- ✔ You can add width to each segment of a polyline. Polyline segment width is similar to lineweight, except that it can be uniform or tapered. The ability to create polyline segments with line widths was more important in the old days before AutoCAD had lineweight as an object property. People used to draw polylines with a small amount of width to show the segments as somewhat heavier than normal on plots. Nowadays, it's easier and more efficient to achieve this effect with object lineweights (as described in Chapter 4) or plot styles (as described in Chapter 12).

After you create a polyline, you can adjust its segments by grip editing any of the vertex points. (The little squares on the vertices in Figure 5-2 are called *grips;* see Chapter 6 for details on grip editing.) For more complicated polyline editing tasks, you can use the PEdit command to edit the polyline, or you can convert the polyline to a collection of line and arc segments by using the eXplode command — although you lose any width defined for each segment when you explode a polyline.

Drawing polylines composed of straight segments is pretty much like drawing with the Line command, as demonstrated in the following procedure. Watch the command prompts carefully because the PLine command has a lot of options! Remember that you can right-click in the drawing area to select one of the options, but reading the command prompts is your ticket to knowing what the options are at any moment.

Polyline (all segments form one object)

Figure 5-2:
Results of
drawing
with the
Line and
PLine
commands.

Line (each segment is a separate object)

To draw a polyline composed of straight segments, follow these steps:

1. **Set object properties to the layer and other properties that you want applied to the polyline object that you'll draw.**

2. **Click the Polyline button — the one that looks like a fishhook — on the Draw toolbar.**

   AutoCAD starts the PLine command and prompts you at the command line:

   ```
   Specify start point:
   ```

3. **Specify the starting point by clicking a point or typing coordinates.**

   AutoCAD displays the current polyline segment line-width and prompts you to specify the other endpoint of the first polyline segment:

   ```
   Current line-width is 0.0000
   Specify next point or [Arc/Halfwidth/Length/Undo/Width]:
   ```

4. **If the current line-width isn't zero, change it to zero by typing** W, **Enter,** 0, **Enter,** 0 **(as shown in the following command line sequence).**

```
Specify next point or [Arc/Halfwidth/Length/Undo/Width]:
      W
Enter Specify starting width <0.0000>: 0
Enter Specify ending width <0.0000>: 0
Enter Specify next point or
      [Arc/Halfwidth/Length/Undo/Width]:
```

Despite what you may think, a zero width polyline segment is not the AutoCAD equivalent of writing with disappearing ink. "Zero width" means "display this segment, using the normal, thin line-width on the screen." AutoCAD still applies object property or plot style lineweights when you plot.

5. **Specify additional points by clicking or typing.**

After you specify the second point, AutoCAD adds the Close option to the command line prompt:

```
Specify next point or
      [Arc/Close/Halfwidth/Length/Undo/Width]:
```

In addition, you can view and choose options from the right-click menu, as shown in Figure 5-3.

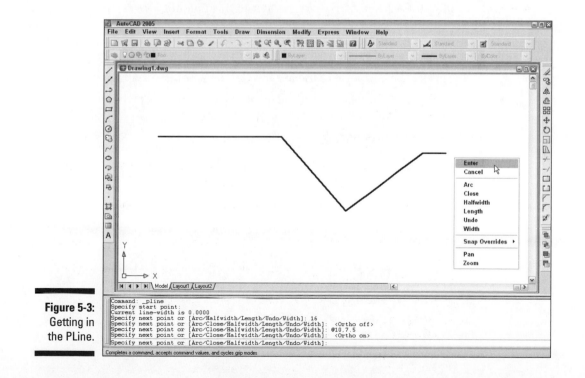

Figure 5-3:
Getting in
the PLine.

6. **After you finish drawing segments, either press Enter (to leave the figure open) or type C and press Enter (to close it).**

   AutoCAD draws the final segment and returns to the Command prompt, indicating that the PLine command is finished:

   ```
   Command:
   ```

In the following procedure, I spice things up a bit and give you a preview of coming (curvy) attractions by adding an arc segment to a polyline.

Just so you know, curved segments in polylines are *circular arcs* — pieces of circles that you can draw with the AutoCAD Arc command. AutoCAD can draw other kinds of curves, including ellipses and splines, but not within the PLine command.

To draw a polyline that includes curved segments, follow these steps:

1. **Repeat Steps 1 through 5 of the previous procedure.**

2. **When you're ready to add one or more arc segments, type A and press Enter to select the Arc option.**

   The command line prompt changes to show arc segment options. Most of these options correspond to the many ways of drawing circular arcs in AutoCAD; see "Arc-y-ology," later in this chapter.

   ```
   Specify endpoint of arc or
           [Angle/CEnter/CLose/Direction/Halfwidth/Line/
           Radius/Second pt/Undo/Width]:
   ```

3. **Specify the endpoint of the arc by clicking a point or typing coordinates.**

   AutoCAD draws the curved segment of the polyline. The command line prompt continues to show arc segment options.

   ```
   Specify endpoint of arc or
           [Angle/CEnter/CLose/Direction/Halfwidth/Line/
           Radius/Second pt/Undo/Width]:
   ```

   Your options at this point include

   • Specifying additional points to draw more arc segments

   • Choosing another arc-drawing method (such as CEnter or Second pt)

   • Returning to drawing straight-line segments with the Line option

   In this example, I return to drawing straight-line segments.

Perhaps the most useful of the alternative arc-drawing methods is Second pt. You can use it to gain flexibility in the direction of the arc, but at the cost of losing tangency of contiguous segments. Sometimes it's best not to go off on a tangent, anyway.

4. **Type** L **and press Enter to select the** Line **option.**

```
Specify endpoint of arc or
       [Angle/CEnter/CLose/Direction/Halfwidth/Line/
       Radius/Second pt/Undo/Width]: L
```

The command line prompt changes back to showing straight-line segment options.

```
Specify next point or
       [Arc/Close/Halfwidth/Length/Undo/Width]:
```

5. **Specify additional points by clicking or typing.**

6. **After you're finished drawing segments, either press Enter or type** C **and press Enter.**

```
Command:
```

Figure 5-4 shows some of the things that you can draw with the PLine command by using straight segments, arc segments, or a combination of both.

Figure 5-4:
A plethora
of polylines.

The Line and PLine commands work well for drawing a series of end-to-end single lines, but what if you want to draw a series of double lines to represent, for example, the edges of a wall or roadway? Here are three options:

✔ Use the AutoCAD MLine command to draw *multilines* — series of two or more parallel, straight lines. The AutoCAD multiline feature was full of limitations and bugs when it debuted ten years ago. It hasn't improved significantly since then. Look up the MLine and MLSTYLE commands in AutoCAD's online help system if you'd like to tangle with this feature, but be prepared to spend time experimenting and struggling.

✔ In AutoCAD LT only, use the DLine (Double Line) command to draw pairs of parallel line and/or arc segments. AutoCAD LT doesn't include the MLine command, which, given MLine's problems, probably is more of a blessing than a limitation. AutoCAD, on the other hand, doesn't include the DLine command. (Score one for the little brother!)

✔ Use the PLine command to draw a single set of connected line and/or arc segments, and then use the Offset command to create one or more sets of parallel segments. Chapter 6 covers the Offset command.

Square off with rectangle

You can use the PLine or Line command to draw a rectangle segment by segment. In most cases, though, you'll find it easier to use the special-purpose RECtang command. The following procedure demonstrates how:

1. **Set object properties to the layer and other properties that you want applied to the rectangle that you'll draw.**

2. **Click the Rectangle button on the Draw toolbar.**

   AutoCAD starts the RECtang command and prompts you at the command line to specify a point for one corner of the rectangle:

   ```
   Specify first corner point or
           [Chamfer/Elevation/Fillet/Thickness/Width]:
   ```

   You can add fancy effects with the additional command options. The default options work best for most purposes. Look up "RECTANG command" in the AutoCAD help system if you want to know more about the options.

3. **Specify the first corner by clicking a point or typing coordinates.**

   The command line prompts you to specify the other corner of the rectangle — the one that's diagonally opposite from the first corner:

   ```
   Specify other corner point or [Dimensions]:
   ```

4. **Specify the other corner by clicking a point or typing coordinates.**

If you know the size of the rectangle that you want to draw (for example, 100 units long by 75 units high), type relative coordinates to specify the dimensions (for example, @100,75). (Chapter 4 describes how to type coordinates.)

AutoCAD draws the rectangle.

Choose your sides with polygon

Rectangles and other closed polylines are types of *polygons*, or closed figures with three or more sides. The AutoCAD POLygon command provides a quick way of drawing *regular polygons* — polygons in which all sides and angles are equal. (If regular polygons seem a little square, maybe that's because a square is a special case of a regular polygon!)

The following procedure demonstrates the POLygon command:

1. **Set object properties to the layer and other properties that you want applied to the polygon that you'll draw.**

2. **Click the Polygon button on the Draw toolbar.**

   AutoCAD starts the POLygon command and prompts you at the command line to enter the number of sides for the polygon:

   ```
   Enter number of sides <4>:
   ```

3. **Type the number of sides in the polygon that you want to draw and press Enter.**

   The command line prompts you to specify the center point of the polygon:

   ```
   Specify center of polygon or [Edge]:
   ```

   You can use the Edge option to draw a polygon by specifying one side, instead of the center and radius of an imaginary inscribed or circumscribed circle. The imaginary circle method is much more common.

4. **Specify the center point by clicking a point or typing coordinates.**

   The command line prompts you to specify whether the polygon will be inscribed in or circumscribed about an imaginary circle whose radius you will specify in the following step:

   ```
   Enter an option [Inscribed in circle/Circumscribed about
         circle] <I>:
   ```

5. **Type I or C and press Enter.**

   The command line prompts you to specify the radius of imaginary circle:

   ```
   Specify radius of circle:
   ```

6. **Specify the radius by typing a distance or clicking a point.**

   AutoCAD draws the polygon.

If you type a distance or you click a point with Ortho turned on, the polygon will be aligned orthogonally, as shown in Figure 5-5. If you click a point with Ortho turned off, the polygon most likely won't be aligned orthogonally.

Figure 5-5 shows the results of drawing plenty of polygons — a practice known as "polygony," and which, as far as I know, remains legal in most states.

Rectangles and polygons in AutoCAD are really just polylines that you specify in a way that's appropriate to the shape you're creating. You'll notice this when you grip edit a rectangle or polygon and move one of the vertexes: Only the selected vertex moves. AutoCAD doesn't make the entire rectangle or polygon larger or smaller. (See Chapter 6 for information about grip editing.)

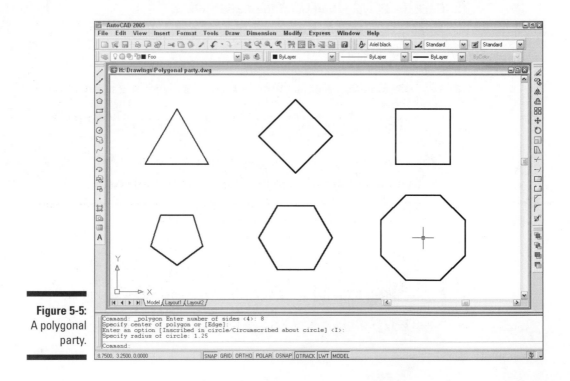

Figure 5-5:
A polygonal party.

(Throwing) Curves

Although straight line segments predominate in many CAD drawings, even the most humdrum, rectilinear design is likely to have a few curves. And if you're drawing car bodies or Gaudí buildings, your drawings will be almost nothing but curves! This section shows you how to use the following AutoCAD curve-drawing commands:

- **Circle:** Draws circles (you were expecting rectangles, maybe?)

- **Arc:** Draws circular arcs — arcs cut from circles, not from ellipses, parabolas, or some other complicated curve

- **ELlipse:** Draws ellipses and elliptical arcs

- **SPLine:** Draws smoothly flowing curves of a variety of shapes

- **DOnut:** Draws filled-in annular rings and circles

- **REVCLOUD:** Draws free-form "clouds," the most common application of which is to indicate revised areas in the drawing

The following sections describe each command.

Going full circle

AutoCAD offers an easy way to draw circles, and it also offers . . . *other* ways. The easy way is to define the center point of the circle and then to define the radius or diameter. You can also define a circle by entering one of the following options of the command (for those "other" ways):

- **3P (3-Point):** Specify any three points on the circumference.

- **2P (2-Point):** Specify the endpoints of a diameter of the circle.

- **Ttr (Tangent-Tangent-Radius):** Specify two lines or other objects that are tangent to the circle, and then specify its radius.

Whether these additional circle-drawing methods are useful or superfluous depends on the kinds of drawings that you make and how geometry is defined in your industry. Get familiar with the default center point/radius method and then try the other methods to see whether they may be helpful to you. If you find yourself going around in circles, you can always draw them the default way and move them into position with other geometry.

1. **Set object properties to the layer and other properties that you want applied to the circle that you'll draw.**

2. **Click the Circle button on the Draw toolbar.**

   AutoCAD starts the Circle command and prompts you at the command line to specify the center point of the circle:

   ```
   Specify center point for circle or [3P/2P/Ttr (tan tan
   radius)]:
   ```

   The prompt shows the methods other than "center point plus radius" that you can use to draw circles in AutoCAD. (No, "tan tan radius" is not a mathematician's dance.) Look up "CIRCLE command" in the online help if you think you may have a use for these less common circle-drawing methods.

3. **Specify the center point by clicking a point or typing coordinates.**

   Use one of the precision techniques described in Chapter 4 if you're doing real drafting. Object snap, snap, and typing coordinates all work well for specifying the center point.

   The command line then prompts you to specify the circle's radius:

   ```
   Specify radius of circle or [Diameter]:
   ```

   Type **D** and press Enter if you prefer to enter the diameter rather than the radius and you've forgotten your twos tables — or, more seriously, if the diameter is easier to specify with the cursor or type exactly than the radius is.

4. **Specify the radius by typing a distance or clicking a point.**

   AutoCAD draws the circle, as shown in Figure 5-6.

Arc-y-ology

Arcs in AutoCAD are, quite simply, pieces of circles. As with circles, AutoCAD offers you an easy way to define arcs. Just specify three points on-screen to define the arc, easy as one-two-three. These points tell AutoCAD where to start the arc, how much to curve it, and where to end it.

Sounds pretty easy, right? So where's the problem? The trouble is that you often must specify arcs more exactly than is possible by using this method. AutoCAD helps you specify such arcs, too, but the procedure ain't easy.

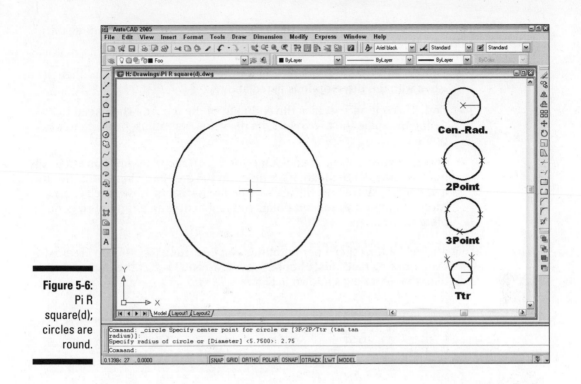

Figure 5-6:
Pi R
square(d);
circles are
round.

You can start your arc by specifying the center of the arc or the start point. If you choose the Center option, AutoCAD prompts you for the center point first and the start point second. AutoCAD defines arcs counterclockwise, so pick a start point in a clockwise direction from the end point. After you specify the center and start point, AutoCAD presents several options you can choose, including the following:

- ✔ **Angle:** This option specifies the included angle that the arc sweeps out. A 180-degree angle, for example, is a semicircle.

- ✔ **Length of chord:** This option specifies the length of an imaginary straight line connecting the endpoints of the arc. Most people use this option seldom or never.

- ✔ **Endpoint:** This option specifies where the arc ends. It's the default option and is often the easiest to use.

If you specify the start point as the first option, you can choose among the following three command line options as well:

- ✔ **Center:** This option prompts you for the arc's center point and then finishes with the three options listed above.

- ✔ **End:** This option specifies the endpoint of the arc. You then need to define the angle the arc covers, its direction, its radius, or its center point.

- ✔ **Second point:** This is the default option. The second point you choose is not the endpoint; instead, it's a point on the arc that, along with the start and endpoints, defines the arc's *curvature* — that is, how much it curves. After you enter the second point, you must enter an endpoint to complete the arc.

To get a feel for how these permutations can be strung together to create different arc-drawing methods, choose Draw⇨Arc and look at the impressive submenu that unfurls, as shown in Figure 5-7.

Figure 5-7: A deluge of Arc options, with the results of using some of those options.

The following example shows how you draw an arc with the default start point/second point/endpoint method:

1. **Set object properties to the layer and other properties that you want applied to the arc that you'll draw.**

2. **Click the Arc button on the Draw toolbar.**

   AutoCAD starts the Arc command and prompts you at the command line to specify the first endpoint of the arc:

   ```
   Specify start point of arc or [Center]:
   ```

3. **Specify the start point by clicking a point or typing coordinates.**

   The command line prompts you to specify a second point on the arc:

   ```
   Specify second point of arc or [Center/ENd]:
   ```

4. **Specify a second point on the arc by clicking a point or typing coordinates.**

   The second point lies somewhere along the curve of the arc. AutoCAD determines the exact curvature of the arc after you choose the final endpoint in the following step. To align the second point with an existing object, use an object snap mode.

   The command line prompts you to specify the other endpoint of the arc; as you move the cursor around, AutoCAD shows how the arc will look:

   ```
   Specify end point of arc:
   ```

5. **Specify the other endpoint of the arc by clicking a point or typing coordinates.**

   AutoCAD draws the arc, as shown in Figure 5-7.

Ellipses (S. Grant?)

An *ellipse* is like a warped circle with a *major* (long) axis and a *minor* (short) axis. These axes determine the ellipse's length, width, and degree of curvature. An *elliptical arc* is an arc cut from an ellipse. Some kinds of drawing geometry require ellipses or elliptical arcs, but many people use AutoCAD happily for years without ever drawing an ellipse. If you think you're one of those people, skip this section.

The AutoCAD ELlipse command provides a straightforward way of drawing an ellipse: You specify the two endpoints of one of its axes and then specify an endpoint on the other axis. But like the Arc command, the ELlipse command offers a bunch of other options on the command line:

✔ **Arc:** This option generates an elliptical arc, not a full ellipse. You define an elliptical arc just as you do a full ellipse. The following methods for creating an ellipse apply to either.

✔ **Center:** This option requires that you define the center of the ellipse and then the endpoint of an axis. You can then either enter the distance of the other axis or specify that a rotation around the major axis define the ellipse. If you choose the latter, you can enter (or drag the ellipse to) a specific rotation for the second axis that, in turn, completely defines the ellipse.

✔ **Rotation:** With this option, you specify an angle, which defines the curvature of the ellipse — small angles make fat ellipses (0 degrees creates a circle, in fact), and large angles make skinny ellipses. The name of the option, Rotation, has something to do with rotating an imaginary circle around the first axis. If you can figure out the imaginary circle business, then you have a better imagination than I do.

The following example creates an ellipse by using the default endpoints of the axes method. Figure 5-8 shows an ellipse and an elliptical arc.

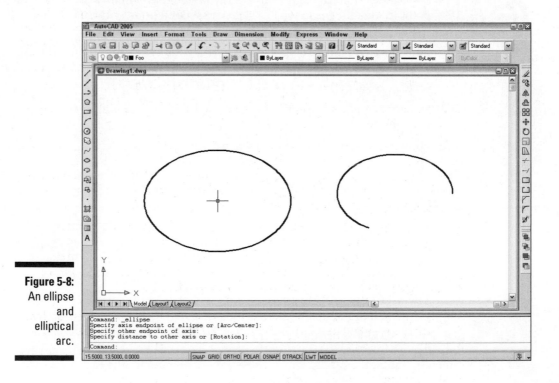

Figure 5-8:
An ellipse and elliptical arc.

```
Command: ELlipse Enter
Specify axis endpoint of ellipse or [Arc/Center]: pick or
        type the first endpoint of one axis
Specify other endpoint of axis: pick or type the other
        endpoint of one axis
Specify distance to other axis or [Rotation]: pick or type
        the endpoint of the other axis
```

You can create elliptical arcs (as opposed to the circular arcs that the AutoCAD Arc command draws) by using the Arc option of the ELlipse command; it's perfect for drawing those cannonball trajectories! Alternatively, you can draw a full ellipse and use the TRIM or BREAK command to cut a piece out of it.

Splines: The sketchy, sinuous curves

Most people use CAD programs for precision drawing tasks: straight lines, carefully defined curves, precisely specified points, and so on. AutoCAD is not the program to free your inner artist — unless your inner artist is Mondrian. Nonetheless, even meticulously created CAD drawings sometimes need free-form curves. The AutoCAD *spline object* is just the thing for the job.

Although PLine is pronounced to rhyme with "beeline," SPLine rhymes with "vine." (If you liked my earlier pronunciation comment, you may want to think about beer before you say "PLine" and about wine before you say "SPLine.")

You can use AutoCAD splines in two ways:

- ✔ Eyeball the location and shape of the curve and don't worry too much about getting it just so. That's the free-form, sketchy, not-too-precise approach that I describe here.

- ✔ Specify their control points and curvature characteristics precisely. Beneath their easy-going, informal exterior, AutoCAD splines are really highly precise, mathematically defined entities called *NURBS curves* (Non-Uniform Rational B-Spline curves). Mathematicians and some mechanical and industrial designers care a lot about the precise characteristics of the curves they work with. For those people, the AutoCAD SPLine and SPlinEdit commands include a number of advanced options. Look up "spline curves" in the AutoCAD online help if you need precision in your splines.

Drawing splines is straightforward, if you ignore the advanced options. The following procedure draws a free-form curve with the SPLine command:

1. **Set object properties to the layer and other properties that you want applied to the spline that you'll draw.**

2. **Click the Spline button on the Draw toolbar.**

   AutoCAD starts the SPLine command and prompts you at the command line to specify the first endpoint of the spline:

   ```
   Specify first point or [Object]:
   ```

3. **Specify the start point by clicking a point or typing coordinates.**

   The command line prompts you to specify additional points:

   ```
   Specify next point:
   ```

4. **Specify additional points by clicking or typing coordinates.**

   After you pick the second point, the command line prompt changes to show additional options:

   ```
   Specify next point or [Close/Fit tolerance] <start tangent>:
   ```

   Because you're drawing a free-form curve, you usually don't need to use object snaps or other precision techniques when picking spline points.

5. **Press Enter after you've chosen the final endpoint of your spline.**

   AutoCAD prompts you to specify tangent lines for each end of the spline:

   ```
   Specify start tangent:
   Specify end tangent:
   ```

   The `Specify start tangent` and `Specify end tangent` prompts can control the curvature of the start and end points of the spline. In most cases, just pressing Enter at both prompts to accept the default tangents works fine.

6. **Press Enter twice to accept the default tangent directions.**

   AutoCAD draws the spline.

Figure 5-9 shows some examples of splines.

After you've drawn a spline, you can grip edit it to adjust its shape. See Chapter 6 for information about grip editing. If you need finer control over spline editing, look up the SPlinEdit command in the AutoCAD online help.

Figure 5-9:
A slew of
splines.

Donuts: The circles with a difference

Creating a *donut* is a simple way to define a single object that consists of two concentric circles with the space between them filled.

When you start the DOnut command, AutoCAD prompts you for the inside diameter and the outside diameter — the size of the hole and the size of the donut, as measured across their widest points. After you've entered these values, AutoCAD prompts you for the center point of the donut. But one donut is rarely enough, so AutoCAD keeps prompting you for additional center points until you press Enter (the AutoCAD equivalent of saying, "no, really, I'm full now!").

The following example draws a regulation-size donut, with a 1.5-inch hole and 3.5-inch outside diameter. Figure 5-10 shows several kinds of donuts.

```
Command: DOnut Enter
Specify inside diameter of donut <0.5000>: 1.5 Enter
Specify outside diameter of donut <1.0000>: 3.5 Enter
Specify center of donut or <exit>: pick or type the center
        point of one or more donuts
Specify center of donut or <exit>: Enter
```

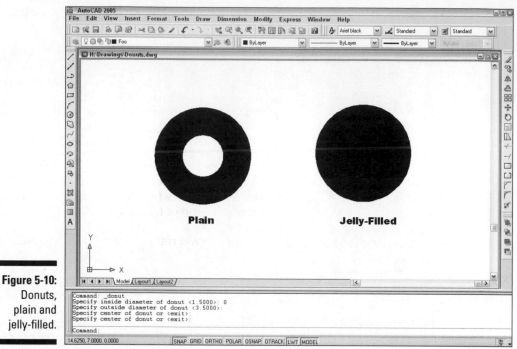

Figure 5-10:
Donuts,
plain and
jelly-filled.

You can use the DOnut command to create a filled circle — also known as a jelly-filled donut. Just specify an inside diameter of 0.

Revision clouds on the horizon

It's customary in many industries to submit a set of drawings at a stage of completion and then submit them again later with *revisions* — corrections, clarifications, and requested changes. Often, the recipients like to locate changed stuff easily. A common drafting convention in many industries is to call attention to revised items by drawing free-form clouds around them. The REVCLOUD command makes quick work of drawing such clouds.

Drawing revision clouds is easy, after you understand that you click with the mouse only once in the drawing area. That one click defines the starting point for the cloud's perimeter. After that, you simply move the cursor around, and the cloud takes shape. When you return to near the point that you clicked in the beginning, AutoCAD automatically closes the cloud.

The following example shows you how to draw a revision cloud. Figure 5-11 shows what revision clouds look like.

```
Command: REVCLOUD
Minimum arc length: 0.5000  Maximum arc length: 0.5000
          Style: Normal
Specify start point or [Arc length/Object/Style] <Object>:
          pick a point along the perimeter of your future
          cloud
Guide crosshairs along cloud path... sweep the cursor around
          to define the cloud's perimeter
```

You don't need to click again. Simply move the cursor around without clicking. AutoCAD draws the next *lobe* of the cloud when your cursor reaches the `Minimum arc length` distance from the end of the previous lobe.

Continue moving the cursor around until you return to the point that you clicked at first.

```
Revision cloud finished.
```

Figure 5-11:
Cloud cover.

Here are a few tips for using revision clouds:

✔ It's a good idea to put revision clouds on their own layer so that you can choose to plot with or without the clouds visible.

✔ You'll probably find it easier to control the shape of revision clouds if you turn off ortho mode before you start the command.

✔ You may need to add a triangle and number, as shown in Figure 5-11, to indicate the revision number. A block with an attribute is a good way to handle this requirement: Chapter 13 covers blocks and attributes.

If the revision cloud's lobes are too small or too large, erase the cloud, restart the REVCLOUD command, and use the command's Arc length option to change the minimum and maximum arc lengths. The default minimum and maximum lengths are 0.5 (or 15 in metric drawings) multiplied by the DIM-SCALE (DIMension SCALE) system variable setting. If you make the minimum and maximum lengths equal (which is the default), the lobes will be approximately equal in size. If you make them unequal, there will be more variation in lobe size — you'll get "fluffier" clouds. Fortunately, of these options are more than most nonmeteorologists will need. If you've set DIMSCALE properly during your drawing setup procedure (see Chapter 3), REVCLOUD should do a pretty good job of guessing reasonable default arc lengths.

Scoring Points

I thought about not covering points in this book, but I didn't want you complaining that *AutoCAD 2005 For Dummies* is pointless.

The word *point* describes two different things in AutoCAD:

✔ A *location* in the drawing that you specify (by typing coordinates or clicking with the mouse)

✔ An *object* that you draw with the POint command

Throughout this chapter and most of the book, I tell you to specify points — that's the location meaning. This section tells you how to draw point objects.

A *point object* in AutoCAD can serve two purposes.

✔ **Points often identify specific locations in your drawing to other people who look at the drawing.** A point can be something that displays on the screen, either as a tiny dot or as another symbol, such as a cross with a circle around it.

✔ **You can use points as precise object snap locations.** Think of them as construction points. For example, when you're laying out a new building, you might draw point objects at some of the engineering survey points and then snap to those points as you sketch the building's shape with the polyline command. You use the NODe object snap mode to snap to AutoCAD point objects. In this guise, points usually are for your use in drawing and editing precisely. Other people who view the drawing probably won't even be aware that the point objects are there.

What makes AutoCAD point objects complicated is their almost limitless range of display options, provided to accommodate the two different kinds of purposes just described (and possibly some others that I haven't figured out yet). You use the Point Style dialog box, shown in Figure 5-12, to specify how points should look in the current drawing.

DDPTYPE is the command that opens the Point Style dialog box. You can access it from the menus by choosing Format➪Point Style. The top portion of the dialog box shows the available point display styles. Most of the choices do pretty much the same thing. Just click one of the squares that says "hey, that's a point!" to you.

Figure 5-12:
The Point Style dialog box controls the way point objects appear on-screen.

The first choice, a single-pixel dot, is hard to see on the screen, and the second choice, invisible (a stealth point?), is impossible to see. Avoid these choices if you want your point objects to show up on the screen and on plots. The single-pixel dot, which is the default display style, works well if you use point objects as object snap locations and don't want the points obtrusive on plots.

The remaining settings in the Point Style dialog box control the size at which points appear on the screen at different zoom resolutions. The default settings often work fine, but if you're not satisfied with them, click the Help button to find out how to change them.

After you specify the point style, placing points on-screen is easy; the following example shows you how.

This is an example of the command-line commands to create a point:

```
Command: POint Enter
Current point modes: PDMODE=0 PDSIZE=0.0000
Specify a point: pick or type the coordinates of a location
                in the drawing
```

PDMODE and PDSIZE in the command prompt are system variables that correspond to the point display mode and display size options in the Point Style dialog box. If you want to know exactly how the system variables correspond to the dialog box choices, you have all the makings of a successful CAD nerd. Click the Help button in the Point Style dialog box to find out more (about the system variables — not about yourself).

If you start the POint command from the Draw toolbar or the Draw⇨Point⇨ Multiple Point menu, it will repeat automatically — that is, it will prompt you repeatedly to Specify a point. When you're finished drawing points, press Esc to finish the command for good. If the command doesn't repeat automatically and you want to draw more points, press the Enter key to repeat the POint command and pick another location on the screen. Repeat as required: Enter, pick, Enter, pick, Enter pick . . . by now you should've gotten the point.

Chapter 6

Edit for Credit

• •

In This Chapter

▶ Using command-first editing

▶ Selecting objects with maximum flexibility

▶ Moving, copying, and stretching objects

▶ Manipulating whole objects

▶ Changing pieces of objects

▶ Editing with grips

▶ Editing object properties

• •

*E*diting objects is the flip side of creating them, and in AutoCAD, you spend a lot of time editing — far more than drawing objects from scratch. That's partly because the design and drafting process is by its nature iterative, and also because CAD programs make it easy to edit objects cleanly.

When you edit objects in AutoCAD, you need to be just as concerned about specifying precise locations and distances as you are when you originally create the objects. Make sure that you're familiar with the precision techniques described in Chapter 4 before you apply the editing techniques from this chapter to real drawings.

Commanding and Selecting

AutoCAD offers two main styles of editing:

✔ Command-first editing

✔ Selection-first editing

Within the selection-first editing style, you have an additional choice of editing that uses actual, named commands and *direct manipulation* of objects without named commands. The following sections cover these editing styles.

Command-first editing

With *command-first editing,* you enter a command and then click the objects on which the command works. This style of editing may seem backwards to you at first unless you're a longtime user of AutoCAD or a veteran of command-line operating systems (where you typically type the name of command and then the names of the files or other objects to which you want to apply the command). Command-first editing works well for power users who are in a hurry and who are willing to memorize most of the commands they need to do their work. It's no surprise that command-first editing is the default style of editing in AutoCAD.

Selection-first editing

In *selection-first editing,* you perform the same steps — in the same order — as in most Windows applications: Select the object first, then choose the command.

Selection-first editing tends to be easier to master, which is why Windows and the Macintosh are easier for most people to use for a variety of tasks than DOS ever was. Selection-first editing makes AutoCAD more approachable for new and occasional users.

Direct manipulation is a refinement of selection-first editing in which you perform common editing operations by using the mouse to grab the selected object and perform an action on it, such as moving all or part of it to a different place in the drawing. No named command is involved; the act of moving the mouse and clicking the mouse buttons in certain ways causes the editing changes to happen. AutoCAD supports direct manipulation through a powerful but somewhat complicated technique called *grip editing.* Grips are the little square handles that appear on an object when you select it. You can use the grips to stretch, move, copy, rotate, or otherwise edit the object. These grip-editing techniques can make selection-first editing almost as powerful as command-first editing. The complications arise from the fact that you can do so many things with an object after you select it.

Choosing an editing style

This chapter emphasizes command-first editing. (I also discuss grip editing at the end of the chapter.) AutoCAD is fundamentally a command-first program. AutoCAD started out offering *only* command-first editing and later added selection-first methods; AutoCAD 2005 inherits this ancestral trait. I emphasize command-first editing for the following reasons:

✔ It's the default AutoCAD editing style.

✔ It works consistently with all editing commands — some editing commands remain command-first only.

✔ It provides added object selection flexibility, which is useful when you work on complicated, busy drawings.

After you know how to do command-first editing, you can simply reverse the order of *many* editing operations to do them selection-first style instead. But if you don't get familiar with command-first editing in the beginning, you'll be completely bewildered by some very useful AutoCAD commands that work only in the command-first style, such as TRim and EXtend. (Commands such as these ignore any already selected objects and prompt you to select objects.)

Much of the information in this chapter assumes that you're using the default AutoCAD selection settings. If object selection or grip editing works differently than I describe in this chapter, check the settings on the Option dialog box's Selection tab. Five check box settings should be turned on (all other check box settings should be turned off):

✔ Noun/Verb Selection

✔ Implied Windowing

✔ Object Grouping

✔ Enable Grips

✔ Enable Grip Tips

Grab It

Part of AutoCAD's editing flexibility comes from its object selection flexibility. For example, command-first editing offers 16 selection modes! (I describe the most useful ones in this chapter.) Don't worry though; you can get by most of the time with three selection modes:

✔ Selecting a single object

✔ Enclosing objects in a window (pick left corner; then right corner)

✔ Including part or all objects in a crossing window (pick right corner; then left corner)

One-by-one selection

The most obvious way to select objects is to pick (by clicking) them one at a time. You can build up a selection set cumulatively with this "pick one object at a time" selection mode. This cumulative convention may be different from what you're used to. In most Windows programs, if you select one object and then another, the first object is deselected, and the second one selected. Only the object you select last remains selected. In AutoCAD, *all* the objects you select, one at a time, remain selected and are added to the set, no matter how many objects you pick. (You can change this behavior to make AutoCAD work like Windows does by turning on 'Use Shift to add to selection' on the Option dialog box's Selection tab, but I suggest you not change it.) Most editing commands affect the entire group of selected objects.

Selection boxes left and right

Selecting objects one at a time works great when you want to edit a small number of objects, but many CAD editing tasks involve editing lots of objects. Do you really want to pick 132 lines, arcs, and circles, one at a time?

Like most Windows graphics programs, AutoCAD provides a selection window feature for grabbing a bunch of objects in a rectangular area. As you may guess by now, the AutoCAD version of this feature is a bit more powerful than the analogous feature in other Windows graphics programs and, therefore, slightly confusing at first. AutoCAD calls its version *implied windowing*.

If you click a blank area of the drawing —, that is, not on an object — you're *implying* to AutoCAD that you want to specify a selection window, or box. If you move the cursor to the right before picking the other corner of the selection box, you're further implying that you want to select all objects that reside completely within the selection box. If you instead move the cursor to the left before picking the other corner of the selection box, you're implying that you want to select all objects that reside completely *or partially* within the selection box.

The AutoCAD terminology for these two kinds of selection boxes gets a little confusing:

- The move-to-the-right, only-select-objects-completely-within-the-box mode is called *Window* object selection.

- The move-to-the-left, select-objects-completely-or-partially-within-the-box mode is called *Crossing* object selection.

You might think of these modes as *bounding box* (to the right) and *crossing box* (to the left). Fortunately, AutoCAD gives you a visual cue that there's a difference. As you move to the right, the bounding box appears as a solid rectangle. As you move to the left, the crossing box appears as a ghosted, or dashed, rectangle.

Figures 6-1 and 6-2 show a bounding box and a crossing box, respectively, in action.

You can mix and match selecting individual objects, specifying a bounding box, and specifying a crossing box. Each selection adds to the current selection set, allowing you to build up an enormously complicated selection of objects and then operate on them with one or more editing commands.

Selection box

Pick point 2

Figure 6-1: A bounding selection box (Window), drawn left to right, selects only objects completely within the box.

Pick point 1

Selection box

Pick point 2

Figure 6-2:
A crossing
selec-
tion box
(Crossing),
drawn right
to left,
selects
objects
that are
completely
or partially
within
the box.

Pick point 1

You can press the Shift key in combination with any of the three standard selection modes — single object, bounding box (Window), and crossing box (Crossing) — to *remove* already selected objects from the selection set. This feature is especially useful when you're building a selection set in a crowded drawing; you can select a big batch of objects by using Window or Crossing, and then hold down the Shift key while selecting to remove the objects that you want to exclude from the editing operation.

Perfecting Selecting

When you edit in command-first mode, you have all the selection options described in the previous section — single object, bounding box (Window), and crossing box (Crossing) — plus a slew of others. If you type ? and press Enter at any Select objects prompt, AutoCAD lists all the selection options:

```
Window/Last/Crossing/BOX/ALL/Fence/WPolygon/CPolygon/Group/
        Add/Remove/Multiple/Previous/Undo/AUto/SIngle
```

Table 6-1 summarizes the most useful command-first selection options.

Table 6-1	Some Useful Command-First Selection Options
Option	*Description*
Window	All objects within a rectangle that you specify by picking two points
Last	The last object you drew that's still visible in the drawing area
Crossing	All objects within or crossing a rectangle that you specify by picking two points
ALL	All objects on layers that aren't frozen and that are in the current space (model space or paper space)
Fence	All objects touching an imaginary polyline whose vertices you specify by picking points
WPolygon	All objects within a polygonal area whose corners you specify by picking points
CPolygon	All objects within or crossing a polygonal area whose corners you specify by picking points
Previous	The previous selection set that you specified

To use any of the command-first selection options at the `Select objects` prompt, type the uppercase letters corresponding to the option and press Enter. After you're finished selecting objects, you must press Enter again to tell AutoCAD that you've finished selecting objects and want to start the editing operation.

The following example demonstrates how to use the Erase command in command-first mode with several different selection options. The selection techniques used in this example apply to most AutoCAD editing commands:

1. **Press Esc to make sure that no command is active and no objects are selected.**

   If any objects are selected when you start an editing command, the command in most cases will operate on those objects (selection-first editing) instead of prompting you to select objects (command-first editing). For the reasons that I describe earlier in this chapter, you should use the command-first editing style until you're thoroughly familiar with it. Later, you can experiment with selection-first editing if you like. (Just reverse the sequence of commanding and selecting that I describe in this chapter.)

2. **Click the Erase button on the Modify toolbar.**

The command line displays the `Select objects` prompt.

3. **Select two or three individual objects by clicking each one.**

AutoCAD adds each object to the selection set. All the objects you select remain ghosted. The command line displays the `Select objects` prompt.

4. **Specify a bounding selection box (Window) that completely encloses several objects.**

Move the cursor to a point below and to the left of the objects, click, release the mouse button, move the cursor above and to the right of the objects, and click again.

All objects that are completely within the box are selected.

5. **Specify a crossing selection box (Crossing) that encloses a few objects and cuts through several others.**

Move the cursor to a point below and to the right of some of the objects, click, release the mouse button, move the cursor above and to the left of some of the objects, and click and release again.

All objects that are completely within or cross through the box are selected.

6. **Type WP and press Enter to activate the WPolygon selection option.**

The command line prompts you to pick points that define the selection polygon.

7. **Pick a series of points and press Enter.**

Figure 6-3 shows an example. After you press Enter, AutoCAD selects all objects that are completely within the polygon.

8. **Press Enter to end object selection.**

AutoCAD erases all the selected objects.

Notice how you were able to use a combination of object selection methods to build up a selection set and then press Enter to execute the command on them. Most AutoCAD editing commands work this way in command-first mode.

If, after erasing a selection set, you immediately realize that you didn't really mean to do away with so many objects, you can use the Undo button on the Standard toolbar to restore all of them. But AutoCAD has one additional un-erase trick up its sleeve — the aptly named OOPS command. When you type **OOPS** and press Enter, AutoCAD restores the last selection set that you erased — even if you've run other commands after Erase.

Figure 6-3:
Lasso-ing
objects
with a
WPolygon.

Ready, Get Set, Edit!

The following sections cover the most important AutoCAD editing commands, using command-first editing mode.

Whether you start an AutoCAD editing command by clicking a toolbar button, choosing a pull-down menu command, or typing a command name, in almost all cases the command prompts you for points, distances, and options at the command line. Read the command line prompts during every step of the command, especially when you're figuring out how to use a new editing command. Otherwise, you're unlikely to complete the command successfully.

As I describe in Chapter 4, maintaining precision when you draw and edit is crucial to good CAD work. If you've used a drawing program and are accustomed to moving, stretching, and otherwise editing objects by eye, you'll need to suppress that habit when you edit in AutoCAD. Nothing ruins a drawing faster than approximate editing, in which you shove objects around until they look okay, without worrying about precise distances and points.

The Big Three: Move, CoPy, and Stretch

Moving, copying, and stretching are, for many drafters, the three most common editing operations. AutoCAD obliges this need with the Move, CoPy, and Stretch commands.

Base points and displacements

The Move, CoPy, and Stretch commands all require that you specify how far and in what direction you want the objects moved, copied, or stretched. After you've selected the objects to be edited and started the command, AutoCAD prompts you for two pieces of information:

```
Specify base point or displacement:
Specify second point of displacement or <use first point as
        displacement>:
```

In a not-so-clear way, these prompts say that two possible methods exist for you to specify how far and in what direction you want the objects copied, moved, or stretched:

- ✔ **The most common way is to pick or type the coordinates of two points that define a displacement vector.** AutoCAD calls these points the *base point* and the *second point* (hence, it's called the "base point method"). Imagine an arrow pointing from the base point to the second point — that arrow defines how far and in what direction the objects get copied, moved, or stretched.

- ✔ **The other way is to type an X,Y pair of numbers that represents a distance rather than a point.** This distance is the absolute displacement that you want to copy, move, or stretch the objects (thus it's called the "displacement method").

How does AutoCAD know whether your response to the first prompt is a base point or a displacement? It depends on how you respond to the second prompt. (Is that confusing, or what?) First, you pick a point on-screen or enter coordinates at the Base point prompt. Next, there are a couple of possibilities:

- ✔ If you then pick or type the coordinates of a point at the second point prompt, AutoCAD says to itself, "Aha — displacement vector!" and moves the objects according to the imaginary arrow pointing from the base point to the second point.

- ✔ If you press Enter at the second prompt (without having typed anything), AutoCAD says, "Aha — displacement distance," and uses the X,Y pair of numbers that you typed at the first prompt as an absolute displacement distance.

What makes this displacement business even more confusing is that AutoCAD lets you pick a point at the first prompt and press Enter at the second prompt. AutoCAD still says, "Aha — displacement distance," but now it treats the coordinates of the point you picked as an absolute distance. If the point you picked has relatively large coordinates, the objects can get moved way outside the normal drawing area as defined by the limits. The objects fly off into space, which you probably won't notice at first because you're zoomed into part of your normal drawing area; it just looks to you like the objects have vanished! In short, be careful when you press Enter during the Move, CoPy, and Stretch commands. Press Enter in response to the second prompt only if you want AutoCAD to use your response to the first prompt as an absolute displacement. If you make a mistake, click the Undo button to back up and try again. You can use Zoom Extents (described in Chapter 7) to look for objects that have flown off into space.

Move

The following steps demonstrate command-first editing with the Move command, using the base point method of indicating how far and in what direction to move the selected objects. This procedure also gives detailed recommendations on how to use precision techniques when you edit:

1. **Press Esc to make sure that no command is active and no objects are selected.**

2. **Click the Move button on the Modify toolbar.**

   The command line displays the `Select objects` prompt.

3. **Select one or more objects.**

   You can use any of the object selection techniques described in the "Perfecting Selecting" section, earlier in this chapter.

4. **Press Enter when you're finished selecting objects.**

   AutoCAD displays the following prompt:

   ```
   Specify base point or displacement:
   ```

5. **Specify a base point by clicking a point or typing coordinates.**

   This point serves as the tail end of your imaginary arrow indicating how far and in what direction you want the objects moved. After you pick a base point, it's fairly easy to see what's going on because AutoCAD displays a temporary image of the object that moves around as you move the cursor. Figure 6-4 shows what the screen looks like.

Displacement vector

Original location   Drag image to new location

Figure 6-4:
Dragging
objects in
the middle
of the MOVE
command.

Specify a base point somewhere on or near the object(s) that you're moving. You can use an object snap mode to choose a point exactly on one of the objects.

AutoCAD displays the following prompt:

```
Specify second point of displacement or <use first point
    as displacement>:
```

6. **Specify the second point by clicking a point or typing coordinates.**

The second point serves as the arrow end of your imaginary displacement arrow. After you specify the second point, AutoCAD moves the objects.

Don't press Enter alone at this prompt! If you do, AutoCAD treats the X,Y coordinates of the first point you picked as an absolute displacement, and the objects fly off in an unpredictable fashion.

These are common precision techniques for specifying the second point:

- ✔ Use an object snap mode to pick a second point exactly on another object in the drawing.

- ✔ Type a relative or polar coordinate, as described in Chapter 4. For example, if you type **@6,2**, AutoCAD moves the objects 6 units to the right and 2 units up. If you type **@3<45**, AutoCAD moves the objects 3 units at an angle of 45 degrees.

- ✔ Use direct distance entry to move objects in an orthogonal or polar tracking direction. See Chapter 4 for instructions.

Copy

The CoPy command works almost identically to the Move command, except that AutoCAD leaves the selected objects in place and moves new copies of them to the new location. The CoPy command also includes a Multiple option for making multiple copies of the same set of objects. You activate the Multiple option by typing **M** and pressing Enter after you finish object selection. As always, you must watch the command line prompts to find out what you can do and when to do it!

Copy between drawings

You can't copy objects from one drawing to another with the CoPy command. Instead, you use the COPYCLIP command, together with its companion command, PASTECLIP. Follow these steps:

1. **Open two drawings that contain geometry you want to copy from one to the other. Arrange the two drawings so that you can see both of them, as shown in Figure 6-5.**

   If you don't have enough screen real estate to arrange the two drawings side by side, you can leave them overlapped and change between the two drawing windows by using the Window menu or by pressing Ctrl+Tab.

2. **In the first drawing, right-click in the drawing area and choose Copy from the cursor menu.**

   Choose Cut if you want to move rather than copy the objects to the other drawing. Choose Copy with Base Point if you want to choose a specific base point rather than let AutoCAD choose a base point.

   The base point that AutoCAD chooses is the lower-left corner of an imaginary rectangle that just barely encloses all the objects you've selected.

3. **If you chose Copy with Base Point in Step 2, pick a base point to use for the copy operation.**

   The base point is like a base point for a block definition, as described in Chapter 13. Choose a useful point such as the endpoint of a line, the lower-left corner of a rectangle, or the center of a circle.

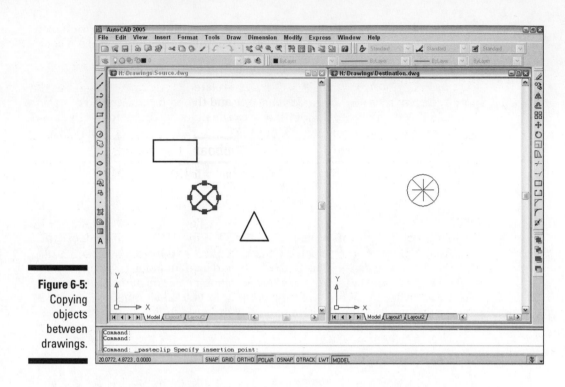

Figure 6-5:
Copying
objects
between
drawings.

4. **Select the objects that you want to copy and then press Enter to end object selection.**

5. **Click in the second drawing's window to make it current.**

6. **Right-click in the second drawing's window and choose Paste from the cursor menu.**

   Choose Paste to Original Coordinates if you want to copy the objects so that they land at the same point (with respect to 0,0) in the second drawing as they were located in the first drawing.

7. **Specify an insertion point for the copied objects by object snapping to a point on an existing object or typing absolute X,Y coordinates.**

   AutoCAD copies the objects.

It's easy to confuse the CoPy and COPYCLIP commands:

✔ CoPy is AutoCAD's primary command for copying objects within a drawing.

✔ COPYCLIP — along with related commands like CUTCLIP and PASTECLIP — is AutoCAD's version of copy and paste via the Windows Clipboard.

(You can use the Windows Clipboard cut-and-paste method to copy or move objects within a single drawing, but using the AutoCAD CoPy and Move commands usually gives you better control and precision.)

Table 6-2 summarizes AutoCAD's Clipboard-related commands, along with the equivalent choices on the right-click menu and the Standard toolbar.

Table 6-2	AutoCAD Clipboard Commands	
Cursor Menu Choice	*Command Name*	*Toolbar Button Name*
Cut	CUTCLIP	Cut to Clipboard (Ctrl+X)
Copy	COPYCLIP	Copy to Clipboard (Ctrl+C)
Copy with Base Point	COPYBASE	none
Paste	PASTECLIP	Paste from Clipboard (Ctrl+V)
Paste as Block	PASTEBLOCK	none
Paste to Original Coordinates	PASTEORIG	none

Stretch

The Stretch command is superficially similar to CoPy and Move; it has the same inscrutable base point and displacement prompts, and it shifts objects — or parts of objects — to other locations in the drawing. But it also has important differences that often confound new AutoCAD users to the point where they give up trying to find out how to use Stretch. That's a mistake, because Stretch is a valuable command. With it, you can perform editing operations in seconds that would take many minutes with other commands. Here are the things you need to know to make Stretch your friend:

✔ To use Stretch, you must select objects by using a crossing selection box (or crossing polygon), as described in the section "Perfecting Selecting," earlier in this chapter. See Figure 6-6.

✔ Stretch operates on the defining points of objects — endpoints of a line, vertices of a polyline, the center of a circle, and so on — according to the following rule: If a defining point is within the crossing selection box that you specify, AutoCAD moves the defining point and updates the object accordingly.

For example, if your crossing selection box surrounds one endpoint of a line but not the other endpoint, Stretch moves the first endpoint and redraws the line in the new position dictated by the first endpoint's new location. It's as though you have a rubber band tacked to the wall with two pins, and you move one of the pins. See Figure 6-7.

Figure 6-6:
Use a crossing selection box to select objects for stretching.

Figure 6-7:
Stretch moves defining points that lie within the crossing selection box.

✔ Stretch can make lines longer or shorter, depending on your crossing selection box and displacement vector. In other words, the Stretch command really combines stretching and compressing.

✔ You usually want to turn on ortho or polar tracking mode before stretching. Otherwise, you'll end up stretching objects in strange directions, as shown in Figure 6-8.

Figure 6-8:
The hazards of stretching without ortho or polar tracking turned on.

The following steps describe how to Stretch lines:

1. **Draw some lines in an arrangement similar to the dark lines shown in Figure 6-9.**

   Start your stretching with simple objects. You can work up to more complicated objects — polylines, circles, arcs, and so on — after you've limbered up with lines.

2. **Press Esc to make sure that no command is active and no objects are selected.**

3. **Click the Stretch button on the Modify toolbar.**

   The command line displays the Select objects prompt, with a warning to use the Crossing or CPolygon object selection mode:

   ```
   Select objects to stretch by crossing-window or crossing-
           polygon...
   Select objects:
   ```

4. **Specify a crossing selection box that encloses some, but not all, endpoints of the lines.**

   Figure 6-9 shows a sample crossing selection box that completely encloses the two vertical lines on the right side of the figure. This crossing selection box cuts through the four horizontal lines, enclosing only one endpoint of each.

   You specify a crossing selection box by picking a point, moving your mouse to the *left*, and picking a second point.

5. **Press Enter to end object selection.**

   AutoCAD displays the following prompt.

   ```
   Specify base point or displacement:
   ```

6. **Specify a base point by object snapping to a point on an existing object or by typing absolute X,Y coordinates.**

   This step is just like Step 5 in the Move procedure earlier in this chapter.

   AutoCAD displays the following prompt.

   ```
   Specify second point of displacement or <use first point
           as displacement>:
   ```

7. **Toggle ortho mode on and then off by clicking the ORTHO button on the status bar; try moving the cursor around first with ortho mode on and then with it off to see the difference.**

   Figure 6-9 shows what the screen looks like as you move the cursor around with ortho off.

Crossing window pick point 1

Original location   Displacement vector

Figure 6-9:
Dragging
objects in
the middle
of the
Stretch
command.

Crossing window pick point 2   Drag image to new location

8. **Toggle ortho mode on and then specify the second point — usually by using direct distance entry, object snapping to a point on an existing object, or typing relative X,Y coordinates.**

   This step is just like Step 6 in the Move procedure earlier in this chapter. After you pick the second point, AutoCAD stretches the objects. Notice that the Stretch command moved the two vertical lines because the crossing selection box contained both endpoints of both lines. Stretch lengthened or shortened the four horizontal lines because the crossing selection box enclosed only one endpoint of each.

The Stretch command takes some practice, but it's worth the effort. Draw some additional kinds of objects and practice stretching with different crossing selection box locations as well as different base points and second points.

More manipulations

The commands in this section — ROtate, SCale, ARray, and OFfset — provide other ways (in addition to Move, CoPy, and Stretch) of manipulating objects or creating new versions of them. The procedures for each command assume that you're familiar with the object selection and editing precision techniques presented in the Move, CoPy, and Stretch procedures (see the previous sections in this chapter).

Rotate

The ROtate command "swings" one or more objects around a point that you specify. Follow these steps to use the ROtate command:

1. **Press Esc to make sure that no command is active and no objects are selected.**

2. **Click the Rotate button on the Modify toolbar.**

3. **Select one or more objects and then press Enter to end object selection.**

    AutoCAD prompts you for the base point for rotating the selected objects:

    ```
    Specify base point:
    ```

4. **Specify a base point by clicking a point or typing coordinates.**

    The base point becomes the point about which AutoCAD rotates the objects. You also have to specify a rotation angle:

    ```
    Specify rotation angle or [Reference]:
    ```

5. **Specify a rotation angle by typing an angle measurement and pressing Enter.**

    Alternatively, you can indicate an angle on the screen by moving the cursor until the Coordinates section of the status bar indicates the desired angle and then clicking. If you choose this alternative, you will need to use ortho mode or polar tracking to indicate a precise angle (for example, 90 or 45 degrees) or an object snap to rotate an object so that it aligns precisely with other objects.

    After you specify the rotation angle by typing or picking, AutoCAD rotates the objects into their new position.

Scale

If you read all my harping on drawing scales and drawing scale factors in Chapter 3, you may think that the SCale command performs some magical scale transformation on your entire drawing. No such luck. It merely scales one or more objects up or down by a factor that you specify. Here's how it works:

1. **Press Esc to make sure that no command is active and no objects are selected.**

2. **Click the Scale button on the Modify toolbar.**

3. **Select one or more objects and then press Enter to end object selection.**

   AutoCAD prompts you for the base point about which it will scale all the selected objects:

   ```
   Specify base point:
   ```

   AutoCAD does not scale each object individually around its own base point (because most AutoCAD drawing objects don't have individual base points). Instead, AutoCAD uses the base point that you specify to determine how to scale *all* objects in the selection set. For example, if you select a circle to scale, pick a point outside the circle as the base point, and then specify a scale factor of 2, AutoCAD not only makes the circle twice as big, but also moves the circle twice as far away from the base point that you specified.

4. **Specify a base point by picking a point or typing coordinates.**

   The base point becomes the point about which the objects are scaled. AutoCAD prompts you for the scale factor:

   ```
   Specify scale factor or [Reference]:
   ```

5. **Type a scale factor and press Enter.**

   AutoCAD then scales the objects by the factor that you type, using the base point that you specified. Numbers greater than one increase the objects' size. Numbers smaller than one decrease the objects' size.

Changing the drawing scale factor of a drawing after you've drawn it is a tedious and complicated process in AutoCAD. In brief, you need to change the scale-dependent system variables described in Chapter 3, and then scale some, but not all, drawing objects. You don't scale the real-world geometry that you've drawn, because its measurements in the real world remain the same. You do scale objects such as text and hatching that have a fixed height or spacing regardless of drawing scale factor. (The SCALETEXT command can help with this operation. See Chapter 9 for more information.) Because of these complications, try to make sure that you choose a proper scale and set up the drawing properly for that scale before you begin drawing. See Chapter 3 for details.

Array

The ARray command is like a supercharged CoPy: You use it to create a rectangular grid of objects at regular X and Y spacings or a polar wheel of objects at a regular angular spacing. For example, you can use rectangular arrays to populate an auditorium with chairs or a polar array to draw bicycle spokes.

The following steps describe how to create a rectangular array, which you'll probably do more often than creating a polar array:

1. **Press Esc to make sure that no command is active and no objects are selected.**

   Alternatively, you can select objects before starting the ARray command and thereby skip Step 3.

2. **Click the Array button on the Modify toolbar.**

   The Array dialog box appears, as shown in Figure 6-10.

Figure 6-10: ARray makes duplicates of objects in a rectangular or polar pattern.

3. **Click the Select Objects button, and then select one or more objects. Press Enter to end object selection and return to the Array dialog box.**

4. **Make sure that the Rectangular Array radio button is selected.**

   If rectangular arrays seem too square, choose the cool Polar Array radio button instead and experiment with the other array option.

5. **Fill in the five edit boxes: Rows, Columns, Row Offset, Column Offset, and Angle of Array.**

The Rows and Columns numbers include the row and column of the original objects themselves. In other words, entries of 1 don't create any new objects in that direction. The Row Offset and Column Offset measurements are the distances between adjacent rows and columns.

6. **Click Preview.**

AutoCAD shows what the array will look like by using your current settings and displays a dialog box with Accept, Modify, and Cancel buttons.

7. **Click the Accept button if you're satisfied with the array, or the Modify button if you want to change the array parameters.**

Offset

You use Offset to create parallel copies of lines, polylines, circles, arcs, or splines. Follow these steps to use OFfset:

1. **Click the Offset button on the Modify toolbar.**

AutoCAD prompts you for the *offset distance* — the distance from the original object to the copy you're creating:

```
Specify offset distance or [Through] <Through>:
```

2. **Type an offset distance and press Enter.**

Alternatively, you can indicate an offset distance by picking two points on the screen. If you choose this method, you normally should use object snaps to specify a precise distance from one existing object to another.

AutoCAD prompts you to select the object from which you want to create an offset copy:

```
Select object to offset or <exit>:
```

3. **Select a single object, such as a line, polyline, or arc.**

Note that you can select only one object at a time with the OFfset command. AutoCAD asks where you want the offset object:

```
Specify point on side to offset:
```

4. **Point to one side or the other of the object and then click.**

It doesn't matter how far away from the object the cursor is when you click. You're simply indicating a direction.

AutoCAD repeats the `Select object` prompt, in case you want to offset other objects by the same distance:

```
Select object to offset or <exit>:
```

5. **Go back to Step 3 if you want to offset another object, or press Enter if you're finished offsetting objects for now.**

Figure 6-11 shows the OFfset command in progress.

Object to offset

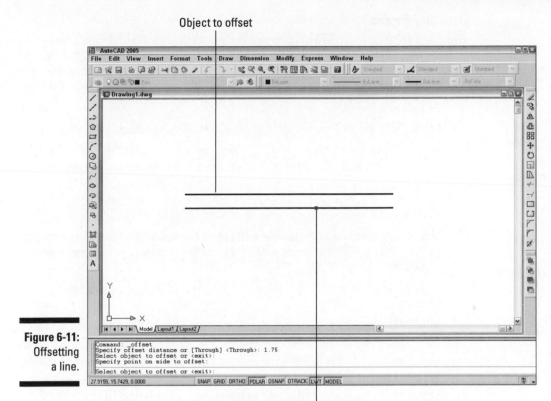

Figure 6-11:
Offsetting
a line.

Point on side of offset

If you want to offset a series of connected lines (for example, a rectangular
house plan outline or one side of a pathway on a map), make sure that you
either draw it as a polyline or convert the individual line and/or arc segments
into a polyline with the PEdit command. If you draw a series of line segments
with the Line command and then try to offset it, you have to pick each segment and offset it individually. Even worse, the corners usually aren't finished
off in the way that you'd expect, because AutoCAD doesn't treat the segments
as connected. You avoid all these problems by offsetting a polyline, which
AutoCAD does treat as a single object. See Chapter 5 for more information
about the differences between lines and polylines.

Slicing and dicing

The commands in this section — TRim, EXtend, BReak, Fillet, and CHamfer —
are useful for shortening and lengthening objects and for breaking them in two.

Trim and Extend

TRim and EXtend are the twin commands for making lines, polylines, and arcs shorter and longer. They're the yin and yang, the Laurel and Hardy, the Jack Sprat and his wife of the AutoCAD editing world. The two commands and their prompts are almost identical, so the following steps cover both. I show the prompts for the TRim command; the EXtend prompts are similar:

1. **Click the Trim or Extend button on the Modify toolbar.**

   AutoCAD prompts you to select cutting edges that will do the trimming (or, if you chose the EXtend command, boundary edges for extending to):

   ```
   Current settings: Projection=UCS, Edge=None
   Select cutting edges ...
   Select objects:
   ```

2. **Select one or more objects that will act as the knife for trimming objects or the wall to which objects will be extended. Press Enter to end object selection.**

   Figure 6-12 shows a cutting edge (for TRim) and a boundary edge (for EXtend).

   AutoCAD prompts you to select objects that you want to trim or extend:

   ```
   Select object to trim or shift-select to extend or
           [Project/Edge/Undo]:
   ```

3. **Select a single object to trim or extend. Choose the portion of the object that you want AutoCAD to trim away or the end of the object that's closer to the extend-to boundary.**

   AutoCAD trims or extends the object to one of the objects that you selected in Step 2. If AutoCAD can't trim or extend the object — for example, if the trimming object and the object to be trimmed are parallel — the command line displays an error message such as `Object does not intersect an edge`.

   TRim and EXtend normally allow you to select only one object at a time for trimming or extending. The one exception is that you can type **F** and press Enter to use the Fence object selection mode (refer to Table 6-1). Fence is useful for trimming or extending a large group of objects in one fell swoop.

   The command line continues to prompt you to select other objects to trim or extend:

   ```
   Select object to trim or shift-select to extend or
           [Project/Edge/Undo]:
   ```

Cutting edge (for trim)   Boundary edge (for extend)

Figure 6-12:
Anatomy of
the TRim
and EXtend
operations.

Objects to trim   Objects to extend

4. Choose additional objects, or press Enter when you're finished trimming or extending.

If you accidentally trim or extend the wrong object and you're still in the TRim or EXtend command, type **U** and press Enter to undo the most recent trim or extend.

The example in Figure 6-12 shows trimming to a single cutting edge, in which the end of the trimmed lines gets lopped off. Another common use of the TRim command is for trimming out a piece of a line between two cutting edges. In the two-cutting-edges scenario, TRim cuts a piece out of the middle of the trimmed line.

The LENgthen command provides other useful ways to make lines, arcs, and polylines longer (or shorter). You can specify an absolute distance (or "delta") to lengthen or shorten by, a percentage to lengthen or shorten by, or a new total length. Look up "LENGTHEN command" in AutoCAD's help system for more information.

Break

The BReak command isn't what you use before heading out for coffee. It's for breaking pieces out of — that is, creating gaps in — lines, polylines, circles, arcs, or splines. BReak also comes in handy if you need to split one object into two without actually removing any visible material.

If you want to create regularly spaced gaps in an object — so that it displays dashed, for instance — don't use BReak. Use an AutoCAD dash-dot linetype instead. See Chapter 4 for more linetype information.

The following example shows how you BReak an object:

1. **Click the Break button on the Modify toolbar.**

   AutoCAD prompts you to select a single object that you want to break:

   ```
   Select object:
   ```

2. **Select a single object, such as a line, polyline, or arc.**

   The point you pick when selecting the object serves double duty: It selects the object, of course, but it also becomes the default first break point (that is, it defines one side of the gap that you'll create). Thus, you should either use one of the AutoCAD precision techniques, such as an object snap, to pick the object at a precise point, or use the First point option (described in the next step) to repick the first break point.

   AutoCAD prompts you to specify the second break point, or to type **F** and press Enter if you want to respecify the first break point:

   ```
   Specify second break point or [First point]:
   ```

3. **If the point that you picked in the preceding step doesn't also correspond to a break point (see the previous tip), type F and press Enter to respecify the first break point, and then pick the point with an object snap or other precision technique.**

   If you do type **F** and press Enter and then respecify the first break point, AutoCAD prompts you now to select the second break point:

   ```
   Specify second break point:
   ```

4. **Specify the second break point by picking a point or typing coordinates.**

   AutoCAD cuts a section out of the object, using the first and second break points to define the length of the gap.

If you want to cut an object into two pieces without removing anything, click the Break at Point button on the Modify toolbar. You first select the object and then choose a second point that defines where AutoCAD breaks the object in two. You can then move, copy, or otherwise manipulate each section of the original object as a separate object.

Fillet and Chamfer

Whereas TRim, EXtend, and BReak alter one object at a time, the Fillet and CHamfer commands require a pair of objects. As Figure 6-13 shows, Fillet creates a curved corner between two lines, whereas CHamfer creates an angled, straight corner. In case you wondered, it's pronounced "fill-et," not "fill-eh." Saying that you know how to "fill-eh" may get you a job in a butcher shop, but it will get you strange looks in a design office.

The following steps describe how to use the Fillet command:

1. **Click the Fillet button on the Modify toolbar.**

   AutoCAD displays the current Fillet settings and prompts you to select the first object for filleting or specify one of three options:

   ```
   Current settings: Mode = TRIM, Radius = 0.0000
   Select first object or [Polyline/Radius/Trim/mUltiple]:
   ```

2. **Type R and press Enter to set the fillet radius.**

   AutoCAD prompts you to specify the fillet radius that it uses for future fillet operations:

   ```
   Specify fillet radius <0.0000>:
   ```

Figure 6-13: Cleaning up those corners with Fillet and CHamfer.

3. **Type a fillet radius and press Enter.**

   The number you type will be the radius of the arc that joins the two lines.

   ```
   Select first object or [Polyline/Radius/Trim/mUltiple]:
   ```

4. **Select the first line of the pair that you want to fillet.**

   AutoCAD prompts you to select the second object for filleting:

   ```
   Select second object:
   ```

5. **Select the second line of the pair that you want to fillet.**

   AutoCAD fillets the two objects, drawing an arc of the radius that you specified in Step 3.

You can fillet two lines and specify a radius of zero to make them meet at a point. If you have lots of lines to fillet, whether with a zero or nonzero radius, use the Fillet command's mUtliple option to speed the process.

The CHamfer command works similarly except that, instead of specifying a fillet distance, you specify either two chamfer distances or a chamfer length and angle.

Get a Grip

Although command-first editing is the most flexible and widespread editing style in AutoCAD, it's not the only way. *Grip editing* is a useful adjunct to command-first editing, especially when you want to modify just one or two objects. You may have encountered grip editing when using other kinds of graphics programs. Even if you're an experienced user of other graphics programs, you've never seen grips used in quite the way that AutoCAD uses them.

Anything that you can do with grip editing can be done with command-first editing as well. In some situations, grip editing is a little more efficient or convenient than command-first editing, but command-first editing always gets the job done. If you master only one style of editing, make it command-first style. In other words, feel free to skip this section — at least until you're comfortable with command-first editing.

About grips

Grips are little square handles that appear on an object after you select it.

In their simplest guise, AutoCAD grips work similar to the little squares on graphical objects in other Windows programs. But in AutoCAD, instead of clicking and dragging a grip, you must click, release the mouse button, move the cursor, and click again at the new location. (By separating the selection of beginning and ending points into two different operations, AutoCAD allows you to use different techniques — such as different object snap modes — to select each point.)

AutoCAD grips are, for sophisticated users, better than the grips found in most other programs, because you can do so much more with them. You can, for example, use AutoCAD grips to move, stretch, or copy an object. You also can use them to rotate an object, scale it to a different size, or *mirror* an object — that is, create one or more backwards copies. Grips also act as *visible object snaps,* or little magnets that draw the cursor to themselves.

A gripping example

The following sections cover in detail the five grip-editing modes — Stretch, Move, Rotate, Scale, and Mirror. Follow these steps to explore the grip-editing modes:

1. **Press Esc to make sure that no command is active and no objects are selected.**

   AutoCAD displays the naked command prompt — that is, no command is currently active:

   ```
   Command:
   ```

2. **Click an object on-screen to select it and display its grips.**

   Grips — solid blue squares on the selected object — appear at various points on the object. Note that the AutoCAD command prompt remains naked; you haven't started a command or grip-editing operation yet.

3. **Click another object.**

   Both the newly selected object and the object that you selected previously display grips.

4. **Click one of the grips on either object.**

   The blue square turns to a red square. This grip is now *hot,* or ready for a grip-editing operation.

   Grip-editing options now appear on the command line. The first option to appear is STRETCH.

5. **Press the spacebar repeatedly to cycle through the five grip-editing options on the command line:**

```
** STRETCH **
Specify stretch point or [Base point/Copy/Undo/eXit]:
** MOVE **
Specify move point or [Base point/Copy/Undo/eXit]:
** ROTATE **
Specify rotation angle or [Base
        point/Copy/Undo/Reference/eXit]:
** SCALE **
Specify scale factor or [Base
        point/Copy/Undo/Reference/eXit]:
** MIRROR **
Specify second point or [Base point/Copy/Undo/eXit]:
```

The grip-editing option displayed on the command line changes as you press the spacebar. If you move the cursor (without picking) in between each press of the spacebar, the appearance of your selected object changes as you display each option. As you can see, each of the grip-editing operations resembles the ordinary AutoCAD command of the same name. Choosing STRETCH, for example, causes a stretched version of the object to appear on-screen.

Pressing the spacebar a bunch of times is a good way to become familiar with the grip-editing modes, but there's a more direct way to choose a particular mode. After you click a grip to make it hot, right-click to display the grip-editing menu. That menu contains all the grip-editing options plus some other choices, as shown in Figure 6-14.

```
Enter
Move
Mirror
Rotate
Scale
Stretch

Base Point
Copy
Reference
Undo

Properties

Exit
```

Figure 6-14:
The grip-editing cursor menu.

6. **Press the spacebar until STRETCH (or the option you want) reappears as the grip-editing option.**

7. **Move the hot grip in the direction in which you want to stretch (or otherwise manipulate) your object.**

   AutoCAD dynamically updates the image of the object to show you what the modified object will look like before you click the final location.

8. **Click again to finish the grip-editing operation.**

   The selected object with the hot grip updates. The object with the cold grips doesn't change.

9. **Click the same grip that you chose in Step 4 (now in a different location) to make it hot.**

10. **This time, move the cursor near one of the grips on the other object. When you feel the magnetic pull of the grip on the other object, click again to connect the hot grip with the other grip.**

   The object point represented by the hot grip now coincides exactly with the grip on the other object.

11. **Press Esc to deselect all objects and remove all grips.**

Figure 6-15 shows a hot (red) endpoint grip of a line being connected to the cold (blue) endpoint grip of another line. The ghosted line shows the original position of the line being edited, and the continuous line shows the new position. Using a grip in this way as a visible object snap offers the same advantage as using single point object snaps, as described in Chapter 4: It ensures precision by making sure that objects meet exactly.

Figure 6-15:
Using grips
to connect
two objects.

You can experiment with all the grip-editing options to find out how they affect a selected object.

Because MOVE and STRETCH are the most useful grip-editing modes, I cover them more specifically.

Move it!

Back in the days of manual drafting, moving objects was a big pain in the eraser. You had to erase the stuff you wanted to move and redraw the objects in their new location. In the process, you usually ended up erasing parts of other stuff that you didn't want to move and left smudged lines and piles of eraser dust everywhere. CAD does away with all the fuss and muss of moving objects, and AutoCAD grip editing is a great way to make it happen. The following steps describe how to move objects:

1. **Select one or more objects.**

   Use any combination of the three editing modes — single object, bounding box, or crossing box — described in the section, "Grab It," earlier in this chapter.

2. **Click one of the grips to make it hot.**

   At this point in your editing career, it doesn't matter which grip you click. As you become more familiar with grip editing, you'll discover that certain grips serve as better reference points than others for particular editing operations.

3. **Right-click anywhere in the drawing area and choose Move from the cursor menu.**

4. **Move the cursor to a different location and click.**

   As you move the cursor around, AutoCAD displays the tentative new positions for all the objects, as shown in Figure 6-16. After you click, the objects assume their new positions.

5. **Press Esc to deselect all objects and remove all grips.**

Copy, or a kinder, gentler Move

If you were paying attention during "A gripping example," earlier in the chapter, you may have noticed while pressing the spacebar that COPY was not among the five grip-editing modes. Why not? Because every grip mode includes a copy option (as the command line prompts shown in "A gripping example," earlier in this chapter indicate). In other words, you can STRETCH with copy, MOVE with copy, ROTATE with copy, SCALE with copy, and MIRROR with copy.

Displacement vector

Original location   Drag image to new location

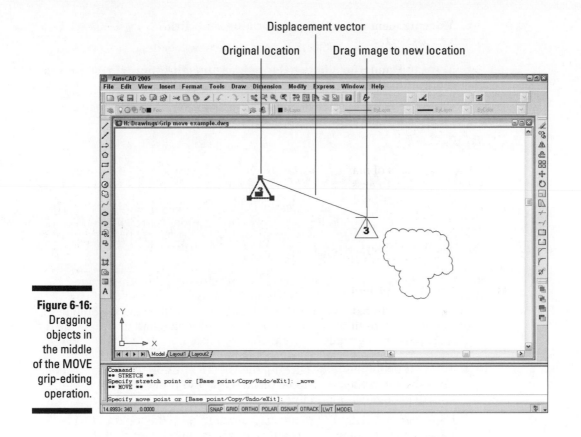

Figure 6-16:
Dragging
objects in
the middle
of the MOVE
grip-editing
operation.

The copy option leaves the selected objects in place and does the editing operation on a new copy of the objects.

By far the most common use for the copy option is with the MOVE grip-editing mode. If you think about "MOVE with copy" for about two seconds, you'll realize that it's just a complicated way of saying "copy." The following steps show how to copy objects quickly by using grip editing:

1. **Select one or more objects.**

2. **Click any one of the grips to make it hot.**

3. **Right-click anywhere in the drawing area and choose Move from the cursor menu.**

    If you want to copy objects in the normal sense of the word "copy," you must choose the MOVE grip-editing mode first. Otherwise, you'll be copying with the STRETCH grip-editing mode.

4. **Right-click again and choose Copy from the cursor menu.**

5. **Move the cursor to a different location and click.**

   After you click, new objects appear in the new location.

6. **Move the cursor to additional locations and click there if you want to make additional copies.**

7. **Press Esc twice — once to end the copying operation and once to deselect all objects and remove all grips.**

A warm-up Stretch

In AutoCAD, stretching is the process of making objects longer *or* shorter. The STRETCH grip-editing operation is really a combination of stretching and compressing, but the programmers probably realized that STRETCHANDCOMPRESS didn't exactly roll off the tongue.

The STRETCH grip-editing mode works differently than the other modes. By default, it affects only the object with the hot grip on it, not all objects with grips on them. You can override this default behavior by using the Shift key to pick multiple hot grips. Follow these steps to get acquainted with using the STRETCH grip-editing mode to stretch one or more objects:

1. **Turn off ortho mode by clicking the ORTHO button on the status bar until the button appears to be pushed out and the words** `<Ortho off>` **appear on the command line.**

   Ortho mode forces stretch displacements to be orthogonal — that is, parallel to lines running at 0 and 90 degrees. During real editing tasks, you'll often want to turn on ortho mode, but while you get acquainted with stretching, leaving ortho mode off makes things clearer.

2. **Select several objects, including at least one line.**

3. **On one of the lines, click one of the endpoint grips to make it hot.**

   All the objects remain selected, but as you move the cursor, only the line with the hot grip changes. Figure 6-17 shows an example.

4. **Click a new point for the hot endpoint grip.**

   The line stretches to accommodate the new endpoint location.

5. **On the same line, click the midpoint grip to make it hot.**

   As you move the cursor, the entire line moves. Using the STRETCH grip-editing mode with a line's midpoint "stretches" the entire line to a new location.

Original location

Displacement vector

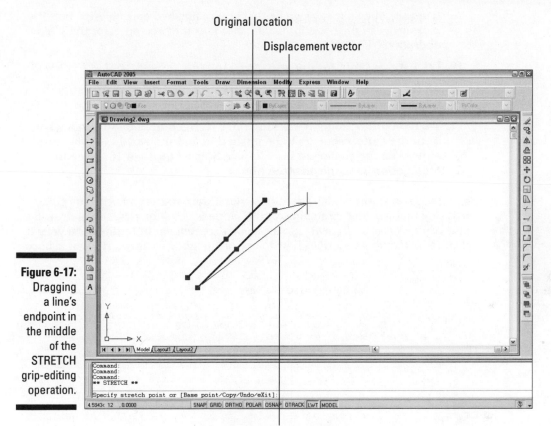

Figure 6-17:
Dragging
a line's
endpoint in
the middle
of the
STRETCH
grip-editing
operation.

Drag image to new location

6. **Click a new point for the hot midpoint grip.**

   The line moves to the new midpoint location.

7. **On one of the lines, click one of the endpoint grips to make it hot.**

8. **Hold down the Shift key, and then click one of the endpoint grips on a different line to make it hot.**

   Two grips on two different lines are now hot because you held down the Shift key and clicked the second grip.

   You can create more hot grips by holding down the Shift key and clicking more grips.

9. **Release the Shift key and re-pick any one of the hot grips.**

Releasing the Shift key signals that you're finished making grips hot. Re-picking one of the hot grips establishes it as the base point for the stretch operation (see Figure 6-18).

10. **Click a new point for the grip.**

    All the objects with hot grips stretch based on the displacement of the grip that you clicked in Step 9.

11. **Turn on ortho mode by clicking the ORTHO button on the status bar until the button appears to be pushed in and the words `<Ortho on>` appear on the command line. Repeat Steps 2 through 10 to see the effect of ortho mode on stretching.**

For most real-world editing situations, you'll want to turn on ortho or polar tracking mode before stretching. Ortho mode is good for all kinds of drawing and editing tasks because it enforces a nice, rectilinear orderliness on your drawing. Chapter 4 describes how to use ortho mode to draw orthogonal lines.

The hot grip used as a base point

Figure 6-18:
Stretching
multiple
objects with
multiple
hot grips.

Multiple hot grips

Polishing those properties

When you think of editing objects, you probably think first about editing their geometry: moving, stretching, making new copies, and so on. That's the kind of editing I cover in this chapter.

Another kind of editing is changing objects' properties. As I describe in Chapter 4, every object in an AutoCAD drawing has a set of non-geometrical properties, including layer, color, linetype, and lineweight. Sometimes, you need to edit those properties — when you accidentally draw something on the wrong layer, for example. Three common ways of editing objects properties in AutoCAD are

- **The Properties palette:** This is the most flexible way to edit properties. Select any object (or objects), right-click in the drawing area, and choose Properties from the cursor menu. The Properties palette displays a tabular grid that lists the names and values of all properties. Click in the value cell to change a particular property.

- **Layers and Properties toolbars:** Another way to change properties is to select objects and then choose from the drop-down lists (Layer, Color, and so on) on the Layers and the Properties toolbars. See Chapter 4 for more information.

- **Match Properties:** You can use the Match Properties button on the Standard toolbar — the button with the paintbrush on it — to paint properties from one object to another. Match Properties works similarly to the Format Painter button in Microsoft applications. Match Properties works even when the objects reside in different drawings.

Chapter 7

A Zoom with a View

*O*ne of the advantages of CAD over manual drawing is its capability of giving you different ways to view your drawing. You can zoom in close, zoom out to a great distance, and pan around. In fact, not only *can* you zoom and pan in your drawing, but in most kinds of drawings, you *must* do it frequently to be able to draw, edit, and view effectively.

Technical drawings are jampacked with lines, text, and dimensions. Zooming and panning frequently enables you to see the details better, draw more confidently (because you can see what you're doing), and edit more quickly (because object selection is easier when there aren't a zillion objects on the screen). This chapter covers AutoCAD's most useful display control features.

Zoom and Pan with Glass and Hand

Moving your viewpoint in to get a closer view of your drawing data is called *zooming in;* moving your viewpoint back to get a more expansive view is called *zooming out.*

Zooming in and out of your drawing is one of the big advantages that AutoCAD offers over manual drawing. You can do detailed work on tiny objects and then zoom out and move around rooms, houses, or neighborhoods from an Olympian perspective.

Panning is closely related to zooming. If you zoom in enough that some of your drawing no longer shows up on-screen, you're going to want to pan around — move left, right, up, and down in your drawing — without zooming in and out. AutoCAD makes panning easy with scroll bars and *real-time* panning.

Both panning and zooming change what is known as the *view*. The view is the current location and magnification of the AutoCAD depiction of your drawing. Each time you zoom or pan, you establish a new view. You can give a name to a specific view to make returning to that view easy, as I demonstrate later in this chapter.

Fortunately, zooming and panning in AutoCAD is as simple as it is necessary. The following steps describe how to use AutoCAD's Zoom and Pan Realtime feature, which is easy to operate and provides a lot of flexibility:

1. **Click the Zoom Realtime button (the one that looks a magnifying glass with a plus/minus sign next to it) on the Standard toolbar.**

   The Realtime option of the Zoom command starts. The cursor changes to a magnifying glass, and AutoCAD prompts you at the command line:

   ```
   Press ESC or ENTER to exit, or right-click to display
                     shortcut menu.
   ```

2. **Move the cursor near the middle of the screen, press and hold down the left mouse button, and drag the cursor up and down until the table almost fills the screen.**

   Dragging up increases the zoom magnification and dragging down decreases it.

3. **Right-click in the drawing area to display the Zoom/Pan Realtime cursor menu, shown in Figure 7-1, and choose Pan from the menu that appears.**

Figure 7-1:
The
Zoom/Pan
Realtime
cursor
menu.

Exit
Pan
✓ Zoom
3D Orbit
Zoom Window
Zoom Original
Zoom Extents

The cursor changes to a hand.

4. **Click and drag to pan the drawing in any direction.**

   You can use the right-click menu to toggle back and forth between Zoom and Pan as many times as you like. If you get lost, choose Zoom Original or Zoom Extents to return to a recognizable view.

5. **Right-click in the drawing area and choose Exit.**

   The cursor returns to the normal AutoCAD crosshairs.

In the preceding example, you started with zooming and ended with panning. You also have the option of doing the reverse: Click the Pan Realtime button (the one showing a hand), and after you've panned, use the right-click menu to switch to zooming. However you start it, the important thing to realize is that Zoom and Pan Realtime is a single AutoCAD function. At any time, you can switch between panning and zooming (or switch to a related function, such as Zoom Window) by using the right-click menu.

You also can pan and zoom by using your mouse's *scroll wheel* (if it has one) or the *middle button* of a three-button mouse:

- To zoom in and out, roll the scroll wheel forward (in) or backward (out).

- To zoom to the extents of your drawing, double-click the scroll wheel or the middle button.

- To pan, hold down the scroll wheel or the middle button as you move the mouse.

The scroll wheel or middle mouse button zoom and pan operations described in the preceding paragraph depend on an obscure AutoCAD system variable named MBUTTONPAN. (See Chapter 2 for a description of what system variables are and how to change them.) When MBUTTONPAN is set to 1 — the default value — you can use the middle button to pan and zoom, as I describe in the preceding tip. If you change MBUTTONPAN to 0, clicking the middle mouse button displays a cursor object snap menu, as it did in older AutoCAD versions. If you're not able to zoom or pan with your middle mouse button, set MBUTTONPAN back to 1. (With MBUTTONPAN set to 1, you use Shift+right-click to display the cursor object snap menu.)

Realtime zooming and panning is the easiest, most interactive way to get around in your drawings. In some situations, though, this method is less efficient or precise than the old-fashioned methods, the most important of which are described in the next section.

Out of the frying pan . . .

Another way to pan in AutoCAD should be familiar from other Windows programs — the scroll bars in the drawing area. Scrolling is the same in AutoCAD as in any other Windows program; click the arrows in the right and bottom borders of the drawing window to scroll, or pan, a step at a time; or click and drag the little square "thumbs" in those borders to pan as little or as much as you want to.

Believe it or not, the realtime and scrollbar panning methods are relatively recent enhancements in AutoCAD's long history. These methods have pretty much replaced the less-intuitive two-point method of panning in older versions of AutoCAD. If you want to see how Grandpa used to pan, enter **–Pan**

(with the leading dash) at the command line and then follow the prompts. This older method remains useful in special situations where you need to pan *orthogonally* by a specific distance — that is, move the display precisely horizontally without wavering up and down or precisely vertically without wavering side to side. This situation sometimes occurs in advanced paper space viewport setup, which I don't cover in this book.

Time to zoom

Because zooming is such a frequent necessity in AutoCAD, it's worth knowing some alternative ways of doing it.

The Zoom command has different options, the most important of which are the following:

- ✔ **All and Extents:** Zoom Extents zooms out just far enough to show all the objects in the current drawing. Zoom All does the same thing, unless the drawings limits are larger than the extents, in which case Zoom All zooms to show the entire rectangular area defined by the limits. If you've defined your limits properly (see Chapter 3), Zoom All is a good way to see your whole drawing area. These two options are especially useful when you zoom in too small or pan off into empty space and want to see your entire drawing again.

  It's a good idea to Zoom All or Zoom Extents and then save before you close a drawing. By performing these steps, you ensure the following:

  - • The next person who opens the drawing — whether it's you or someone else — can see the full drawing from the very beginning.

  - • The drawing preview that displays in the Select File dialog box displays the full drawing, instead of just a tiny, unidentifiable corner of it.

- ✔ **Window:** This option is great for zooming in quickly and precisely. It zooms to a section of your drawing that you specify by clicking two points. The two points define the diagonal of a window around the area you want to look at. (Note that the Zoom command's Window option is not a click-and-drag operation — unlike in some other Windows programs and, confusingly, unlike in the Zoom/Pan realtime Zoom Window option. With the Zoom command's Window option, you click one corner, release the mouse button, and then click the other corner.)

- ✔ **Scale (X/XP):** The X option zooms by a percentage of the current display; values less than 1 cause you to zoom in, values greater than 1 cause you to zoom out. You can also think of the value as a scaling factor: 0.5X causes the screen image to shrink to half its apparent size, and 2X causes the screen image to double its apparent size. (The XP option after a number is for zooming model space objects in a viewport relative to paper space; see Chapter 3 for information about paper space.)

✔ **Realtime:** Realtime zooming, the technique described previously, enables you to zoom in and out by starting a realtime zoom and then moving the cursor up to zoom in or down to zoom out.

✔ **Previous:** This option undoes the last zoom and/or pan sequence. It's like going back in time but without the funny costumes!

Some of the zoom options take some getting used to. I recommend that you use realtime zoom and pan for most of your zooming and panning. Supplement it with Zoom Window to move quickly into a precise area, Zoom Previous to back up in zoom/pan time, and Zoom All or Zoom Extents to view your whole drawing.

A View by Any Other Name . . .

If you find yourself repeatedly zooming and panning to the same area, you probably can get there faster with a named view. A *named view* is a name that you assign to a particular region of your drawing. After you create a named view, you can return to that region quickly by restoring the view. You use the View command, which displays the View dialog box, to create and restore named views. Follow these steps to create a named view:

1. **Zoom and pan until you find the view that you want to assign a name to.**

2. **Choose View➪Named Views.**

   The View dialog box appears.

3. **Click the New button.**

   The New View dialog box appears, as shown in Figure 7-2.

4. **Type a name in the View Name text box.**

5. **(Optional) Type a new category in the View Category box, or select an existing one from the drop-down list.**

View Category is a new view property in AutoCAD 2005. You use it to organize views and certain display characteristics of views in sheet sets, as described in Chapter 14. Until you use the sheet sets feature, you can leave this box blank.

6. **Select the Current Display radio button, if it's not selected already.**

If you want to name a region other than the currently displayed view, select the Define Window radio button instead, click the Define View Window button to the right of it, and pick two corners of the region's rectangle (as though you were zooming windows).

Figure 7-2:
Create a
new view
for you.

7. Confirm or change the choices in the Settings area.

The Store Current Layer Settings with View option is new in AutoCAD 2005. If you leave this setting turned on, then when you later restore the view, AutoCAD also will restore the layer visibility settings (on/off and freeze/thaw) that were in effect when you created the view. (Chapter 4 describes the layer visibility settings.) The two UCS-related settings are primarily for 3D drawings (see Chapter 8). If you're creating 2D drawings, you can ignore the UCS settings.

8. Click OK.

The New View dialog box disappears, and you see your new named view in the list in the View dialog box.

9. Click OK.

The View dialog box disappears.

To restore a named view, choose View➪Named Views or enter View at the command line to display the View dialog box. Click the name of the view that you want to restore, click the Set Current button, and then click OK to close the dialog box.

With the new Update Layers and Edit Boundaries buttons in the main View dialog box, you can change the layer visibility settings that AutoCAD associates with an existing view and revise the view's boundary.

You also can plot the area defined by a named view. See Chapter 12 for instructions on plotting views.

Looking Around in Layout Land

All the zoom, pan, and view operations I describe in this chapter apply to paper space layouts as well as to model space. (Chapter 3 describes the difference between model space and paper space and how to navigate between the two.) One little complication exists, though: In a *paper space layout* — that is, any drawing area tab except for the Model tab — it's possible for the cursor to be either in paper space or in model space inside a viewport. Zooming and panning have a different effect depending on which space your cursor is in at the moment. Experiment with the different effects by following these steps:

1. **Open a drawing that contains at least one paper space layout with a title block and one or more viewports.**

   If you don't have any such drawings handy, try using the AutoCAD sample drawing `\Program Files\AutoCAD 2005\Sample\Wilhome.dwg`.

2. **Click one of the layout tabs — that is, any tab other than the Model tab.**

   AutoCAD displays the paper space layout for that tab, including any title block and viewports.

3. **Click the PAPER/MODEL button on the status bar until it says PAPER.**

   Alternatively, you can double-click in the gray part of the drawing area outside of the layout.

   The cursor is now in paper space, so zooming and panning changes the display of all the objects in the layout, including the title block.

4. **Choose View⇨Zoom⇨All.**

   AutoCAD displays the entire layout, as shown in Figure 7-3.

5. **Zoom and pan by using any of the techniques described in this chapter.**

   Zooming and panning change the appearance of the title block, as shown in Figure 7-4. The effect is similar to moving a plotted sheet in and out and all around in front of your face.

6. **Choose View⇨Zoom⇨All.**

   AutoCAD displays the entire layout again.

7. **Click the PAPER/MODEL button on the status bar until it says MODEL.**

   Alternatively, you can double-click with the cursor over a viewport.

   The cursor is now in model space, inside the viewport, so zooming and panning change only the display of the objects that are visible in the viewport. The display of the title block doesn't change.

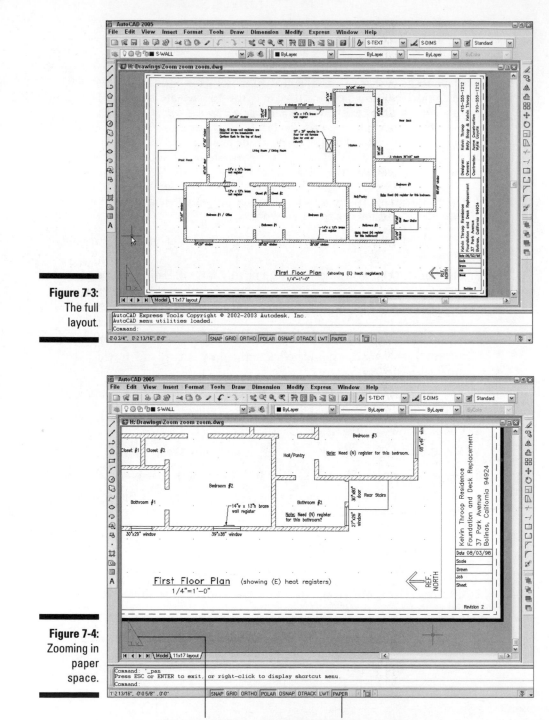

Figure 7-3:
The full
layout.

Figure 7-4:
Zooming in
paper
space.

Paper space icon   Paper/Model button set to Paper

8. **Zoom and pan by using any of the techniques described in this chapter.**

   Zooming and panning don't change the appearance of the title block, as shown in Figure 7-5. The result looks as if you're moving a picture of the model space geometry in and out and all around behind a frame.

   In real drawings, you usually shouldn't zoom and pan inside viewports after they've been set up (see Chapter 3). Doing so changes the scale of the viewport, which messes up plotting. I'm asking you to do it here to illustrate the difference between zooming in paper space and zooming in a model space viewport.

   If the title block is changing when you zoom and pan, someone has locked the viewport to prevent the kind of mischief that I warn against in the previous paragraph. (You also see the command line prompt `Viewport is view-locked. Switching to Paper space.`) See "viewports, floating, locking" in the AutoCAD online help system if you need to lock — or unlock — viewports.

9. **Choose View⇨Zoom⇨Previous one or more times until you've restored the original view.**

10. **Click the PAPER/MODEL button on the status bar until is says PAPER.**

    Always leave the cursor in paper space when you're finished.

Figure 7-5:
Zooming in a model space viewport.

Model space icon

11. **Choose File⇨Close and click the No button to close the drawing without saving changes.**

    In this example, I have you close the drawing without saving changes, just in case you did mess up the viewport zoom scale.

In most cases, you set up a paper space layout once, as described in Chapter 3, and then just return to it to plot. You shouldn't be spending a lot of time zooming and panning in paper space layouts. You zoom and pan to get a better view of what you're drawing and editing, and that's what the Model tab is for. But if you do want to zoom in paper space — to get a better look at part of your title block, for example — make sure that you're doing it with the PAPER/MODEL button set to PAPER.

AutoCAD 2005 includes new VPMAX and VPMIN commands for maximizing and minimizing a viewport in the current layout. These commands provide an alternative to switching between the Model and Layout tabs without the potential problems of zooming inside of paper space viewports. The easiest way to run VPMAX or VPMIN is to click the new Maximize Viewport/Minimize Viewport button located on the status bar, just to the right of the PAPER button.

Degenerating and Regenerating

As you zoom and pan around your drawing, you may wonder how the image that you see on the screen is related to the DWG file that AutoCAD saves on the hard disk. Well, maybe you don't wonder about that, but I'm going to tell you anyway!

When you draw and edit objects, AutoCAD stores all their geometrical properties (that is, location and size) in a highly precise form — technically, *double floating-point precision*. The program always maintains that precision when you save the DWG file. For computer performance reasons, however, AutoCAD does *not* use that high-precision form of the data to display your drawing on the screen. Instead, AutoCAD converts the highly precise numbers in the DWG file into slightly less precise *integers* in order to create the view that you see on the screen.

The happy consequence of this conversion is that zooming, panning, and other display changes are a lot faster than they would be otherwise. The unhappy consequence is that the conversion, which is called a *regeneration* (or *regen* for short), occasionally leaves you with some artifacts to deal with.

In most cases, AutoCAD performs regenerations automatically when it needs to. You sometimes will see command line messages like `Regenerating model` or `Regenerating layout`, which indicate that AutoCAD is taking care of regens for you.

If, on the other hand, you see the command line message Regen queued, then AutoCAD is warning you that it's *not* performing a regeneration, even though one might be advisable now. In addition, you might see a warning dialog box with the message "About to regen — proceed?" These messages are AutoCAD's way of saying, "What your drawing looks like on the screen at the moment may not exactly match the real version of the drawing database that gets stored when you save the drawing. I'll update the display version at the next regeneration."

The REGENAUTO system variable controls whether or not AutoCAD performs most regenerations automatically (see Chapter 1 if you're unfamiliar with system variables or how to change them):

 ✓ The default REGENAUTO setting in new drawings, 1, tells AutoCAD to regenerate your drawing automatically if it's required to synchronize the screen display with the drawing database.

 ✓ The other REGENAUTO setting, 0 (Off), tells AutoCAD not to regenerate automatically, but instead to display Regen queued on the command line and let you force a regeneration with the REgen command if you want to.

The REGENAUTO off option is for the most part a holdover from much slower computers and older versions of AutoCAD. You probably don't need to subject yourself to the mental contortion of trying to avoid REgens unless you work on huge drawings and/or use a painfully slow computer.

Don't confuse the REgen command with the Redraw command. REgen (View⇨Regen) forces the synchronization process described in this section. Redraw (View⇨Redraw) simply repaints the screen, without attempting to synchronize the screen with the drawing database. The Redraw command was useful in the days of very slow computers and older versions of AutoCAD, which didn't handle the display as effectively, but it's essentially a useless command now.

The REgenAll command (View⇨Regen All) regenerates all viewports in a paper space layout. If you run the REgenAll command in model space, it has the same effect as the ordinary REgen command.

Chapter 8

On a 3D Spree

*F*or millennia, people have documented the design and construction of three-dimensional objects by drawing two-dimensional views of them. Most people have continued to use these "classical" methods with CAD because the methods are well understood and work reasonably well. After all, if 2D drawing was good enough for guys like Leonardo da Vinci and Andrea Palladio, it should be good enough for us, right?

Nonetheless, there's a growing trend of using CAD programs to create 3D models and letting the CAD program generate the 2D views more-or-less automatically. This approach seems more logical, especially if the documentation requires numerous, complex views of the same object. 3D modeling also is a virtual necessity (pun intended) when you want to create *rendered* (shaded) views for presentation purposes.

The 3D construction and visualization tools in AutoCAD have improved dramatically over the years to support this 3D modeling approach to CAD, but it's still a complex process that requires sophistication on the part of the CAD user. Although 3D modeling requires only one more dimension than 2D drafting, developing 3D CAD models is considerably more complicated. Users must master new techniques and contend with the 2D limitations of most display screens and input devices.

This chapter introduces you to the concepts, tools, and techniques for AutoCAD 3D modeling and visualization. Be prepared to spend some additional time wading around in the AutoCAD online help system and experimenting if you want to become proficient at 3D modeling. And if 3D CAD makes you feel a little wobbly at first, Figure 8-1 shows that you're not alone.

Figure 8-1:
Leaning
toward 3D.

Full 3D support is one of the main differentiators between full AutoCAD and AutoCAD LT. If you're using AutoCAD LT, you can look at and plot 3D models created in AutoCAD, but you can't do much 3D object creation or editing yourself. Also, viewing 3D models is less flexible in AutoCAD LT because it lacks AutoCAD's 3DOrbit command.

Is 3D for Me?

The concept of 3D hardly seems to need introduction. We live in a three-dimensional world, and most of the objects that you represent in your 2D AutoCAD drawings are three-dimensional.

Traditional 2D drawings provide clues to help the viewer's mind construct a 3D model from the 2D image on paper. Multiple views from different view-points in 3D space give experienced designers, drafters, and builders the information they need to make 3D sense of 2D drawings. Design and drafting have succeeded pretty well by using 2D representations as the guide to creating 3D objects. But at some point, nothing can replace a true 3D model, such as in helping someone understand how a building will look when constructed or how two parts fit together.

What does using 3D in CAD mean? Fundamentally, it means creating models instead of views. Rather than create cross sections of an object or individual views of it from certain perspectives, you create a fully three-dimensional model of the object. This 3D depiction of each object includes all the necessary information for AutoCAD to create a view from any point of view. With a properly constructed 3D model, AutoCAD can output commands to machines to create actual 3D objects, whether plastic prototypes carved from a tank of jelly by lasers or an actual bolt, valve, or piston created by computer-controlled machine tools.

AutoCAD, like most 3D CAD programs, enables you to create three different kinds of 3D models of objects:

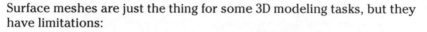

✔ **Wireframes:** A wireframe model is like a skeleton of a 3D object; it shows the edges of the object, not any of its surfaces. You create a set of 2D objects that represent an outline of each part of the object and then connect them three-dimensionally to make the wireframe. It's like building a model from wire coat hangers. One of the biggest limitations of wireframe models is that you can't shade them; there aren't any surfaces "inside" the wire edges to catch the light — imagine shining a flashlight on a coat hanger.

✔ **Surfaces:** A surface model represents the "skin" of an object but not the solid mass inside. AutoCAD uses objects called *meshes* to create surfaces. A mesh is a faceted surface that represents the edges and surfaces of a 3D object. You also can create a surface mesh by sweeping a 2D object such as a polyline around an axis. Creating a surface model is like building a physical model out of thin sheets of balsa wood. A surface model is one step up from a wireframe model because you can apply material properties and shading to its surfaces.

Surface meshes are just the thing for some 3D modeling tasks, but they have limitations:

• Some 3D objects are awkward to build by pasting surfaces together.

• You can't check mass properties or interferences of a surface model. (AutoCAD doesn't recognize that there's any solid mass inside the surfaces.)

✔ **Solids:** A solid model is as close to true 3D as you can get without whipping out some Play-Doh and building a real-world model yourself. You build solid models by constructing basic 3D shapes and then combining them — adding, subtracting, or finding their intersections — and modifying them. It's like using lots of fancy saws, drills, and glue to build a model made out of wooden blocks. You can render a solid model, as well as check mass properties and interferences.

In most practical applications of 3D, you select one type of representation — wireframe, surface, or solid — for all or most of the objects in the drawing, based on ease of construction and intended use of the model. However, AutoCAD doesn't prevent you from mixing all three types of 3D objects in the same drawing.

3D thumbs up

Using 3D takes time to master, creates additional work, and slows down your computer. Why bother using it? Here are four key reasons why anyone in his or her right mind would bother with 3D:

✔ **It's the wave of the future.** As CAD pursues greater realism and production efficiency, 3D is becoming important for more tasks in more professions. Drafters and designers who want to keep up with how CAD is likely to be used in the future should become familiar with 3D now.

✔ **Sometimes it's nice.** Drawing in 3D is useful for several tasks, including creating shaded renderings to help sell a design to a client, and fit-and-finish testing to find potential problems before a design is put into construction or manufacturing.

✔ **Sometimes it's needed.** Drawing in 3D is required for a small but growing number of tasks. Many mechanical designs are done in 3D or converted into 3D at some point in the design process. 3D perspective views make drawings easier to understand. And the shaded renderings used for both designing and selling are becoming a practical necessity in some fields.

✔ **Sometimes it's faster.** The fastest way to create a single view of something usually is to draw that view in 2D. If you need multiple views, it may be faster to create a 3D model and then slice and render it as needed for the views you want to create.

After you determine the type of 3D representation to use, you decide on the appropriate level of detail and construct the model, using the commands and techniques introduced in this chapter. Finally, you create the required 2D and/or rendered views for plotting or viewing on the screen.

You can do some experimentation with 3D on any computer system that can run AutoCAD. If you want to pursue serious work in 3D AutoCAD, pay attention to the following prerequisites:

✔ **Know AutoCAD well.** You need to be pretty comfortable using AutoCAD for 2D work before doing much with 3D. You should be able to control object properties, use precision techniques, draw and edit 2D objects, and zoom and pan — in other words, all the stuff covered in Chapters 4 through 7 of this book. If you aren't comfortable with these techniques in 2D drafting, you're likely to find 3D modeling in AutoCAD a real struggle.

✔ **Get a fast computer.** For beginning 3D work, any AutoCAD-adequate system will do the job. For serious work with 3D models, you need a fast computer, lots of memory, and lots of disk space.

✔ **Get and master additional software.** In addition to AutoCAD, you may need other programs — either AutoCAD add-ons or separate packages — to do work that AutoCAD isn't as good at. Specialized 3D modeling and rendering programs are among the tools of the trade of most people who do a lot of 3D work. Illustration packages can help you jazz up the appearance of your drawing.

Many of Autodesk's newer software products — AutoCAD-based ones like Architectural Desktop and Mechanical Desktop and non-AutoCAD ones like Revit and Inventor (see Chapter 1 for more information) — use 3D modeling as their fundamental approach to CAD. If you intend to use 3D on real projects, you'll probably use 3D-centric programs such as these, not plain AutoCAD. The information in this chapter will get you started on the right track, especially if you eventually use one of the AutoCAD-based applications.

✔ **Do a real project.** Real work is the best motivation for discovering 3D. If you don't have an actual work assignment, create a task. Something as "simple" as creating a 3D model of your chair will make the difference between really finding out something useful about 3D and just reading about it in the manuals.

3D thumbs down

Consider these issues before you decide how much to use 3D on a particular project:

✔ **2D input and editing:** The mouse, keyboard, and drawing tablet are all 2D devices; the more complex the 3D object you're trying to model, the more complicated it is to construct the object with these devices. In addition, the AutoCAD 3D editing tools are fairly limited in scope — especially for solids. For most heavy-duty 3D work, you need a third-party application, a discipline-specific version of AutoCAD (such as Architectural Desktop), or a special-purpose solid modeling program.

✔ **2D output:** Most of the currently available output methods, notably paper and the computer screen, are 2D. Presenting your 3D model in its full, three-dimensional glory requires extra work by you or the viewer.

✔ **Performance:** Today's personal computers are adequate for the task of storing fairly complex 2D models and displaying them on-screen and on plots; if the model is 3D, the difficulty increases geometrically, and performance seems to slow geometrically as well. You may need a faster computer and more memory to meet these demands. You may also find yourself taking longer coffee breaks as you wait for your computer to load or render complex 3D models.

Getting Your 3D Bearings

The first challenge in 3D modeling is being able to see your three-dimensional model on a two-dimensional computer screen. The normal model space view on the Model tab in the drawing area shows a single, projected 2D view of your model — the top-down, "plan" view by default.

AutoCAD provides two model space capabilities that enable you to escape this visual flatland:

✔ With *viewports,* you can carve the model space drawing area into smaller rectangular areas, each of which shows a different view of the model.

✔ With *viewpoints,* you can change the point in 3D space from which you look at the model. By setting a different viewpoint in each viewport, you can look at several sides of your model at the same time. It's like looking at one of Picasso's cubist paintings, only more orderly.

If you want to experiment with viewports and viewpoints in an existing 3D drawing, try one of the AutoCAD2005 samples, such as `\Program Files\ AutoCAD 2005\Sample\Welding Fixture Model.dwg`. To remove shading and make the model faster to work with, choose View⇨Shade⇨2D Wireframe.

Model space viewports left and right

Chapter 3 discusses viewports in paper space, which are useful for creating layouts for use in plots and presentations in both 2D and 3D. *Model space viewports,* cousins of paper viewports, are less powerful but simpler and are intended to help you construct 3D models.

Model space viewports divide the screen into separate rectangles with no gaps between them. Unlike with paper space viewports, you can't move, stretch, or overlap them. You can't plot multiple model space viewports; that's what paper space is for. And, unlike in layouts, a layer that's visible in one model space viewport always is visible in all of them.

You may hear or read references to *tiled viewports,* which is just another name for model space viewports. *Tiled* refers to the way in which model space viewports always fill the drawing area, with no gaps and no overlapping allowed. Conversely, paper space viewports are sometimes called *floating viewports* because you can move them around, leave gaps between them, and overlap them.

Model space viewports enable you to see several views of your model at one time, each from a different viewpoint. For this reason, model space viewports are especially useful when you're creating and editing objects in 3D. As you draw and edit, the different views help ensure that you're picking points that are located correctly in 3D space.

To set up model space viewports, use the Viewports dialog box:

1. **Choose View⇨Viewports⇨New Viewports.**

   The Viewports dialog box appears.

2. **Choose one of the Standard Viewport arrangements and choose 3D in the Setup drop-down list.**

3. **Click OK.**

Figure 8-2 shows the dialog box and the model space result of choosing the Four Right Standard Viewport arrangement and the 3D Setup. This arrangement, along with the Four Equal, and Four Left standard viewport arrangements, works well for creating viewports that show top, front, right, and isometric views of a 3D model.

Figure 8-2:
The Viewport dialog box makes setting up model space viewports and different viewpoints easy.

To return to a single viewport later, click in the one whose view you want to use, then open the Viewports dialog box and choose Single in the Standard Viewports list.

Seeing the world from new viewpoints

When you choose 3D in the Viewports dialog box's Setup drop-down list, you direct AutoCAD to change the *viewpoint* in each viewport. The default viewpoints when you choose a four viewport arrangement are top, front, right, and isometric. These viewpoints work well for viewing and constructing simple models, but eventually, you'll probably want to specify your own, custom viewpoint in a particular viewport.

The easiest way to change viewpoints is to use the View➪3D Views submenu (shown in Figure 8-3) to switch to one of the standard orthographic 3D views or an isometric view:

- ✔ The six standard orthographic (straight-on) views are Top, Bottom, Left, Right, Front, Back.

- ✔ The four standard isometric views are SW (left-front), SE (right-front), NE (right-back), and NW (left-back). An isometric view is one in which you see the object from above, but not too high above — as though you were hovering in a low-flying helicopter.

These ten views are called standard because they're often used in manual drafting and rendering work. They work well for showing 3D models of common objects such as mechanical components and buildings. (You can also change to plan view, which is a top-down view of either the world coordinate system or a user coordinate system. I describe coordinate systems in "A Cartesian Orientation," later in this chapter.)

You can specify nonstandard viewpoints by choosing View➪3D Views➪ Viewpoint Presets. In the Viewpoint Presets dialog box that appears, specify the following settings:

- ✔ A viewing angle in the XY plane (imagine moving a camera on a dolly around an object, while keeping the camera at the same elevation)

- ✔ An angle from the XY plane (imagine using a boom to swoop the camera up to a different height so that you're looking at the object from increasingly steep angles)

Figure 8-3:
The 3D
Views
submenu.

By default, AutoCAD shows 3D models in 2D wireframe mode, even if you've created surface or solid objects. If you want to better visualize which objects are in front of which other objects, especially in an isometric or other non-orthogonal view, you have a couple of options:

- Choose View⇨Shade and then choose Hidden or any of the Shaded options.

- Render the model, as described later in this chapter.

Dynamic viewpoints with 3DOrbit

Standard views and the Viewpoint Presets dialog box are fine for many 3D construction tasks, but if you really want to have fun with a model, 3DOrbit is your ticket to it.

AutoCAD LT doesn't include the 3DOrbit command. In LT, you can use the DDVPOINT and DView commands to look at a model from different points of view.

The 3DOrbit command displays an *arcball* on the screen — a circle representing a sphere around your object. You click various places inside, outside, and on the arcball and then drag to change the 3D view. The idea is that you're spinning the imaginary sphere containing your model. As you drag the cursor, AutoCAD updates the screen dynamically.

3DOrbit provides many other options through its right-click shortcut menu. You can change the shading mode and projection type, and you can turn on several visual aids that help you understand where you are in 3D space. Additional shortcut menu options enable you to pan, zoom, and restore standard or named views.

The following steps show some of the things that you can do with 3DOrbit:

1. **If you've divided model space into two or more viewports, click in the viewport in which you want to change the viewpoint.**

2. **Choose View⇨3D Orbit.**

   The 3DOrbit arcball appears, as shown in Figure 8-4.

3. **Move the cursor inside the arcball.**

   The 3DOrbit *full orbit cursor* appears: two oval arrows circling a sphere.

4. **Click and drag, keeping the cursor inside the arcball.**

   You can rotate the model in all directions. Imagine that the cursor is your finger pushing on a globe that rotates freely in all directions.

Full orbit

Horizontal rotation   Vertical rotation   Roll

Figure 8-4:
The 3DOrbit
arcball and
right-click
menu.

TIP

Pay attention to the shaded UCS (user coordinate system) icon at the lower-left corner of the drawing area as you change the view. The UCS icon helps you visualize how each orbiting operation works. (The next section of this chapter tells more about UCSs.)

5. Release the mouse button and move the cursor outside the arcball.

The 3DOrbit *roll cursor* appears: a circular arrow circling a sphere.

6. Click and drag, keeping the cursor outside the arcball.

You can rotate the model around an axis at the center of the circle, coming out of the screen. Imagine that you're turning the steering wheel on a car, with the steering column pointing into the screen.

7. Release the mouse button and move the cursor over one of the small circles at the quadrant points (that is, 12 o'clock, 3 o'clock, 6 o'clock, and 9 o'clock) of the arcball.

The 3DOrbit *horizontal or vertical rotation cursor* appears: an elliptical arrow circling a sphere.

8. **Click and drag away from the small circle.**

   You can rotate the model around a horizontal axis (if you clicked the circle at 3 o'clock or 9 o'clock) or a vertical axis (if you clicked the circle at 12 o'clock or 6 o'clock) passing through the little circle. Imagine that you're turning a piece of meat on a spit, with the spit located horizontally or vertically in the plane of the screen.

9. **Release the mouse button and right-click in the drawing area.**

   The 3DOrbit shortcut menu, shown in Figure 8-4, appears.

10. **Experiment with the additional options, such as Shading Modes and Projection.**

    Here's the lowdown on some of these options:

    - Gouraud Shaded usually looks more realistic than Flat Shaded.

    - Hidden removes hidden lines but doesn't shade.

    - Wireframe is the default wireframe view, without hidden lines removed.

    - Parallel projection is the default AutoCAD projection — lines that are parallel in the 3D object remain parallel in the projected view on the screen.

    - Perspective projection makes objects look more realistic (for example, train tracks appear to converge in the distance), but lines that are parallel in the model don't remain parallel in perspective projection.

    If you manage to 3DOrbit out of control so that you no longer see your model, right-click to display the 3DOrbit shortcut menu and choose More⇨Zoom Extents. The Zoom, Pan, and Preset Views options offer other ways of getting your model back in your sights.

11. **When you're finished orbiting, right-click in the drawing area and choose Exit.**

Choose More⇨Adjust Clipping Planes on the 3DOrbit right-click menu (or the 3DCLIP command outside of 3DOrbit) to slice away part of your model temporarily to view what's inside the surfaces or solid boundaries. See "clipping, 3D objects" in the AutoCAD online help for more information.

You can control the camera point and target point that 3DOrbit uses (the point that you're looking from and the point that you're looking towards). Before you start the 3DOrbit command, type **CAMERA** at the command prompt and press Enter. Click or type the coordinates of the desired camera point target points.

A Cartesian Orientation

Viewing your model from different viewpoints in multiple viewports is all well and good, but unless your 3D spree is limited to looking at other people's models, you need to know how to specify points and distances in 3D. To do that, you need to understand AutoCAD's coordinate systems and conventions for entering 3D points and distances.

Coordinate systems: The WCS and UCS

AutoCAD stores the locations of all the objects that you draw as 3D Cartesian coordinates (X, Y, and Z) in the *world coordinate system* (or WCS). The WCS defines the origin (0,0,0) point for the drawing and the orientation of the X, Y, and Z axes. A particular point in the Cartesian coordinate system is defined by its X, Y, and Z coordinates, where the coordinate indicates the distance from the origin (0,0,0) point along the X, Y, or Z axis.

The WCS is the default XYZ coordinate system when you start a new drawing. X is horizontal on the screen, Y is vertical on the screen, and Z extends out of the screen, towards your face.

The X-Y plane (the set of points where Z = 0) is the *construction plane* in which you create 2D objects. It's also important for creating 3D objects, because many commands operate with respect to the X-Y plane.

When you're drawing and editing 3D objects, it's often useful to be able to move or rotate the construction plane. You do so in AutoCAD by defining a *user coordinate system* (UCS). A UCS can have a different origin (0,0,0) point and can have its X, Y, and Z axes point in different directions than they do in the WCS.

Choose Tools⇨Orthographic UCS⇨Preset to run the UCSMAN command, which opens the UCS dialog box, shown in Figure 8-5. This dialog box simplifies the job of changing to common UCSs, such as Top, Front, and Right. The Tools⇨New UCS submenu runs the UCS command, which provides additional options. Look up "UCS command" in AutoCAD's online help to find out more about UCSs and how to work with them.

To keep you informed about which coordinate system is current in each viewport, AutoCAD displays a UCS (user coordinate system) icon in each viewport by default. The icon looks like two or three little arrows (depending on the viewpoint), each of which represents the direction of the positive X, Y, or Z axis. This icon shows the working construction plane — the plane in which AutoCAD places 2D objects when you draw them. Use the View⇨Display⇨UCS Icon submenu to turn the icon off or on or to change its properties.

Figure 8-5:
Get with the
UCSMAN.

Don't confuse viewpoints and coordinate systems:

✔ The viewpoint controls what you *see* in a particular viewport, but doesn't control what you *do* to objects — that is, the viewpoint doesn't dictate the results of drawing and editing commands.

✔ The current coordinate system defines the construction plane in a particular viewport — that is, the UCS (or WCS) dictates how the points that you specify during drawing and editing commands influence the specific locations and orientations of objects. The UCS icon shows the current coordinate system, not the current viewpoint.

Specifying coordinates in 3D

As I indicate in Chapter 4, you specify points in 2D drafting by typing a pair of numbers in the format *X,Y* for absolute coordinates (with respect to the point 0,0) or @*X,Y* for relative coordinates (with respect to the previous point that you specified). In both cases, you ignore the Z coordinate, but AutoCAD still stores it — as zero.

When you create 3D models, you no longer can ignore the Z axis. You need to worry about three coordinates for each point that you pick or type. AutoCAD provides several ways of specifying 3D points. These are the most common:

✔ **Typed coordinates:** When you type coordinates, you simply add a Z coordinate: *X,Y,Z* for absolute coordinates (with respect to the point 0,0,0) or @*X,Y,Z* for relative coordinates.

There are 3D analogues to 2D polar coordinates (@*distance<angle*), too. See "polar coordinates, entering, cylindrical" and "polar coordinates, entering, spherical" in the AutoCAD online help.

✔ **Object snaps:** Happily, the object snap techniques described in Chapter 4 for picking precise locations on existing objects work equally well in 3D. You can object snap to endpoints, intersections, midpoints, and so on, without having to worry about the current construction plane as defined by the WCS or UCS.

In practice, you'll have to be more careful when using object snaps in 3D work. Remember that there are now three coordinates instead of two to be precise about. If you're viewing a 3D model from just one viewpoint, it's easy to osnap to a point that looks right in that view but in fact lies "deeper" or "shallower" in 3D space that you realize. Thus it's a good idea to display your model from several different points of view, as described in the "Getting Your 3D Bearings" section, earlier in this chapter. The different points of view help you predict which location in 3D space a given object snap mode will grab and make any object snap mistakes more obvious.

An additional object snap mode, Apparent Intersection, is useful when you want to snap to the imaginary intersection of two objects that appear on the screen to intersect, but don't in fact intersect because they lie in different planes.

✔ **Coordinate filters:** You'll sometimes need to pick a point some of whose coordinates (for example, the X and Y coordinates) match one object snap point and some of whose coordinates (for example, the Z coordinate) match another object snap point. Coordinate filters — also called *point filters* — solve this problem handily. With coordinate filters, you use the coordinates of points on existing objects to help specify new points. You use coordinate filters together with object snaps to "build up" a point one or two coordinates at a time. When AutoCAD prompts you to pick a point, you activate a coordinate filter before you pick the point. The coordinate filter tells AutoCAD which coordinates of the subsequent point to use.

You activate a coordinate filter by clicking one of the six choices on the object snap cursor menu's Point Filters submenu (shown in Figure 8-6): .X, .Y, .Z, .XY, .YZ, or .XZ. (You display the object snap cursor menu by pressing Shift+right-click; see Chapter 4 for more information.) For example, if you select .XY and then pick a point, AutoCAD remembers only the X and Y coordinates of that point. AutoCAD then prompts you to pick another point and combines the Z coordinate of that second point with the X and Y coordinates of the first point to determine the 3D location of the new point. Look up "coordinate filters" in AutoCAD's online help for more information and an example.

At this point, you may be feeling less then completely 3D-coordinated, despite the WCS, UCSs, and XYZs. All this stuff will become clearer after you create some viewports and draw some objects. The next section gives you some specific instructions, but don't be afraid to experiment with typing Cartesian coordinates, object snapping in 3D, and working with different predefined UCSs. Or, you can console yourself with the following paragraph's geometrical trivia and vile pun.

Figure 8-6:
The object
snap cursor
menu's
Point Filters
submenu.

In case you're wondering, the Cartesian coordinate system is named after its inventor, the French mathematician René Descartes. (Yes, he of "I think therefore I am" and the *Monty Python* Philosophers' Drinking Song fame.) He did not, however, invent the cart. The cart came earlier, and the horse came earlier still. It's for that reason that we know not to put Descartes before de horse.

Drawing in 3D

This section introduces four techniques for creating 3D objects: drawing 3D lines and polylines, extruding 2D objects, creating surface meshes, and creating solids.

When you draw 3D objects, just like when you draw 2D objects, put them on appropriate layers and use precision techniques to specify each point and distance. See Chapter 4 for more information.

Drawing 3D lines and polylines

The most straightforward way to draw objects for a 3D wireframe model is to use the Line or 3DPOLY (3D Polyline) command and specify 3D coordinates. The 3DPOLY command is similar to the PLine (Polyline) command, which is described in Chapter 5. Both commands draw a series of connected line segments, but they have different capabilities:

✔ The 3DPOLY command accepts 3D points for the line segments' vertices. The PLine command requires that all vertices be in the same plane.

✔ 3DPOLY is limited to straight line segments. PLine can draw arc segments and create segments with uniform or tapered width.

✔ Segments created with 3DPOLY can't display dash-dot linetypes; 3D polyline segments always display as continuous lines.

The command sequence for drawing 3D segments with the Line or 3DPOLY command is the same as for drawing 2D segments with the Line command; see Chapter 5 for details. The only difference is that you specify 3D coordinates instead of 2D ones. Figure 8-7 shows an example.

Creating 2D representations in this way is straightforward, though tedious for all but the simplest objects. More important, a wireframe model becomes increasingly difficult to decipher as the complexity of the model increases. You see a mass of lines representing the edges, and you have difficulty telling which parts of which edges are in front of others. To reduce this visual confusion, you need to graduate to a surface or solid modeling commands, as described earlier and in the subsequent sections of this chapter.

Extruding from 2D to 3D

One way to create a surface model is to extrude, or thicken, 2D objects. For example, if you give thickness to a circle, it becomes a cylinder. If you give thickness to a 2D polyline or a series of lines segments, it looks like a fence.

AutoCAD calls this depth *thickness,* which is not to be confused with other characteristics that you may be tempted to call "thickness" — linewidths that you add for plotting and uniform or tapered widths that you can add to polyline segments. Linewidths and polyline segment widths make objects fatter but leave them in the 2D plane. Thickness pushes objects out of the plane, giving them a new dimension.

Folks who do heavy-duty 3D modeling somewhat derisively refer to the result of adding thickness to 2D objects as $2\frac{1}{2}$D — a bit more than 2D, but not quite 3D. That's because extrusion is a limited 3D technique compared to creating real surface meshes and solids, as described in the following two sections. You can't model most objects in a detailed way with extrusion alone. Imagine a set of wooden blocks in which every block has a uniform thickness, with no tapering allowed — kind of dull, huh? Even AutoCAD LT, despite its advertised 3D limitations, can do extrusion (although only the simple kind of extrusion described in the following steps). Nonetheless, extrusion is a fun and fairly low-stress way to get started with 3D, and it's adequate for some simple modeling tasks. It's also a good warm-up exercise for full 3D solid extrusion, which I describe later in this chapter.

Figure 8-7:
Drawing
3D line
segments.

The following steps show the general procedure for creating "2½D" extruded objects.

1. **Define a suitable UCS (user coordinate system), as described earlier in "Coordinate systems: The WCS and UCSs."**

   The extrusion direction will be perpendicular to the UCS, so think about the orientation of the 2D object and which way you want it to "pop out" into 3D space.

2. **Draw a 2D object.**

   See Chapter 5 for more information.

3. **Open the Properties palette.**

   See Chapter 6 for more information.

4. **Press Esc to make sure that no objects are selected.**

5. **Click the object to select it.**

6. **In the Thickness field, type an extrusion thickness and press Enter.**

   AutoCAD extrudes the object perpendicular to the UCS in which you created it, as shown in Figure 8-8.

Figure 8-8:
Just add
thickness
and voilà —
instant 3D!
(Or 2½D,
anyway.)

If you extrude closed polylines and then shade or render them, the extruded shapes appear *hollow* — that is, without any tops or bottoms on them. You can work around this limitation by using the 3DFACE command to add three-sided or four-sided surfaces as "lids." You can build up irregular shapes by using a combination of three-sided and four-sided faces. A better approach in most cases is to use the EXTrude command, which creates a true solid out of closed polylines and other closed shapes. (EXTrude requires AutoCAD — it's not included in AutoCAD LT.)

Meshing around with surface meshes

For surface models that are more complex than simple extrusions of 2D objects, you can use a variety of AutoCAD commands that draw *3D meshes*. One set of commands draws surface model representations of 3D primitives: box, pyramid, wedge, dome, sphere, cone, torus, dish, and mesh. (In this case, the word primitive isn't a pejorative. A *3D primitive* is a relatively simple shape that can be used alone or as a subcomponent of a more complex 3D object.)

To create these objects, choose Draw⇨Surfaces⇨3D Surfaces, select a primitive shape from the image tile menu (shown in Figure 8-9), and follow the command line prompts. It's like constructing your own set of wooden blocks, except that they don't take up any space in your closet after you're finished playing with them!

Figure 8-9:
A torus
mesh —
the perfect
3D surface
snack.

The Surfaces submenu of the Draw menu includes commands for creating complex 3D surfaces from 2D lines and curves. For example, with the Revolved Surface menu choice (the REVSURF command), you revolve a set of 2D line and arc segments around an axis of revolution to "sweep out" a 3D surface. But in most cases, you're better off using solid modeling commands such as REVolve instead.

A solid(s) foundation

Solid modeling is in many ways the culmination of 3D CAD. Solids more accurately represent most real-world objects than do wireframes or surfaces. And even when representational accuracy isn't the main issue, it's easier to construct many kinds of models with solids.

Solid modeling also places more serious demands on computer software and hardware. It takes a sophisticated program and fast computer — not to mention a capable human being running all this stuff — to create useful solid models. That's why solid modeling historically has lagged behind wireframe and surface modeling and only recently become common on ordinary PCs. AutoCAD's solid modeling capabilities have improved steadily over the years, but most people who do real solid modeling use AutoCAD add-on applications or separate, stand-alone programs that have been created with this task in mind. Examples include Inventor from Autodesk and SolidWorks from SolidWorks Corporation.

Many special-purpose solid modeling programs use a combination of solid and surface modeling techniques for maximum flexibility in constructing and editing 3D models. These kinds of programs — and solid modeling in general — are becoming especially popular in mechanical design.

Constructing the basic building blocks — or *solid primitives* — for a solid model in AutoCAD isn't difficult. As with wireframe and surface objects, you follow these steps:

1. **Define a suitable UCS (user coordinate system).**

   See "Coordinate systems: The WCS and UCSs," earlier in this chapter. The UCS controls the construction plane and basic 3D orientation of the solid.

2. **Choose Draw⇨Solids and then choose a solid from the top half of the submenu.**

   As shown in Figure 8-10, your choices are Box, Sphere, Cylinder, Cone, Wedge, and Torus. (These are similar to the surface mesh choices shown in Figure 8-9. In this case, though, you're creating solid instead of surface versions.)

When you see a 3D object in a drawing, you can't tell by looking whether it's a 2D extruded object, surface mesh, or solid. If you want to find out, open the Properties palette and select the object. The drop-down list at the top of the palette shows the type of object that you selected.

Figure 8-10:
Everything you need for a solid foundation.

Constructing solid primitives is pretty simple and immediately gratifying. For example, you can quickly put together a virtual cityscape by populating your drawing with boxes, cylinders, cones, and wedges representing buildings. For additional gratification, you'll want to shade or render them (see the "Ending with Rendering" section, later in this chapter). If you have any questions about any of the 3D solid primitive commands, choose Contents⇨User's Guide⇨ Create and Modify Objects⇨Draw Geometric Objects⇨Create 3D Objects⇨ Create 3D Solids in the AutoCAD online help.

After the solid primitives, the next pair of commands on the Draw⇨Solids submenu is Extrude and Revolve:

✔ Extruding is similar to adding thickness (see "Extruding from 2D to 3D," earlier in this chapter) except that it creates true solids rather than "2½D" objects. In addition, you can specify tapers with the EXTrude command.

✔ Use the REVolve command to create a solid by rotating a closed object around an axis.

The commands described in this section are the building blocks of solid modeling. Developing useful 3D models takes a lot more than just knowing the basics. You can model simple objects by using solid primitives, extrusion and revolution, and the editing techniques discussed in the next section. But for most real-world solid modeling work, you'll want additional software and learning resources.

Editing in three dimensions

When you're ready to modify wireframes or surfaces, you can use most of the editing commands described in Chapter 6. Grip editing also works well on most wireframe and surface objects.

As with 3D drawing, you need to be a more careful when editing in 3D to make sure that the editing transformations you apply occur correctly in all three spatial dimensions. Display your model in multiple viewports from different viewpoints so that you can see what's going on and catch mistakes right away.

Modifying 3D solids is trickier. Simple editing commands like Move, CoPy, and ROtate work fine, but most of the commands that alter an object's shape (for example, Stretch, Trim, and Break) don't work on solids. You can use grips to move and copy solids, but not to stretch them.

Instead, AutoCAD provides a set of specialized commands on the Modify⇨ Solids Editing menu, shown in Figure 8-11. The first three choices — Union, Subtract, and Intersect — perform the so-called *Boolean operations*, which create new 3D solids by combining and removing parts of existing ones. Look up "composite 3D solids" in the AutoCAD online help system for more information about these commands. Also see Contents⇨User's Guide⇨Create and

Modify Objects⇨Change Existing Objects⇨Modify 3D Solids for a description of the other options on the Modify⇨Solids Editing menu.

Figure 8-11:
Specialized
solids
editing
commands.

Modify	
Properties	
Match Properties	
Object ▶	
Clip ▶	
Xref and Block Editing ▶	Union
	Subtract
Erase	Intersect
Copy	
Mirror	Extrude faces
Offset	Move faces
Array...	Offset faces
	Delete faces
Move	Rotate faces
Rotate	Taper faces
Scale	Color faces
Stretch	Copy faces
Lengthen	
	Color edges
Trim	Copy edges
Extend	
Break	Imprint
Chamfer	Clean
Fillet	Separate
	Shell
3D Operation ▶	Check
Solids Editing ▶	
Explode	

Ending with Rendering

To my mother, who grew up on a farm in Iowa, rendering was what you did to fat to make it into lard. But in CAD, rendering is the process of illuminating a set of 3D objects with one or more imaginary lights and then creating a more-or-less realistic picture of the results. (No, computer programmers didn't have lard on their minds when they borrowed the word *rendering*. Hand-drawn pictures of building facades were called renderings long before computers got into the act.)

A single example of this technique is called a *still rendering*. Multiple frames strung together produce computer *animation*. The objects that you see in movies such as *Toy Story* or *A Bug's Life* are first created as 3D models and then rendered frame by frame — a process that can take immense amounts of time even on ultrafast graphics workstations — to produce the beautifully, well-rendered images you see.

AutoCAD creates still renderings only. If you want to create animations, you need to use other software programs such as Discreet's 3DS Max. Even if you use animation programs, AutoCAD can be useful for developing the initial 3D models.

Rendering has steadily improved in speed and usability as PCs have become faster, and programmers have improved their rendering algorithms. Rendering of simple scenes is now practical on a mainstream PC, and a fast personal computer can create some impressive images in a reasonable amount of time. Rendered images are useful for previewing how your models will work in real life and also can be powerful tools for sales and marketing communications for your company. A (rendered) picture can be worth quite a bit more than a thousand words.

To see how rendering works with the default options in AutoCAD, use the steps that follow. When you're ready to get fancy, choose User's Guide⇨ Create Realistic Images and Graphics⇨Render 3D Objects for Realism in the AutoCAD online help system.

1. **Create one or more 3D objects.**

   Use the steps in the previous section or use one of the sample 3D drawings in `\Program Files\AutoCAD 2005\Sample`.

   Unless you want a monochromatic rendering, create the objects on several different layers that you've assigned different colors.

2. **Choose View⇨Render⇨Render.**

   The Render dialog box appears, as shown in Figure 8-12.

Figure 8-12: The Render dialog box and a rendered object.

 3. **Ignore all the options and click the Render button.**

 You can get okay results without changing the options. When you click Render, AutoCAD renders the 3D objects. See Figure 8-12 for an example.

To make rendered images look less cartoonish, you need to apply materials to 3D objects and define different light sources. For more information, navigate to the Render 3D Objects for Realism help page mentioned just before the preceding steps and then look at Create Rendered Images⇨Use Materials in Rendering and Create Rendered Images⇨Use Lights in Rendering.

The SHADE command offers a simpler alternative to the RENDER command, without all the lighting, surface materials, and other options. To experiment with shading, choose any of the options on the View⇨Shade menu. (To return to an unshaded view, choose View⇨Shade⇨2D Wireframe.) As I mention earlier in this chapter, the 3DOrbit command's right-click menu includes shaded modes that you can see even while navigating around your model in real time.

In addition to viewing rendered and shaded views on the screen, you can plot them, whether they're in a paper space layout or in model space. Use the Shaded Viewport Options area of the expanded Plot dialog box to control this feature. Chapter 12 contains more information about plotting.

If you want to plot multiple rendered views (or a rendered view plus other nonrendered views), create a paper space layout with multiple viewports, as described in Chapter 3. As I mention earlier in this chapter, tiled model space viewports are great for creating and viewing 3D models, but you can plot only one model space viewport at a time. Use paper space layouts to compose multiple viewports for plotting purposes.

People who do a lot of rendering and want higher quality, photorealistic results usually use programs other than AutoCAD to render their models. Discreet 3DS Max, Autodesk VIZ, and McNeel's are three popular photorealistic rendering programs. Most rendering programs can import 3D models from AutoCAD DWG files, but some people use specialized 3D modeling programs to do their modeling as well.

Part III
If Drawings Could Talk

The 5th Wave   By Rich Tennant

BRAIN TWISTER PUZZLE

"That reminds me. I have to figure out exploding
the block with AutoCAD."

In this part . . .

Text, dimensions, and hatching have long been important clarifying elements in drafting. In AutoCAD, these elements are flexible almost to a fault, and you can edit and update them quickly as you change the geometry beneath them. The text, dimension, and hatching annotations that you add "speak" about the geometry so that others can understand exactly what, how big, and how far.

After you've made some drawings that talk, you'll probably send the message around by printing — or as CAD users call it, plotting — them. AutoCAD 2005 introduces a redesigned, streamlined Plot dialog box, which makes the often-complex task of plotting a little less daunting. Chapter 12 in this section is your passport to navigating the revised plot process, understanding how the legacy of AutoCAD plotting influences current practice, and most of all getting a good-looking, properly scaled plot onto paper.

Chapter 9

Text with Character

- -

- -

Although it's often true that "A picture is worth a thousand words," it's also true that adding a few words to your drawing can save you from having to draw a thousand lines and arcs. It's a lot easier to write "Simpson A35 framing clip" next to a simple, schematic representation of a clip than to draw one in photorealistic detail and hope that the contractor can figure out what it is!

Most CAD drawings include some text in the form of explanatory notes, objects labels, and titles. This chapter demonstrates how to add text to drawings and shows you how to take advantage of AutoCAD text styles and the spelling checker. Chapter 10 covers text that's connected with dimensions and leaders.

In most cases, adding text, dimensions, and other descriptive symbols is something that you should do later in the drafting process, after you've drawn at least some of the geometry. In CAD drawings, text and other annotations usually are intended to complement the geometry, not to stand alone. Thus, you generally need to have the geometry in place before you annotate it. Many drafters find that it's most efficient to draw as much geometry as possible first, and then add text labels and dimensions to all the geometry at the same time. In this way, you develop a rhythm with the text and dimensioning commands, instead of bouncing back and forth between drawing geometry and adding annotations. (It helps if you hum "I've got rhythm . . ." while sliding the mouse back and forth in time.)

Getting Ready to Write

In AutoCAD, adding text to a drawing is only slightly more complicated than adding it to a word processing document. Here are the steps:

1. **Create a new AutoCAD text style, or select an existing style, that includes the font and other text characteristics you want to use.**

2. **Make an appropriate text layer current.**

3. **Run *one* of these commands to draw text:**

   • mText draws paragraph (also called multiline) text.

   • TEXT draws single-line text.

4. **Specify the text alignment points, justification, and height.**

5. **Type the text.**

You're probably familiar with most of these steps already — especially if you've ever used a word processor. In the next few sections of this chapter, I review the particularities of AutoCAD text styles, the two kinds of AutoCAD text, and ways of controlling height and justification.

Simply stylish text

AutoCAD assigns text properties to individual lines or paragraphs of text based on *text styles*. These text styles are similar to the paragraph styles in Microsoft Word: They contain font and other settings that determine the look and feel of text. An AutoCAD text style includes

✔ The font

✔ A font height, which you can set or leave at 0 for later flexibility

✔ Special effects such as italic

✔ *Really* special effects such as vertical and upside down, which almost nobody uses

Before you add text to a drawing, use the Text Style dialog box to select an existing style or create a new one with settings that are appropriate to your purpose. Your AutoCAD notes may generate strange responses (or no response at all) if they appear in Old Persian Cuneiform or the Cyrillic alphabet.

Most drawings require very few text styles. You can create one style for all notes, object labels, and annotations, and another one for special titles. A title block may require one or two additional fonts, especially if you want to mimic the font used in a company logo or project logo.

As with layers, your office may have its own text style standards. If so, you'll make everyone happy by following those standards. One of the best ways to make your use of text styles efficient and consistent is to create them in a template drawing that you use to start new drawings. (If your office is well organized, it may already have a template drawing with the company-approved styles defined in it.) See Chapter 3 for information about creating and using templates. Another handy technique is to copy existing text styles from one drawing to another by using the DesignCenter palette. See Chapter 4 for instructions.

Font follies

When you create a text style in AutoCAD, you have a choice of a huge number of fonts. AutoCAD can use two different kinds of fonts: native AutoCAD SHX (compiled SHape) fonts and Windows TTF (TrueType) fonts:

- **SHX:** In the Text Style dialog box, SHX font names appear with a drafting compass to the left of the name. SHX fonts usually provide better performance because they're optimized for AutoCAD's use.

- **TTF:** In the Text Style dialog box, TrueType font names appear with a TT symbol to the left of name. TTF fonts give you more and fancier font options, but they slow down AutoCAD when you zoom, pan, and select and snap to objects. TrueType fonts also can cause greater complications when you exchange drawings with other AutoCAD users. Chapter 16 describes the special procedure that you need to use in order to install custom TrueType fonts.

It's okay to use a TrueType font sparingly for something like a title block logo, but in general, you should stick with standard AutoCAD SHX fonts whenever possible.

The most popular AutoCAD font is ROMANS.SHX (Roman Simplex). (You may also run into SIMPLEX.SHX, an older version of Roman Simplex.) ROMANS.SHX is a good, general-purpose font for drafting in AutoCAD. Avoid complicated, thick fonts. They can slow down AutoCAD, and they're usually more difficult to read than the simpler fonts. Remember, you're doing CAD here — not fancy graphic design or reproduction of medieval manuscripts!

Whenever possible, avoid *custom fonts,* which are font files that don't come with AutoCAD or AutoCAD LT (both programs come with the same fonts). AutoCAD installs its standard SHX fonts into the C:\Program Files\AutoCAD 2005\Fonts folder — as long as you haven't added any custom fonts to that folder, you can refer to it for a list of standard fonts. If you use a custom font, exchanging your drawings with other people will be more complicated. If you're compelled to use a custom font, make a note of it and remember either to send it whenever you send the DWG file (assuming that the font isn't copyrighted, which many custom fonts are) or to warn the recipients that the text will appear different on their systems. It's far less hassle to eschew custom fonts altogether. See Chapter 16 for additional information about how to deal with fonts when you send and receive drawings.

Get in style

The following steps describe how to select an existing text style or create a new one before you enter text into a drawing. (If you want to experiment with an existing drawing that contains a variety of text styles, you can use \Program Files\AutoCAD 2005\Sample\Hummer Elevation.dwg.)

1. **Choose Format⇨Text Style.**

   The Text Style dialog box appears, as shown in Figure 9-1.

2. **In the Style Name drop-down list, select each style in turn to see what text styles have been created in this drawing.**

   Note the font name and look at the Preview panel to get a feel for what the different fonts look like.

3. **If you find a suitable text style, select it in the Style Name drop-down list and then skip to Step 9.**

   What constitutes a suitable text style depends on industry practices, office standards, and personal preferences about how the text should look. The information in preceding sections may help you decide. If not, ask an experienced drafter in your office or look at some printed drawings and try to match the text on those.

   The selected text style name becomes the current style.

4. **If you don't find a suitable text style, or if you prefer to create your own text style, click New.**

   The New Text Style dialog box appears, with an edit box for you to type a name.

Figure 9-1:
Text with
style.

5. **Type a name for your new text style and then click OK.**

   Your new text style is added to the Style Name list and becomes the current style.

6. **Choose a font from the Font Name list.**

   ROMANS.SHX is the best all-purpose font for most drafting work. If you'd like to use a different font, review the font suggestions and warnings in the previous section.

   The font that you choose becomes the font that's assigned to your new text style.

7. **Set the remaining text style settings as shown in Figure 9-1: Height = 0.0, Width Factor = 1.0, Oblique Angle = 0.0, and all four check boxes unchecked.**

   A text style height of 0.0 makes the style *variable height,* which means that you can specify the height separately for each single-line text object. Assigning a *fixed* (that is, nonzero) height to a text style forces all single-line text using the style to be the same height. Variable height styles are more flexible, but fixed height styles usually make it easier to draw text of consistent height. The decision to use variable height versus fixed height styles is another aspect of text that depends on office practice, so if you work with other AutoCAD users, ask around.

8. **Click Apply.**

9. **Click Close.**

   The Text Style dialog box closes, and the text style that you selected or created is now the current style for new text objects.

Taking your text to new heights

In Chapter 3, I describe the importance of choosing an appropriate drawing scale when you set up a drawing. I warn you that you need to know the drawing scale factor for tasks described in other chapters of this book. This is one of those chapters, and I'm about to explain one of those tasks!

Drawing scale is the traditional way of describing a scale with an equal sign or colon — for example ¼" = 1'–0", 1:20, or 2:1. The *drawing scale factor* represents the same relationship with a single number such as 48, 20, or 0.5. The drawing scale factor is the multiplier that converts the first number in the drawing scale into the second number.

One of the things that distinguishes knowledgeable CAD users is that they *always* know the drawing scale factor of any drawing they're working on. Make it a point to determine the drawing scale factor of a drawing before you add text to it.

Attack of the giant text strings

"Why do I need to know the drawing scale factor in order to draw text?," you may ask — especially if you've spent time "on the boards," as we grizzled old-timers like to call manual drafting. You need to know the drawing scale factor because you handle scaling of objects and text in CAD opposite from the way you do in manual drafting.

In manual drafting, you squeeze real-world objects (the building, widget, or whatever) down by a specific scale factor, like 10 or 48, so that they fit nicely on a sheet of paper. Naturally, you always draw text the size that you want it to appear on the paper (for example, ⅛ inch or 3 mm high), regardless of the scale of the drawing.

In CAD drafting, you draw objects as if they were at their actual size. Then, when you plot, you shrink — or, if you make drawings of tiny things such as microprocessor circuitry, expand — the entire drawing by that same scale factor (for example, 10 or 48) to fit on the paper. When you shrink the whole drawing to fit on the paper, text shrinks, too. To avoid indecipherably small text,

or incredibly large text, you must create text at a size that's scaled appropriately by the drawing scale factor. (If you're an architect, imagine that your text is neon lettering on the side of the building. If you're a mechanical designer, think of a brand name stamped on the side of a screw.)

For example, assume that someone has drawn a widget at a scale of 1:20 (corresponding to a drawing scale factor of 20), and you want your notes to appear 3 mm high when the drawing is plotted to scale. You need to create text that's 20 times 3 mm, or 60 mm, high. In a building plan drawn at a scale of ¼" = 1'–0" (drawing scale factor equals 48), text that will appear ⅛ inch when plotted needs to be ⅛ inch times 48, or 6 inches, high.

This "tiny text"/"enormous text" approach seems peculiar at first, especially if you were schooled in manual drafting. But it's a consequence of CAD's ability to let you draw and measure the geometry in real-world units. After all, the geometry of what you're representing, not the ancillary notes, usually is the main point of the drawing.

Plotted text height

Most industries have plotted text height standards. A plotted text height of ⅛ inch or 3 mm is common for notes. Some companies use slightly smaller heights (for example, ³⁄₃₂ inch or 2.5 mm) to squeeze more text into small spaces.

Calculating AutoCAD text height

To calculate AutoCAD text height, you need to know the drawing scale factor, the desired plotted text height, and the location of the multiplication button on your calculator. Use the following steps to figure out text height:

1. **Determine the drawing's drawing scale factor.**

   If you set up the drawing, you should know its drawing scale, as described in Chapter 3. If someone else set up the drawing, try the suggestions in the sidebar, "Figuring out a drawing's scale factor."

2. **Determine the height that your notes should appear when you plot the drawing to scale.**

   See the "Plotted text height" section for suggestions.

3. **Multiply the numbers that you figured out in Steps 1 and 2.**

Table 9-1 lists some common drawing scales and text heights for drawings in imperial and metric units. You should know how to calculate the drawing scale factors and text heights, but you're allowed to use the table to check your work. (*Hint:* Multiply the number in the second column by the number in the third column to get the number in the fourth column!) The Cheat Sheet tables include some additional drawing scales and text heights.

Table 9-1	Common Drawing Scales and Text Heights		
Drawing Scale	*Drawing Scale Factor*	*Plotted Text Height*	*AutoCAD Text Height*
⅛" = 1'–0"	96	⅛"	12"
¼" = 1'–0"	48	⅛"	6"
¾" = 1'–0"	16	⅛"	2"
1" = 1'–0"	12	⅛"	1½"
1 = 100 mm	100	3 mm	300 mm
1 = 50 mm	50	3 mm	150 mm
1 = 20 mm	20	3 mm	60 mm
1 = 10 mm	10	3 mm	30 mm

Figuring out a drawing's scale factor

If you're adding text to a drawing that someone else created, you may not immediately know its drawing scale factor. In some cases, making the determination is trivial, whereas in other cases it's tricky indeed. Here are some methods you can use:

✔ Ask the creator of the drawing.

✔ Look for text or a scale bar on the drawing that indicates the scale.

✔ Use an architectural or engineering scale to measure distances on the plotted drawing, if you have one.

✔ Check the value of the DIMSCALE (DIMension SCALE) system variable, as described in Chapter 10.

None of these methods is infallible by itself, but by comparing the evidence, you usually can figure out the drawing scale factor with reasonable certainty.

After you know the AutoCAD text height, you can use it to define the height of a text style or of an individual text object. If you assign a nonzero height to a text style (Step 7 in the "Get in style" section, earlier in this chapter), all single-line text strings that you create with that style will use the fixed height. If you leave the text style's height set to zero, AutoCAD asks you for the text height when you draw each single-line text object.

This discussion of text height assumes that you're adding text in model space, which is the most common practice. You may want to add text to a paper space layout — for example, when you draw text in a title block or add a set of sheet notes that doesn't directly relate to the model space geometry. When you create text in paper space, you specify the actual, plotted height, instead of the scaled-up height.

One line or two?

For historical reasons (namely, because the AutoCAD text capabilities used to be much more primitive than they are now), AutoCAD offers two different kinds of text objects and two corresponding text-drawing commands. Table 9-2 explains the two options.

Table 9-2		The Two Kinds of AutoCAD Text
Text Object	*Command*	*Comments*
Paragraph text	mText	Designed for multiple lines, with word-wrapping. AutoCAD keeps the multiple lines together as a single object. Other special formatting, such as hanging indents, is possible.
Single-line text	TEXT	Designed for creating single lines. Although you can press Enter to create more than one line of text, each line becomes a separate text object.

Although you may be inclined to ignore the older single-line text option, it's worth knowing how to use both kinds of text. The TEXT command is a bit simpler than the mText command, so it's still useful for entering short, single-line pieces of text such as object labels and one-line notes. And it's the command of choice for CAD comedians who want to document their one-liners!

Your text will be justified

Both the TEXT and mText commands offer a bewildering array of text *justification* options — in other words, which way the text flows from the justification point or points that you pick in the drawing. For most purposes, the default

Left justification for single-line text or Top Left justification for paragraph text works fine. Occasionally, you may want to use a different justification, such as Centered for labels or titles. Both commands provide command-line options for changing text justification. I point out these options when I demonstrate the commands later in this chapter.

Using the Same Old Line

Despite its limitations, the TEXT command is useful for labels and other short notes for which mText would be overkill. The following procedure shows you how to enter text by using the AutoCAD TEXT command.

You can use TEXT for multiple lines of text: Just keep pressing Enter after you type each line of text, and TEXT puts the new line below the previous one. The problem is that TEXT creates each line of text as a separate object. If you later want to add or remove words in the multiple lines, AutoCAD can't do any word-wrapping for you; you have to edit each line separately, cutting words from one line and adding them to the adjacent line.

The AutoCAD 2005 TEXT command was called DTEXT (Dynamic TEXT) in older versions of AutoCAD (Release 14 and earlier). You may hear AutoCAD old-timers refer to the DTEXT command instead of TEXT. And you thought they called it DTEXT because it wasn't good enough to be A, B, or C text. . . .

The TEXT command does all of its prompting on the command line, so be sure to read the command line prompts at each step along the way.

Here's how you enter text with the TEXT command:

1. **Set an appropriate layer current, as described in Chapter 4.**

2. **Set an appropriate text style current, as described in the section "Simply stylish text," earlier in this chapter.**

3. **Use the OSNAP button on the status bar to turn off running object snap mode.**

   You usually don't want to snap text to existing objects.

4. **Choose Draw⇨Text⇨Single Line Text from the menu bar to start the TEXT command.**

   The Text button on the Draw toolbar starts the multiline text command, mText, which I cover in the next section.

   AutoCAD tells you the current text style and height settings and prompts you to select a starting point for the text, or to choose an option for changing the text justification or current text style first:

```
Current text style: "Standard" Text height: 0.2000
Specify start point of text or [Justify/Style]:
```

5. **If you want to change justification from the default (lower left), type** J, **press Enter, and choose one of the other justification options.**

    Look up "single-line text, aligning" in the online help system if you need help with the justification options.

6. **Specify the insertion point for the first text character.**

    You can enter the point's coordinates from the command line, use the mouse to click a point on-screen, or press Enter to locate new text immediately below the most recent single-line text object that you created.

    AutoCAD prompts you at the command line for the text height:

    ```
    Specify height <0.2000>:
    ```

7. **Specify the height for the text.**

    This prompt doesn't appear if you're using a text style with a fixed (that is, nonzero) height. See "Simply stylish text," earlier in this chapter, for information about fixed versus variable text heights.

    AutoCAD prompts you at the command line for the text rotation angle:

    ```
    Specify rotation angle of text <0>:
    ```

8. **Specify the text rotation angle by entering the rotation angle from the command line and pressing Enter or by rotating the line on-screen with the mouse.**

    AutoCAD prompts you at the command line to type the text:

    ```
    Enter text:
    ```

9. **Type the first line of text and press Enter.**

10. **Type additional lines of text, pressing Enter at the end of each line.**

    Figure 9-2 shows text appearing on-screen as you type it.

11. **To complete the command, press Enter at the start of a blank line.**

    AutoCAD adds the new line text object — or objects, if you typed more than one line — to the drawing.

To align lines of text exactly, make sure that you type in all the lines in one invocation of the TEXT command, pressing Enter after each line to make the next line appear just after it. Otherwise, aligning different lines of text precisely is harder to do (unless you set your snap just right or use a complicated combination of object snaps and point filters).

To edit single-line text after you've created it, select the text, right-click, and choose Text Edit. The Edit Text dialog box appears, enabling you to edit the contents of the text string. If you want to edit other text properties, such as text height, select the text, right-click, and choose Properties to display the Properties palette. Use the Properties palette to change parameters as needed.

Figure 9-2:
Single-line
text.

Saying More in Multiline Text

When you just can't shoehorn your creative genius into one or more one-line pieces of text, the AutoCAD multiline text object gives you room to go on and on and on. The following procedure shows you how to create text paragraphs with the mText (multiline Text) command.

Making it with mText

The first part of the mText command prompts you for various points and options on the command line. The order is a bit confusing, so read these steps and the command line prompts carefully.

Here's how you use the mText command:

1. **Set an appropriate layer and text style current and turn off running object snaps, as in Steps 1 through 3 in the previous section.**

2. **Click the Multiline Text button on the Draw toolbar.**

   The command line displays the current text style and height settings and prompts you to select the first corner of an imaginary rectangle that will determine the word-wrapping width for the text object:

   ```
   Current text style: "S-NOTES"  Text height:  0.125
   Specify first corner:
   ```

3. **Pick a point in the drawing.**

   The command line prompts you for the opposite corner of the text rectangle that will determine the word-wrapping width and gives you the option of changing settings first:

   ```
   Specify opposite corner or [Height/Justify/Line
             spacing/Rotation/Style/Width]:
   ```

4. **Type H and press Enter to change the default text height.**

   The command line prompts you for a new default text height:

   ```
   Specify height <0.2000>:
   ```

5. **Type an appropriate text height.**

   See the "Taking your text to new heights" section, earlier in this chapter, for information. If you're adding text in model space, remember to use the scaled AutoCAD text height, not the plotted text height.

   The command line prompt for the opposite corner of the mText rectangle reappears:

   ```
   Specify opposite corner or [Height/Justify/Line
             spacing/Rotation/Style/Width]:
   ```

6. **If you want to change justification from the default (top left), type J, press Enter, and choose one of the other justification options.**

   Look up "multiline text, aligning, Justify Multline Text" in the index of the online help system if you want an explanation of the other justification options.

7. **Pick another point in the drawing.**

   Don't worry about the height of the rectangle that you create by choosing the second point; the width of the rectangle is all that matters. AutoCAD adjusts the height of the text rectangle to accommodate the number of lines of word-wrapped text. Don't worry too much about the width, either; you can adjust it later.

   The Multiline Text Editor frameless window appears with the tab and indent ruler above it and the Text Formatting toolbar above that, as shown in Figure 9-3.

Multiline text editor frameless window

Text formatting toolbar   Tab and indent ruler

If you want to see multiline text at its final height as you type it, zoom to a reasonable resolution before you start the mText command. If the text would be very small (because you're zoomed way out) or very large (because you're zoomed way in), AutoCAD temporarily adjusts the size of the text in the frameless editor to show what you're typing. When you finish entering the text (as in Step 11), AutoCAD places it in the drawing at the height that you specified.

8. **Verify the text font and height.**

   The text font and height should be right if you correctly performed Steps 1, 4, and 5. If not, you can change these settings in the Font drop-down list and the Font Height edit box in the Text Formatting toolbar.

9. **Type text into the text area of the dialog box.**

   AutoCAD word wraps multiline text automatically. If you want to force a line break at a particular location, press Enter.

10. **If you want other formatting, select text, right-click, and select the appropriate option from the right-click menu (as in Figure 9-4).**

Undo	Ctrl+Z
Redo	Ctrl+Y
Cut	Ctrl+X
Copy	Ctrl+C
Paste	Ctrl+V
Insert Field...	Ctrl+F
Indents and Tabs...	
Justification	▶
Find and Replace...	Ctrl+R
Select All	Ctrl+A
Change Case	▶
AutoCAPS	
Remove Formatting	Ctrl+Space
Combine Paragraphs	
Symbol	▶
Import Text...	
Background Mask...	
Help	
Character Set	▶

Figure 9-4:
More
multiline
text
formatting
options in
the right-
click menu.

11. Click OK in the Text Formatting toolbar (or press Ctrl+Enter).

The Multiline Text Editor window closes, and AutoCAD adds your text to the drawing.

As you can tell by looking at the Text Formatting toolbar and multiline text right-click menu, the mText command gives you plenty of other options. The Text Formatting toolbar includes a Stack/Unstack button for fractions. The right-click menu includes access to the Indents and Tabs feature, a Find and Replace utility, tools for changing between lower- and uppercase, a special Symbol submenu (including some new symbols in AutoCAD 2005), and an Import Text option for importing text from a TXT (ASCII text) file or RTF (Rich Text Format) file. If you think you may have a use for these additional features, choose Contents⇨Command Reference⇨Commands⇨M Commands⇨MTEXT in AutoCAD's online help.

New mText might in AutoCAD 2005

AutoCAD 2005 adds two more options to the multiline text right-click menu: Insert Field and Background Mask.

mText dons a mask

When you turn on background masking, AutoCAD hides the portions of any objects that lie underneath the text. Use these steps to turn on and control this feature:

1. **Right-click in the Multiline Text Editor window and choose Background Mask from the context menu.**

2. **Click the Use Background Mask check box so that this option is turned on.**

3. **Either click Use Background (to make the mask the same color as the drawing area's background color) or choose a color from the drop-down list (to make the text appear in a solid rectangle of the specified color).**

4. **Click OK to return to the Multiline Text Editor window.**

If you've turned on background masking but it isn't having the desired effect, use the DRaworder or TEXTTOFRONT command to move text "on top of" other objects.

mText plays the field

Insert Field creates a text field that updates automatically every time you open, save, plot, or regenerate the drawing. These fields can contain data such as the date, filename, or author. Fields draw information from the operating system settings, Drawing Properties dialog box, sheet sets feature, and AutoCAD system variables (see Chapter 2). Use the following procedure to add a field while you're creating mtext:

1. **Right-click in the Multiline Text Editor window and choose Insert Field from the context menu.**

2. **Choose a Field Name in the left column.**

3. **Choose a Format in the right column, or, for date fields, type a format in the Date Format box.**

4. **Click OK.**

AutoCAD adds the field to the mText object that you're creating or editing.

If you see four dashes instead of a valid field value, you probably need to do one of the following things:

✔ Regenerate the drawing (see Chapter 7).

✔ Save the drawing.

✔ Fill in Drawing Properties dialog box values (see Chapter 3) and then regenerate the drawing.

✔ Configure sheet sets (see Chapter 14).

Figure 9-5 shows fields and background masking in action.

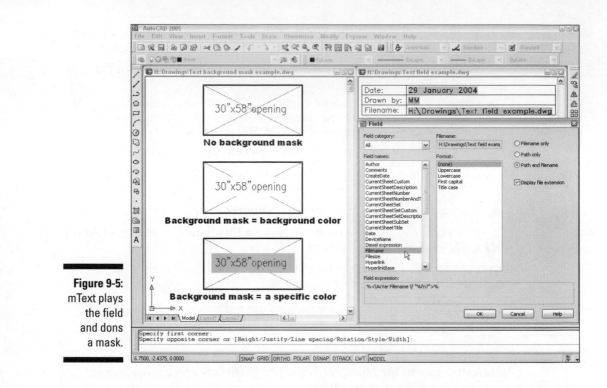

Figure 9-5:
mText plays
the field
and dons
a mask.

Keeping tabs (and indents) on your mText

Another advantage of mText is that it supports tabs and indents. This feature
is especially useful for creating hanging indents — the kind of indents that
push an entire paragraph to the right of a number or bullet, as shown in
Figure 9-5. (Before AutoCAD 2004, there was no straightforward way to perform this feat.) The procedure isn't as straightforward as in most word processing programs, but at least you *can* create numbered and bulleted lists
with hanging indents. Here's how:

1. **Follow Steps 1 through 8 in the preceding section, "Making it with
   mText."**

2. **In the tab and indent ruler, drag the lower slider (the triangle pointing up) to the right a small distance.**

   The lower slider controls the indentation of the second and subsequent
   lines in each paragraph. (The upper slider controls the indentation of
   the first line in each paragraph.) An indent of two to four of the short,
   vertical tick marks usually works well.

3. **Click in the ruler just above the lower slider.**

   A small *L* appears above the lower slider. The L shows the tab stop.

Make sure that the corner of the *L* aligns horizontally with the point of the lower slider triangle. If not, click and drag the *L* until it aligns.

4. **Type a number followed by a period or parenthesis (for example, 1.) or a character that represents a bullet (for example, *).**

5. **Press the Tab key.**

   The cursor jumps to the tab stop that you added in Step 3.

6. **Type the text corresponding to the current number or bullet.**

   As AutoCAD wraps the text, the second and subsequent lines align with the beginning of the text in the first line, as in Figure 9-6.

7. **Press Enter to finish the current numbered or bulleted item.**

8. **Press Enter again if you want to leave a blank line between numbered or bulleted items.**

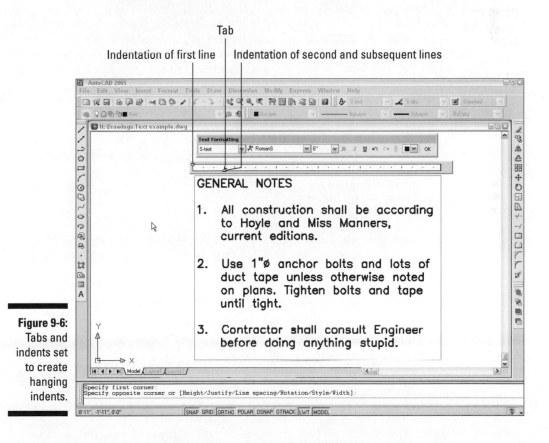

Figure 9-6:
Tabs and indents set to create hanging indents.

9. **Repeat Steps 4 through 8 for each subsequent numbered or bulleted item.**

   If you find that your indents aren't quite the right size, select all the text and adjust the lower slider and tab stop.

10. **Resume with Step 9 in the section, "Making it with mText."**

If you prefer to type tab and indent distances, not adjust them with the cursor, use the Indents and Tabs choice on the mText right-click menu. Whichever way you do it, if you select text first, the tab and indent changes apply to the selected text. If you don't select text first, the changes apply to new text from that point in the multiline text object forward.

The AutoCAD text commands are designed for the kinds of text that most people add to drawings: short, single-line notes or longer blocks of a paragraph or two. If you want sophisticated formatting or long stretches of text, you're likely to bump up against the fact that AutoCAD lacks the capabilities of even the most basic word processing programs. If you're contemplating adding pages of text or fancy text formatting to a drawing, consider putting the text in a separate word processing document instead. If you absolutely must place the text from a long document on a drawing (on a general notes sheet, for example), you'll have to break it up into several columns, each of which is a separate mText object. Get the text right in a word processor first and then copy and paste it into AutoCAD.

If you're tempted to circumvent my warning by pasting a word processing document directly into an AutoCAD drawing, please read Chapter 17 first.

Modifying mText

After you create a multiline text object, you edit it like a single-line text object: Select the object, right-click, and choose Mtext Edit or Properties.

- ✔ The Mtext Edit option opens the Multiline Text Editor window so that you can change the text contents and formatting.
- ✔ The Properties option opens the Properties palette, where you can change overall properties for the text object.

The easiest way to change the word-wrapping width of a paragraph text object is to *grip edit* it. Select the text object, click one of the corner grips, release the mouse button, move the cursor, and click again. Chapter 6 describes grip editing in detail.

AutoCAD includes two text modification commands that may be useful to you when you become an AutoCAD textpert. SCALETEXT scales a group of text objects, similar to the SCale command. The difference is that SCALETEXT scales each text object around its own base point, whereas SCale uses a single base point for scaling all objects. SCALETEXT is especially useful when you have to change the scale of a drawing. JUSTIFYTEXT changes the justification of one or more text strings without causing the text to move. Both of these commands are available on the Modify⇨Object⇨Text submenu.

Setting the Text Table

My vote for the best new feature in AutoCAD 2005 without a doubt goes to tables. You don't know the meaning of the word "tedious" unless you've tried to create a column-and-row data table in previous versions of AutoCAD with the Line and TEXT commands. AutoCAD 2005's new table object and the TableStyle and TaBle commands for creating it make the job almost fun.

Tables have style, too

You control the appearance of tables — both the text and the gridlines — with *table styles* (just as you control the appearance of stand-alone text with text styles). Use the TableStyle command to create and modify table styles. Follow these steps to create a table:

1. **Choose Format⇨Table Style.**

   The Table Style dialog box appears.

2. **In the Styles list, select the existing table style whose settings you want to use as the starting point for the settings of your new style.**

   For example, select the default table style named Standard.

3. **Click the New button to create a new table style that's a copy of the existing style.**

   The Create New Table Style dialog box appears.

4. **Enter a New Style Name and click Continue.**

   The New Table Style dialog box appears as shown in Figure 9-7.

5. **On the Data tab, specify settings for the data text and gridlines (that is, for all cells except the column heads and the table title).**

   The settings you are likely to want to change are Text Style, Text Height, and perhaps either Text Color or Grid Color. (If you leave colors set to ByBlock, then the text and grid lines will inherit the color that's current when you create the table. That color will be the current layer's color, if you follow my advice in the "Accumulating properties" section of Chapter 4.)

Figure 9-7:
Setting the
table.

6. **Repeat Step 5 for the Column Heads tab and the Title tab.**

7. **Click OK to close the New Table Style dialog box.**

   The Table Style dialog box reappears.

8. **(Optional) Select your new table style from the Styles list, and then click Set Current.**

   Your new table style becomes the current table style that AutoCAD uses for future tables in this drawing.

9. **Click Close.**

   The Table Style dialog box closes. Now you're ready to create a table, as described in the next section.

AutoCAD stores table styles in the DWG file, so a style that you create in one drawing isn't immediately available in others. You can copy a table style from one drawing to another with DesignCenter. (Use the "Borrowing existing dimension styles" procedure in Chapter 10, but substitute Table Styles for DimStyles.)

Creating and editing tables

After you create a suitable table style, adding a table to your drawing is easy with the TaBle command. Here's how:

1. **Set an appropriate layer current.**

   Assuming that you leave the current color, linetype, and lineweight set to ByLayer, as I recommend in Chapter 4, the current layer's properties will control the properties of any parts of the table that you left set to ByBlock when you defined the table style. (See Step 5 in the "Tables have style, too" section.)

2. **Choose Draw⇨Table.**

   The Insert Table dialog box appears.

3. **Choose a table style from the Table Style Name drop-down list.**

4. **Choose an Insertion Behavior.**

   Specify Insertion Point is the easiest method and means that you'll pick the location of the table's upper-left corner (or lower-left corner if you set Table Direction to Up in the table style). With this method, you specify the default column width and number of rows in the Insert Table dialog box.

   Specify Window means that you'll pick the upper-left corner and then the lower-right corner. With this method, AutoCAD automatically scales the column widths and determines how many rows to include.

5. **Specify Column & Row Settings.**

   If you chose Specify Window in Step 4, AutoCAD sets the Column Width and number of Data Rows to Auto, which means that AutoCAD will figure them out based on the overall size of the table that you specify in Steps 7 and 8.

6. **Click OK.**

   AutoCAD prompts you to specify the insertion point of the table.

7. **Click a point or type cooordinates.**

   If you chose Specify Insertion Point in Step 4, AutoCAD draws the table grid lines, places the cursor in the title cell, and displays the Text Formatting toolbar.

8. **If you chose Specify Window in Step 4, specify the diagonally opposite corner of the table.**

   AutoCAD draws the table. Based on the table size that you indicated, AutoCAD chooses the column width and number of rows.

9. **Type a title for the table.**

10. **Press the arrow keys or tab key to move among cells, and type values in each cell.**

    The cell right-click menu offers many other options, including copying contents from one cell to another, merging cells, inserting rows and columns, changing formatting, and inserting a block (that is, a graphical symbol — see Chapter 13 for information about blocks).

The new AutoCAD 2005 fields feature described earlier in this chapter works for table text, too — you can insert a field into a table cell. For example, you might use this feature to create part of a title block, with fields serving as the "date" and "drawn by" data.

11. Click OK on the Text Formatting toolbar.

Figure 9-8 shows a completed table, along with the Insert Table dialog box.

You can edit cell values later simply by double-clicking in a cell. To change column width or row height, click on the table grid and then click and move the blue grips. (To change the width of one column without altering the overall width of the table, hold down the Ctrl key while you move the grip.) If you want to change other aspects of a table or individual cells in it, select the table or cell and use the Properties palette to make changes.

You can import tables from Microsoft Excel instead of using the Insert Table dialog box. To import Excel data, select the desired cells and choose Edit➪ Copy in Excel. Then in AutoCAD, choose Edit➪Paste Special and choose AutoCAD Entities in the Paste Special dialog box. AutoCAD attempts to copy the Excel spreadsheet's formatting along with the cell data, but you'll probably have to adjust column widths and perform other cleanup on the imported table.

Figure 9-8:
The Insert
Table dialog
box, and
the result
of using it.

You can go the other direction — from AutoCAD to Excel or another program — via a CSV (Comma Separated Value) file. Look up "TABLEEXPORT command" in AutoCAD's online help.

Checking Out Your Spelling

AutoCAD, like almost every other computer program on this planet — and possibly on other planets and moons in our solar system — has a spelling checker.

Unlike Microsoft Word, AutoCAD's spelling checker doesn't make those little red squiggles under your errors, but it does let you search for spelling errors in most of the text objects in your drawing. This feature checks single-line text, paragraph text, and attribute text (described in Chapter 13), but not dimension text (described in Chapter 10). The following procedure demonstrates how to use the spell checker:

1. **Press the Esc key to unselect any selected objects.**

2. **Choose Tools⇨Spelling to start the SPell command.**

   This is text spell-checking, not casting a spell. (That's the EYEOFNEWT command.) The command line prompts you to select objects.

3. **Select the objects you want to check.**

   You can use any of the standard AutoCAD object selection methods to select text to check. (See Chapter 6 if you're unfamiliar with object selection.) Type **ALL** and press Enter if you want to check the spelling of all text in the drawing. Don't worry if you select objects other than text; the spelling checker ignores any objects that aren't text. When you're finished selecting objects, press Enter to start the spelling check.

   If a misspelling is found, the Check Spelling dialog box appears with the first misspelled or unrecognized word. Figure 9-9 shows an example.

4. **Click the dialog box buttons to tell AutoCAD how to handle a misspelling.**

   You probably know which buttons to click from having used other spelling checkers. If not, use the dialog box help to find out: Click the question mark on the Check Spelling dialog box's title bar, and then click the button that you want to know more about.

   AutoCAD continues with spell-checking until it has checked all the selected text objects. When it finds no further misspellings, the dialog box disappears, and the Spelling check complete alert appears.

Figure 9-9:
It's good to
sue your
spelling
checker.

Check Spelling

Current dictionary: American English

Current word
lawsoot!   Cancel

                                       Help

Suggestions:
lawsuit!   Ignore   Ignore All

lawsuit!   Change   Change All
law soot!
laws!   Add   Lookup

                  Change Dictionaries...

Context
Draft with precision - avoid a lawsoot!

Every industry has its own abbreviations and specialized vocabulary. At first,
AutoCAD complains about perfectly good words (from a drafter's point of
view) such as *thru* and *S.A.D.* (which stands for See Architectural Drawing).
Be prepared to click the Add button frequently during the first few weeks to
tell AutoCAD which words and abbreviations are acceptable in your industry
and office. If you're patient with it, AutoCAD, like an errant puppy, will gradually become more obedient. Then you'll be thru feeling S.A.D.

Chapter 10

Entering New Dimensions

*I*n drafting — either CAD or manual drafting — *dimensions* are special text labels with attached lines that together indicate unambiguously the size of something. Although it's theoretically possible to draw all the pieces of each dimension by using AutoCAD commands such as Line and mText, dimensioning is so common a drafting task that AutoCAD provides special commands for doing the job more efficiently. These dimensioning commands group the parts of each dimension into a convenient, easy-to-edit package. Even better, as you edit an object — by stretching it for example — AutoCAD automatically updates the measurement displayed in the dimension text label to indicate the object's new size, as shown in Figure 10-1.

AutoCAD controls the look of dimensions by means of *dimension styles*, just as it controls the look of text with text styles. (AutoCAD also uses text styles to control the appearance of the text in dimensions.) But dimension styles are much more complicated than text styles, because dimensions have so many more pieces that you need to control. After you find or create an appropriate dimension style, you use one of several dimensioning commands to draw dimensions that point to the important points on an object (the two endpoints of a line, for example).

WARNING!

AutoCAD dimensioning is a big, complicated subject. (It's so complicated, in fact, that Autodesk has an especially wise person in charge of dimensioning in AutoCAD — this person is called the "DimWit.") Every industry has its own dimensioning conventions, habits, and quirks. As usual, AutoCAD tries to support them all and, in so doing, makes things a bit convoluted for everyone. This chapter covers the essential concepts and commands that you need to know to start drawing dimensions. Be prepared to spend some additional time studying how to create any specialized types of dimensions that your industry uses.

Dimension updates when you change the object

Figure 10-1:
Changing
objects
automati-
cally
updates
dimensions.

Original dimension

You may be able to avoid getting too deeply into the details of dimensioning just by copying dimension styles from existing drawings in your office. (I show you how later in this chapter.) This may also be a good time to get some advice and coaching from the AutoCAD geek in the cubicle across from yours.

You add dimensions to a drawing *after* you've drawn at least some of the geometry; otherwise, you won't have much to dimension! Your dimensioning and overall drafting efficiency improve if you add dimensions in batches, rather than draw a line, draw a dimension, draw another line, draw another dimension. . . .

Why dimensions in CAD?

You may think that CAD would have rendered text dimensions obsolete. After all, you comply with all my suggestions about using AutoCAD precision techniques when you draw and edit, and you're careful to draw each object at its true size, right? The contractor or machinist can just use AutoCAD to query distances and angles in the CAD DWG file, right? Sorry, but no (to the

last question, anyway). Here are a few reasons why the traditional dimensioning that CAD drafting has inherited from manual drafting is likely to be around for a while:

✔ **Some people need to or want to use paper drawings when they build something.** We're still some time away from the day when contractors haul computers around in their tool belts (never mind mousing around a drawing while hanging from scaffolding).

✔ **In many industries, paper drawings still rule legally.** Your company may supply both plotted drawings and DWG files to clients, but your contracts probably specify that the plotted drawings govern in the case of any discrepancy. The contracts probably also warn against relying on any distances that the recipient of the drawings measures — using measuring commands in the CAD DWG file or a scale on the plotted drawing. The text dimensions are supposed to supply all the dimensional information that's needed to construct the object.

✔ **Dimensions sometimes carry additional information besides the basic length or angle.** For example, dimension text can indicate the allowable construction tolerances or show that a particular distance is typical of similar situations elsewhere on the drawing.

✔ **Even conscientious CAD drafters rarely draw *every* object its true size.** Drafters sometimes exaggerate distances for graphical clarity. For example, they might draw a small object larger than its true size so that it shows up clearly on a scaled plot. In addition, drafters sometimes settle for approximate distances because time pressures (especially late in a project) make it difficult to be completely accurate.

So remember the old rule of drafting prowess: "It's not the size of the drawn object that matters, but the dimensions that are on it."

Discovering New Dimensions

Before digging into the techniques that you use to create dimension styles and dimensions, I review some AutoCAD dimensioning terminology. If you're already familiar with CAD dimensioning lingo, just skim this section and look at the figures in it. Otherwise, read on.

Anatomy of a dimension

AutoCAD uses the names shown in Figure 10-2 and described in the following list to refer to the parts of each dimension:

✔ **Dimension text:** Dimension text usually is the number that indicates the actual distance or angle. Dimension text can also include other text information in addition to or instead of the number. For example, you can add a suffix such as TYP. to indicate that a dimension is typical of several similar configurations, or you can insert a description such as See Detail 3/A2.

✔ **Dimension lines:** The dimension lines go from the dimension text outward (parallel to the direction of the object being measured), to indicate the extent of the dimensioned length. AutoCAD's default dimension style settings center the dimension text vertically and horizontally on the dimension lines (see Figure 10-2), but you can change those settings to cause the text to appear in a different location — riding above an unbro-ken dimension line as shown in Figure 10-1, for example. See the section "Adjusting style settings," later in this chapter, for instructions.

✔ **Dimension arrowheads:** The dimension arrowheads appear at the ends of the dimension lines and clarify the extent of the dimensioned length. AutoCAD's default arrowhead style is the closed, filled type shown in Figure 10-2, but you can choose other symbols, such as tick marks, to indi-cate the ends of the dimension lines. (Don't get ticked off, but AutoCAD calls the line ending an *arrowhead* even when, as in the case of a tick mark, it doesn't look like an arrow.)

✔ **Extension lines:** The extension lines extend outward from the extension line origin points that you select (usually by snapping to points on an object) to the dimension lines. By drafting convention, a small gap usu-ally exists between the extension line origin points and the beginning of the extension lines. The extension lines usually extend just beyond where they meet the dimension lines.

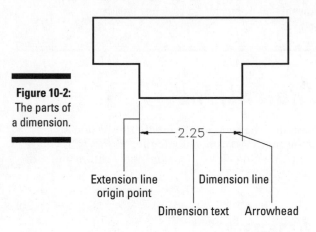

Figure 10-2:
The parts of
a dimension.

Extension line
origin point

Dimension line

Dimension text   Arrowhead

A field guide to dimensions

AutoCAD provides several types of dimensions and commands for drawing them. Figure 10-3 shows the most common types, and the following list describes them:

✔ **Linear dimensions:** A linear dimension measures the linear extent of an object or the linear distance between objects. Most linear dimensions are either *horizontal* or *vertical,* but you can draw dimensions that are *rotated* to other angles, too. An *aligned* dimension is similar to a linear dimension, but the dimension line tilts to the same angle as a line drawn through the origin points of its extension lines.

✔ **Radial dimensions:** A *radius* dimension calls out the radius of a circle or arc, and a *diameter* dimension calls out the diameter of a circle or arc. You can position the dimension text inside or outside the curve, as shown in Figure 10-3. If you position the text outside the curve, AutoCAD by default draws a little cross at the center of the circle or arc.

✔ **Angular dimensions:** An *angular* dimension calls out the angular measurement between two lines, the two endpoints of an arc, or two points on a circle. The dimension line appears as an arc that indicates the sweep of the measured angle.

Figure 10-3: Common types of dimensions.

Other types of AutoCAD dimensions include ordinate, tolerance, center mark, and leader dimensions. See the "Pointy-Headed Leaders" section at the end of this chapter for instructions on how to draw leaders. Look up "dimensions, creating" on the Index tab in the AutoCAD online help system for more information about other kinds of dimensions.

Dimension associativity

By default, AutoCAD groups all the parts of each dimension — the extension lines, dimension lines, arrowheads, and text — into a special *associative dimension* object. *Associative* means two things:

✔ The different parts of the dimension function as a single object. When you click any part of the dimension, AutoCAD selects all of its parts.

✔ The dimension is connected with the points on the object that you specified when you drew the dimension. If you change the size of the object (for example, stretch a line), the dimension updates appropriately — the lines and arrows move, and the text changes to reflect the line's new size.

I call dimensions with both of these characteristics *geometry-driven associative dimensions,* because the geometry "drives" the location of the parts of the dimension and what the text says.

For historical reasons, AutoCAD also is capable of creating dimensions that possess just the first type of associativity — that is, the dimension functions as a single, grouped object but isn't directly connected with the object whose size it shows. Autodesk now calls these kinds of dimensions *nonassociative,* which is pretty confusing to AutoCAD veterans, because AutoCAD used to call them *associative!* AutoCAD also is capable of creating dimensions that possess no type of associativity at all — no grouping of the bits and pieces and no connection to the dimensioned object. Autodesk now calls these *exploded* dimensions, but before AutoCAD 2002, they were called *nonassociative!*

I mention the conflicting use of associative and nonassociative in case you find yourself discussing dimensions with AutoCAD veterans, most of whom will use the terms in their older sense. To avoid confusion, I always use the term *geometry-driven associative dimensions* (or simply *geometry-driven dimensions*) in this book to refer to dimensions that possess both types of associativity. For more information about how to determine which kind of dimension AutoCAD draws, see "Controlling and editing dimension associativity," later in this chapter.

Pulling out your dimension tools

The AutoCAD Dimension menu provides access to dimensioning commands. If you find yourself adding dimensions in batches, the Dimension toolbar is more efficient because it makes the dimensioning commands more accessible. You toggle the Dimension toolbar off and on by right-clicking any AutoCAD toolbar icon and choosing Dimension from the cursor menu. As with other toolbars, you can move the Dimension toolbar to a different location on the screen or dock it on any margin of the drawing area.

All dimensioning commands have long command names (such as DIMLINEAR and DIMRADIUS) and corresponding shortened abbreviations (DLI and DRA) that you can type at the command prompt. If you do lots of dimensioning and don't want to toggle the Dimension toolbar on and off repeatedly, memorize the abbreviated forms of the dimension commands that you use frequently. You'll find a list of the long command names on the Contents tab in the AutoCAD online help system. Choose Command Reference⇨Commands⇨ D Commands. The short names are the first, fourth, and fifth letters of the long names. (In other words, take the first five letters of the long name and remove *IM.*)

Doing Dimensions with Style(s)

Creating a usable dimension style that gives you the dimension look you want is the biggest challenge in using AutoCAD's dimensioning features. Each drawing contains its own dimension styles, so changes you make to a dimension style in one drawing affect only that drawing. However, after you get the dimension styles right in a drawing, you can use it as a template or starting point for later drawings.

A dimension style is a collection of drawing settings called *dimension variables,* which are a special class of the *system variables* that I introduce in Chapter 2.

If you want to see a list of the dimension variable names and look up what each variable controls, see Contents⇨Command Reference⇨System Variables⇨ D System Variables in the AutoCAD online help system. All the system variables that begin with DIM are dimension variables.

AutoCAD users, like all computer nerds, like to shorten names. You may hear them refer to dimstyles and dimvars instead of dimension styles and dimension variables. You can tell them that doing so makes you think of them as dimwits — which is actually an honorable title at Autodesk, as I mention earlier in this chapter.

Borrowing existing dimension styles

If you're lucky enough to work in an office where someone has set up dimension styles that are appropriate for your industry and project, you can skip the pain and strain of creating your own dimension styles. If the ready-made dimension style that you need lives in another drawing, you can use the DesignCenter palette to copy it into your drawing, as described in the following steps:

1. **Open the drawing that contains the dimension style you want to copy (the *source* drawing).**

2. **Open the drawing to which you want to copy the dimension style (the *destination* drawing).**

   If you already had both drawings open, make sure that you can see the destination drawing. If you can't, choose the Window menu and then choose the destination drawing in order to bring it to the foreground.

3. **Click the AutoCAD DesignCenter button on the Standard toolbar.**

   The DesignCenter palette appears. (Chapter 4 describes this palette in detail.)

4. **In the DesignCenter palette, click the Open Drawings tab.**

   DesignCenter's navigation pane displays a list of drawings that you currently have open in AutoCAD.

5. **In the left pane of the DesignCenter palette, click the plus sign next to the name of the drawing that you opened in Step 1.**

   A list of copyable objects, including Dimstyles, appears.

6. **Click and drag the desired dimension style from the right pane of the DesignCenter palette into the window containing the drawing that you opened in Step 2, as shown in Figure 10-4.**

   If the name of the dimension style that you copy duplicates the name of an existing dimension style in the destination drawing, AutoCAD refuses to overwrite the existing dimension style. In that case, you must first rename the existing dimension style in the destination drawing by using the information in the following section, "Creating and managing dimension styles."

7. **Change the Use Overall Scale Of factor on the Fit tab of the Modify Dimension Style dialog box so that it matches the drawing scale factor of the current drawing.**

   See Chapter 3 for detailed instructions.

Drag from source drawing's Dimstyles in AutoCAD DesignCenter

Figure 10-4:
Copying a
dimension
style from
one drawing
to another.

Drop in destination drawing

If you want a dimension style to be available in new drawings, copy the style to a template drawing and use that template to create your new drawings. See Chapter 3 for more information about template drawings.

Creating and managing dimension styles

If you *do* need to create your own dimension styles, or you want to tweak ones that you copied from another drawing, you use the Dimension Style Manager dialog box, shown in Figure 10-5.

Figure 10-5: Yet another manager, this one for dimension styles.

Every drawing comes with a default dimension style named Standard (for nonmetric drawings) or ISO-25 (for metric drawings). Although you can use and modify the Standard or ISO-25 style, I suggest that you leave it as is and create your own dimension style(s) for the settings that are appropriate to your work. This approach ensures that you can use the default style as a reference. More important, it avoids a potential naming conflict that can change the way your dimensions look if the current drawing gets inserted into another drawing. (Chapter 13 describes this potential conflict.)

The following steps describe how to create your own dimension style(s):

1. **Choose Format⇨Dimension Style from the menu bar, or click the Dimension Style Manager button on the Styles toolbar.**

   The Dimension Style Manager dialog box appears.

2. **In the Styles list, select the existing dimension style whose settings you want to use as the starting point for the settings of your new style.**

   For example, select the default dimension style named Standard or ISO-25.

3. **Click the New button to create a new dimension style that's a copy of the existing style.**

   The Create New Dimension Style dialog box appears.

4. **Enter a New Style Name and click Continue.**

   The New Dimension Style dialog box appears, which is the same as the Modify Dimension Style dialog box shown in Figure 10-6.

5. **Modify dimension settings on any of the six tabs in the New Dimension Style dialog box.**

   See the descriptions of these settings in the next section of this chapter. In particular, be sure to set the Use Overall Scale Of factor on the Fit tab to set the drawing scale factor.

6. **Click OK to close the New Dimension Style dialog box.**

   The Dimension Style Manager dialog box reappears.

7. **Select your new dimension style from the Styles list, and then click Set Current.**

   Your new dimension style becomes the current dimension style that AutoCAD uses for future dimensions in this drawing.

8. **Click Close.**

   The Dimension Style Manager dialog box closes.

9. **Draw some dimensions to test your new dimension style.**

Avoid changing existing dimension styles that you didn't create, unless you know for sure what they're used for. When you change a dimension style setting, all dimensions that use that style change to reflect the revised setting. Thus, one small dimension variable setting change can affect a large number of existing dimensions! When in doubt, ask the dimension style's creator what the dimension style is for and what the consequences of changing it are. If that's not possible, instead of modifying an existing dimension style, create a new style by copying the existing one, and then modify the new one.

A further variation on the already baroque dimension style picture is that you can create dimension *secondary styles* (also called *substyles* or *style families*) — variations of a main style that affect only a particular type of dimension, such as radial or angular. You probably want to avoid this additional complication if you can, but if you open the Dimension Style Manager dialog box and see names of dimension types indented beneath the main dimension style names, be aware that you're dealing with secondary styles. Look up "dimension styles, secondary styles" on the Index tab in the AutoCAD online help system for more information.

Adjusting style settings

After you click New or Modify in the Dimension Style Manager dialog box, AutoCAD displays a tabbed New/Modify Dimension Style subdialog box with a mind-boggling — and potentially drawing-boggling, if you're not careful — array of settings. Figure 10-6 shows the settings on the first tab, which I've modified from the AutoCAD defaults to conform to one office's drafting standards.

Figure 10-6: Modifying dimension settings.

Fortunately, the dimension preview that appears on all tabs — as well as on the main Dimension Style Manager dialog box — immediately shows the results of most setting changes. With the dimension preview and some trial-and-error changing of settings, you usually can home in on an acceptable group of settings. For more information, use the dialog box help: Click the question mark button on the title bar and then click the setting that you want to know more about.

Before you start messing with dimension style settings, it's important to know what you want your dimensions to look like when they're plotted. If you're not sure how it's done in your industry, ask others in your office or profession or look at a plotted drawing that someone in the know represents as being a good example.

The following sections introduce you to the more important New/Modify Dimension Style tabs and highlight useful settings. Note that whenever you specify a distance or length setting, you should enter the desired *plotted* size. AutoCAD scales all these numbers by the overall scale factor that you enter on the Fit tab.

Following Lines and Arrows

The settings on the Lines and Arrows tab control the basic look and feel of all parts of your dimensions except text. Use this tab to change the type and size of arrowheads or the display characteristics of the dimension and extension lines.

Tabbing to Text

Use the Text tab to control how your dimension text looks — the text style and height to use (see Chapter 9) and where to place the text with respect to the dimension and extension lines. You'll probably want to change the Text Style setting to something that uses a more pleasing font than the dorky default Txt.shx font, such as the Romans.shx font. The default Text Height is too large for most situations — set it to ⅛", 3mm, or another height that makes sense. Figure 10-7 shows one company's standard text settings.

Figure 10-7: Whip your dimension text into shape.

The text style that you specify for a dimension style must be a variable height style — that is, the height that you specify in the Text Style dialog box must be zero. (See Chapter 9 for more information about variable height and fixed height text styles.) If you specify a fixed height text style for a dimension style, the text style's height will override the Text Height setting in the New/Modify Dimension Style subdialog box. This behavior is confusing at best and unacceptable at worst. Use a variable height style to avoid the problem.

Enter the desired *plotted* text height. Don't multiply it by the drawing scale factor, as you do for ordinary text.

Industry or company standards usually dictate the size of dimension text. (For example, ⅛ inch is common in the architectural industry.) In any case, make sure you pick a height that's not too small to read on your smallest check plot.

AutoCAD 2005's new background mask feature, described in Chapter 9, works for dimension text, too. To turn on masking, choose either Background or a specific color from the Fill Color drop-down list. When you do, AutoCAD hides the portions of any objects that lie underneath dimension text. (To ensure that dimension text lies on top of other objects, use the DRaworder or TEXTTOFRONT command — see Chapter 9 for more information.

Getting Fit

The Fit tab includes a bunch of confusing options that control when and where AutoCAD shoves the dimension text if it doesn't quite fit between the dimension lines. The default settings leave AutoCAD in "maximum attempt at being helpful mode" — that is, AutoCAD moves the text, dimension lines, and arrows around automatically so that things don't overlap. If these guesses seem less than satisfactory to you, try the modified settings shown in Figure 10-7: Select the Over the Dimension Line, without a Leader radio box under Text Placement and the Always Draw Dim Line between Ext Lines check box under Fine Tuning. (You can always move the text yourself by grip editing it, as I describe later in this chapter.)

Most important, the Fit tab includes the Use Overall Scale Of setting, as noted in Figure 10-8. This setting acts as a global scaling factor for all the other length-related dimension settings. Always set Use Overall Scale Of to the drawing scale factor of the current drawing.

Drawing scale factor goes here

Figure 10-8:
Keep Fit and don't forget the Scale.

If your drawing includes areas of different scales, you can create multiple dimension styles, one for each scale. Alternatively, you can set the Use Overall Scale Of setting to 1.0 and draw dimensions in a paper space layout, rather than in model space. See the "Trans-spatial dimensioning" section, later in this chapter, for more information.

The Use Overall Scale Of setting corresponds to the DIMSCALE system variable, and you'll hear AutoCAD drafters refer to it as such. AutoCAD accepts zero as a special DIMSCALE setting for dimensioning in paper space layouts. Look up the DIMSCALE system variable in the AutoCAD online help system for more information about additional dimension scale options.

Using Primary Units

The Primary Units tab gives you incredibly — or maybe overly — detailed control over how AutoCAD formats the characters in the dimension text string. You usually want to set the Unit format and Precision and maybe specify a suffix for unit-less numbers, such as **mm** for millimeters. You may also change the Zero Suppression settings, depending on whether you want dimension text to read 0.5000, .5000, or 0.5. ("Zero Suppression!" also makes a great rallying cry for organizing your fellow AutoCAD drafters.)

Other style settings

If your work requires that you show dimensions in two different units (such as inches and millimeters), use the Alternate Units tab to turn on and control alternate units. If your work requires listing construction tolerances (for example, 3.5 mm +/–0.01), use the Tolerances tab to configure the tolerance format that you want.

The New/Modify Dimension Style dialog box Tolerance tab settings are for adding manufacturing tolerances (for example, **+0.2** or **-0.1**) to the text of ordinary dimensions — the kind of dimensions I cover in this chapter. AutoCAD also includes a separate TOLERANCES *command* that draws special symbols called *geometric tolerances.* If you need these symbols, you probably know it; if you've never heard of them, just ignore them. Look up "Geometric Tolerance dialog box" on the Index tab in the AutoCAD online help system for more information.

Drawing Dimensions

After you've copied or created a suitable dimension style, you're ready to dimension. Fortunately, adding dimensions to a drawing with existing dimension styles is usually pretty straightforward.

When you want to dimension something in AutoCAD, you can either select the object, such as a line or polyline segment, or select *points* on that object, such as the endpoints of the line or polyline segment. If you select an object,

AutoCAD finds the most obvious points on it to dimension, such as the end-points of a line. If you choose to select individual points instead, use object snaps (see Chapter 4). The points that you pick — or that AutoCAD finds for you — are called the *origins* of the dimension's extension lines. When you change the size of the object (for example, by stretching it), AutoCAD automatically moves the dimension's origin points and updates the dimension text to show the new length.

If you don't use object snaps or another AutoCAD precision technique to choose dimension points, the dimension text probably won't reflect the precise measurement of the object. This lack of precision can cause serious problems. When in doubt, osnap to it!

When you set up a new drawing, make sure that you change the Use Overall Scale Of setting on the Fit tab in the New/Modify Dimension Style dialog box so that it matches the drawing scale factor. Before you draw any dimensions in a drawing that you didn't set up, check this setting to make sure it's correct.

The AutoCAD dimension drawing commands prompt you with useful information at the command line. Read the command line prompts during every step of the command, especially when you're trying a dimensioning command for the first time.

Lining up some linear dimensions

Linear dimensions are the most common type of dimensions, and horizontal and vertical are the most common of those. The following example demonstrates all the important techniques for creating horizontal and vertical linear dimensions, as well as aligned dimensions (which are similar to linear dimensions):

1. **Use the LINE command to draw a nonorthogonal line — that is, a line segment that's not horizontal or vertical.**

   An angle of about 30 degrees works well for this example.

   If you want to apply dimensioning to an object other than a line, use these steps as a general guideline, filling in the appropriate commands and data as applicable to your drawing.

2. **Set a layer that's appropriate for dimensions current.**

   See Chapter 4 for details.

3. **Set a dimension style that's appropriate for your needs current.**

   Choose an existing dimension style from the Dim Style Control drop-down list on the Styles toolbar, or create a new style by using the procedure in the section, "Creating and managing dimension styles," earlier in this chapter.

4. **Choose Dimension⇨Linear or click the Linear Dimension button on the Dimension toolbar.**

   AutoCAD prompts you:

   ```
   Specify first extension line origin or <select object>:
   ```

5. **To specify the origin of the first extension line, snap to the lower-left endpoint of the line by using endpoint object snap.**

   If you don't have endpoint as one of your current running object snaps, specify a single endpoint object snap by holding down the Shift key, right-clicking, and choosing Endpoint from the cursor menu. (See Chapter 4 for more about object snaps.)

   AutoCAD prompts you:

   ```
   Specify second extension line origin:
   ```

6. **To specify the origin of the second extension line, snap to the other endpoint of the line by using endpoint object snap again.**

   AutoCAD draws a *horizontal* dimension — the length of the displacement in the left-to-right direction — if you move the cursor above or below the line. It draws a *vertical* dimension — the length of the displacement in the up-and-down direction — if you move the cursor to the left or right of the line.

   AutoCAD prompts you:

   ```
   Specify dimension line location or
   [Mtext/Text/Angle/Horizontal/Vertical/Rotated]:
   ```

7. **Move the mouse to generate the type of dimension you want, horizontal or vertical, and then click wherever you want to place the dimension line.**

   When you're specifying the dimension line location, you usually *don't* want to object snap to existing objects — you want the dimension line and text to sit in a relatively empty part of the drawing rather than bump into existing objects. If necessary, temporarily turn off running object snap (for example, click the OSNAP button on the status bar) in order to avoid snapping the dimension line to an existing object.

   AutoCAD draws the dimension.

   If you want to be able to align subsequent dimension lines easily, turn on Snap and set a suitable snap spacing — more easily done than said! — before you pick the point that determines the location of the dimension line. See Chapter 4 for more information about snap.

8. **Repeat Steps 4 through 7 to create another linear dimension of the opposite orientation (vertical or horizontal).**

9. **Choose Dimension⇨Aligned or click the Aligned Dimension button on the Dimension toolbar.**

   The prompt includes an option to select an object instead of picking two points (you can use this technique with the Linear Dimension command, too):

   ```
   Specify first extension line origin or <select object>:
   ```

10. **Press Enter to choose the select object option.**

    AutoCAD prompts you:

    ```
    Select object to dimension:
    ```

11. **Select the line or other object that you want to dimension.**

    AutoCAD automatically finds the endpoints of the line and uses them as the extension line origin points, as shown in Figure 10-9.

AutoCAD uses endpoints as dimension origin points

Figure 10-9:
Drawing a linear dimension by selecting an object.

Select a line

Specify dimension line placement

AutoCAD prompts you:

```
Specify dimension line location or
[Mtext/Text/Angle]:
```

12. **Click wherever you want to place the dimension line.**

    AutoCAD draws the dimension.

Drawing other kinds of dimensions

After you have the hang of ordinary linear dimensions, you should be able to master other common dimension types quickly. Draw some lines, arcs, and circles, and try the other dimension commands on the Dimension toolbar or menu.

Although AutoCAD includes special commands for dimensioning the diameter or radius of a circle or arc, you can use the linear dimension techniques described in the previous section to dimension these objects.

To draw a series of side-by-side dimensions whose dimension lines are perfectly aligned, use the DimCOntinue command. To draw an overall dimension above one or more smaller dimensions, use DimBAseline. If you use these commands often in your work, you may find that the QDIM (Quick DIMension) command provides a quick way to draw lots of dimensions in one fell swoop.

Figure 10-10 shows some results of using the more common additional dimensioning commands.

Trans-spatial dimensioning

Trans-spatial dimensioning may sound like the latest New Age fad — after all, most of Autodesk's programmers do work in California — but actually it's just a relatively new (circa AutoCAD 2002) dimensioning feature. There's an age-old argument about whether to draw dimensions in model space, where the geometry that you're dimensioning usually resides, or paper space. (See Chapter 3 for information about model space and paper space.) Most people have settled on dimensioning in model space, but sometimes dimensioning in paper space offers advantages — for example, when you want to dimension different parts of the same geometry in different paper space viewports.

Since AutoCAD 2002, the program works much better for dimensioning in paper space layouts — when you set the DIMSCALE system variable to 1.0 and then draw dimensions in paper space, AutoCAD can associate them with objects in model space.

Figure 10-10:
Examples of
additional
dimen-
sioning
commands.

DimRAdius DimDIameter DimANgular DimCOntinue

DimLInear DimBAseline

Get comfortable with dimensioning in model space first. If you later want to try dimensioning in paper space, look up "dimensioning, methods" in the AutoCAD online help system.

Editing Dimensions

After you draw dimensions, you can edit the position of the various parts of each dimension and change the contents of the dimension text. AutoCAD groups all the parts of a dimension into a single object.

Editing dimension geometry

The easiest way to change the location of dimension parts is to use grip editing, which I describe in Chapter 6. Just click a dimension, click one of its grips, and maneuver away. You'll discover that certain grips control certain directions of movement. Experiment a few minutes to see how they work.

If you want to change the look of a dimension part (for example, substitute a different arrowhead or suppress an extension line), use the Properties palette. (See Chapter 6 for more on the Properties palette.) All the dimension settings in the New/Modify Dimension Style dialog box (see "Adjusting style settings," earlier in this chapter) are available in the Properties palette when you select one or more dimensions.

If you select one or more dimensions and right-click, the cursor menu displays a number of useful options for overriding dimension settings or assigning a different style.

When you change a setting in the Properties palette, you're *overriding* the default style setting for that dimension. If you need to make the same change to a bunch of dimensions, it's better to create a new dimension style and assign that style to them. You can use the Properties palette or the right-click menu to change the dimension style that's assigned to one or more dimensions.

You can use the Properties palette to turn on AutoCAD 2005's new background mask feature, described in Chapter 9, for the text of individual dimensions: Select the dimensions, display the Text area in the Properties palette, and choose either Background or a specific color from the Fill Color drop-down list. Note that turning on background mask in the Multiline Text Editor window, as Chapter 9 tells you to do for regular (nondimension) text, does *not* work for dimension text. You must use the Fill Color setting on either the Text tab of the New/Modify Dimension Style dialog box (as described earlier in this chapter) or the Properties palette.

The AutoCAD eXplode command on the Modify toolbar will blow a dimension apart, into a bunch of line and multiline text objects. Don't do it! Exploding a dimension makes it much harder to edit cleanly and eliminates AutoCAD's capability of updating the dimension text measurement automatically.

Editing dimension text

In most cases, you shouldn't have to edit dimension text. Assuming that you drew your geometry accurately and picked the dimension points precisely, AutoCAD displays the right measurement. If you change the size of the associated object, AutoCAD updates the dimension and its measurement. However, you occasionally may need to *override* the dimension text (that is, replace it with a different measurement) or *add* a prefix or a suffix to the true measurement.

AutoCAD creates dimension text as a multiline text (mText) object, so dimension text has the same editing options as ordinary text. Unfortunately, the right-click menu for dimension objects doesn't include a Text Edit option. You can use the Text Override field in the Properties palette, or type ED (the keyboard shortcut for the ddEDit command) to edit dimension text in the Multiline Text Editor window.

The default text is <> (that is, the left and right angled bracket characters), which acts as a placeholder for the true length. In other words, AutoCAD displays the true dimension length as text in the actual dimension (and keeps the text up-to-date if you change the distance between the dimension's origin points). You can override the true length by typing a specific length or other text string. You can preserve the true length but add a prefix or suffix by typing it before or after the left- and right-angled bracket characters. In other words, if you enter **<> Max.**, and the actual distance is 12.00, AutoCAD displays 12.00 Max. for the dimension text. If you later stretch the object so that the actual distance changes to 14.50, AutoCAD automatically changes the dimension text to read 14.50 Max. Now you can appreciate the importance of drawing and editing geometry precisely!

Avoid the temptation to override the default dimension text by replacing the angled brackets with a numeric value. Doing so eliminates AutoCAD's capability of keeping dimension measurements current, but even worse, you get no visual cue that the default distance has been overridden (unless you edit the dimension text). If you're overriding dimension text a lot, it's probably a sign that the creator of the drawing didn't pay enough attention to using precision techniques when drawing and editing. I'm not going to point any fingers, but you probably know whom to talk to.

Controlling and editing dimension associativity

When you add dimensions by selecting objects or picking points on the objects by using object snap modes, AutoCAD normally creates geometry-driven associative dimensions, which are connected to the objects and move with them. This is the case in new drawings that were originally created in any version of AutoCAD starting with 2002. (Autodesk introduced geometry-driven dimensions in AutoCAD 2002. Before that, AutoCAD normally created dimensions whose parts functioned as a single grouped object but that weren't connected with the dimensioned object.)

In drawings that were created originally in versions older than AutoCAD 2002, you must set the new DIMASSOC system variable to 2 before AutoCAD 2005 will create geometry-driven associative dimensions. An easy way to make this change for the current drawing is to open the Options dialog box (choose Tools⇨Options), click the User Preferences tab, and turn on the Make New Dimensions Associative setting. Be aware that this setting affects only new dimensions that you draw from now on. Thus, you'll end up with geometry-driven associative new dimensions and less than fully associative existing dimensions in your old drawing. Look up "DIMASSOC system variable" in the AutoCAD online help system for more information.

You aren't likely to need any of these three commands very often, but if you do, look up the command name in the online help system.

- **DIMREASSOCIATE:** If you have dimensions that aren't currently geometry-driven (probably because they were created in older versions of AutoCAD) or are associated with the wrong objects, you can use the DIMREASSOCI-ATE command (Dimensions⇨Reassociate Dimensions) to associate them with points on the objects of your choice.

- **DIMDISASSOCIATE:** You can use the DIMDISASSOCIATE command to sever the connection between a dimension and its associated object.

- **DIMREGEN:** In a few special circumstances, AutoCAD doesn't automatically update geometry-driven associative dimensions (maybe Autodesk should call them "usually geometry-driven but occasionally asleep at the wheel associative dimensions"). In those cases, the DIMREGEN command will fix things.

Pointy-Headed Leaders

No, I'm not talking about your boss (or about you, if you happen to be the boss). I'm talking about arrows that point from your comment to the object or area about which you're commenting. AutoCAD treats leaders as a special kind of dimension object (no jokes about dimwitted leaders, now). You can draw leaders and text at the same time easily by using the qLEader (Quick Leader) command, as described in the following steps.

qLEader is an improved version of the old LEADER command, which remains in AutoCAD 2005 for compatibility reasons. I recommend that you use qLEader instead of LEADER. Fortunately, the AutoCAD 2005 Dimension menu and tool-bar choices run the qLEader command.

qLEader is another one of those annoying AutoCAD commands that prompts you for some information on the command line and some in a dialog box. Pay close attention to the command line prompts throughout this example:

1. **Set a layer that's appropriate for dimensions current.**

   See Chapter 4 for details.

2. **Set a dimension style that's appropriate for your needs current.**

   Choose an existing dimension style from the drop-down list on the Styles toolbar, or create a new style by using the procedure in the section, "Creating and managing dimension styles," earlier in this chapter.

3. **Choose Dimension⇨Leader or click the Quick Leader button on the Dimension toolbar.**

   The command line prompts you to select the first leader point — that is, the arrowhead point — and gives you the option of changing leader settings first:

   ```
   Specify first leader point, or [Settings] <Settings>:
   ```

   If you want to draw curved rather than straight leader lines or choose a different leader arrowhead style, press Enter now to open the Leader Settings dialog box.

4. **Pick a point that you want to point to.**

   If you use an object snap mode, such as Nearest or Midpoint, to pick a point on an object, AutoCAD associates the leader with the object. If you later move the object, AutoCAD updates the leader so that it points to the new location.

   The command line prompts you for the next point — AutoCAD draws a shaft from the arrowhead to this point:

   ```
   Specify next point:
   ```

5. **Pick a second point.**

   If you pick a second point that's too close to the arrowhead point, AutoCAD doesn't have enough room to draw the arrowhead, and thus omits it.

   AutoCAD repeats the next point prompt so that you can draw a multisegment shaft if you want to:

   ```
   Specify next point:
   ```

6. **Pick one more point if you want to, or press Enter if you want a leader with a single shaft.**

   Pressing Enter tells the qLEader command that you're finished selecting the points that define the leader shaft. By default, the qLEader command lets you pick up to three points (the arrowhead point and two more points). You can change this behavior in the Leader Settings dialog box (refer to Step 3).

   The command line prompts you to specify the width for word-wrapping the text that you'll attach to the leader:

   ```
   Specify text width <0.0>:
   ```

   The default text width, 0.0, turns off word-wrapping and displays your text on a single line. You can type a width or point and click with the mouse.

Turning off word-wrapping works fine for short notes that fit on one line. If you think your note may be longer, specify a width instead of accepting the default value of 0.0.

7. **Press Enter to suppress word-wrapping, or move the cursor to the right or left to specify a width for word-wrapping; then click.**

The command line prompts you to type a short note directly at the command line, or press Enter to type your note in the Multiline Text Editor window:

```
Enter first line of annotation text <Mtext>:
```

8. **Press Enter to open the Multiline Text Editor window.**

9. **Enter your comment.**

10. **Click OK.**

The Multiline Text Editor window closes and adds your comment to the drawing, next to the leader.

Figure 10-11 shows several different leaders with notes.

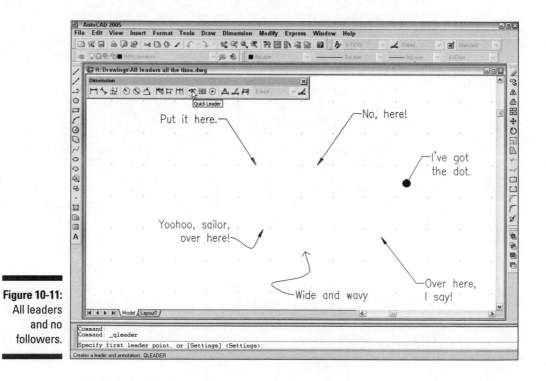

Figure 10-11:
All leaders
and no
followers.

If both the leader arrowhead and the text are the wrong size or appear to be missing entirely, the dimension scale isn't set correctly in the drawing. (As I warn you earlier, AutoCAD treats leaders as a special kind of dimension object.) See Chapter 3 for detailed instructions on how to set the dimension scale. After you set the dimension scale properly, erase and re-create the leader and text.

If you add a comment to a drawing and later decide that the comment merits a leader, you can use the qLEader command to draw the leader so that the end of the shaft ends up in the vicinity of the existing text object. Then, when the Multiline Text Editor window appears (Step 8 in the previous steps), click OK without entering any new text.

A leader and the text that you draw with it are partially associated with each other. When you move the text, the leader's shaft follows. Unfortunately, the converse isn't true — moving the leader or one of its vertices doesn't cause the text to follow.

Chapter 11

Down the Hatch

● ●

In This Chapter

▶ Adding hatching to your drawings

▶ Copying existing hatches

▶ Using predefined and user-defined hatch patterns

▶ Making solid and gradient fills

▶ Scaling hatches properly

▶ Choosing hatching boundaries

▶ Editing hatches

● ●

*I*f you were hoping to hatch a plot (or plot a hatch), see Chapter 12 instead. If you want to hatch an egg, buy my companion book, *Raising Chickens For Dummies*. If you need to fill in closed areas of your drawings with special patterns of lines, this is your chapter.

Drafters often use hatching to represent the type of material that makes up an object, such as insulation, metal, concrete, and so on. In other cases, hatching helps emphasize or clarify the extent of a particular element in the drawing — for example, showing the location of walls in a building plan, or highlighting a swampy area on a map so you know where to avoid building a road. Figure 11-1 shows an example of hatching in a structural detail.

An AutoCAD hatch is a separate object that fills a space, that has an appearance dictated by the hatch pattern assigned to it, and that is associated with the objects that bound the space, such as lines, polylines, or arcs. If you move or stretch the boundaries, AutoCAD normally updates the hatching to fill the resized area.

Don't go overboard with hatching. The purpose of hatching is to clarify, not overwhelm, the other geometry in the drawing. If your plots look like a patchwork quilt of hatch patterns, it's time to simplify.

Hatching is another kind of annotation of your geometry, similar in purpose to text and dimensions. As I describe at the beginning of Chapter 9, you'll usually be more efficient if you save annotation for later in the drafting process. Draw as much geometry as possible first, and *then* hatch the parts that require it. In other words, batch your hatch.

Hatch . . . Hatch . . . Hatchoo

This section outlines the steps you use to add hatching to a drawing with the Boundary Hatch and Fill dialog box, shown in Figure 11-2. You can use this information to get started quickly with hatching. When you need more information about any part of the process, jump to the relevant sections of "Pushing the Boundary (of) Hatch," later in this chapter.

The following steps show you how to hatch an enclosed area by using the "pick points" method of selecting the hatch area:

1. **Open a drawing containing geometry that forms fully closed boundaries, or draw some boundaries by using the drawing commands I describe in Chapter 5.**

   The areas you want to hatch must be completely enclosed. The Circle, POLygon, and RECtang commands, and the Line and PLine commands with the Close option, make great hatch boundaries (see Chapter 5 for details).

Boundary Hatch and Fill

Hatch | Advanced | Gradient

Type: Predefined

Pattern: GRAVEL

Swatch:

Custom pattern:

Angle: 0

Scale: 3

☐ Relative to paper space

Spacing: 1"

ISO pen width:

Pick Points

Select Objects

✕ Remove Islands

🔍 View Selections

Inherit Properties

Draw Order
Send behind boundary

Composition
○ Associative
● Nonassociative

☐ Double

Preview | OK | Cancel | Help

Figure 11-2:
The Hatch
tab of the
Boundary
Hatch
and Fill
dialog box.

2. **Set an appropriate layer current, as described in Chapter 4.**

    It's usually best to put hatching on its own layer.

3. **Start the bHatch command by clicking the Hatch button on the Draw toolbar.**

    The Boundary Hatch and Fill dialog box appears.

    For historical reasons, AutoCAD 2005 also has a HATCH command, which prompts you at the command line instead of opening a dialog box. Trust me — you want the bHatch command's dialog box.

4. **Choose Predefined, User Defined, or Custom from the Type drop-down list.**

    Predefined or User Defined works best for most purposes. See the next section for details.

5. **If you chose Predefined or Custom in the previous step, select any predefined or custom hatch pattern from the Pattern drop-down list or the Pattern button just to the right of it. If you chose User Defined, you don't need to choose a pattern.**

6. **Specify an Angle and Scale for the hatch pattern (or, if you chose User Defined in Step 4, specify Angle and Spacing).**

    See "Getting it right: Hatch angle and scale," later in this chapter, for more information.

7. **Click the Pick Points button.**

   The Boundary Hatch and Fill dialog box (temporarily) disappears, and your drawing reappears with the following prompt at the command line:

   ```
   Select internal point:
   ```

8. **Select a point inside the boundary within which you want to hatch by clicking it with the mouse.**

   AutoCAD analyzes the drawing and decides which boundaries to use. In a complex drawing, this analysis can take several seconds. AutoCAD highlights the boundary that it finds.

   If AutoCAD highlights the wrong boundary, right-click, choose Clear All from the cursor menu, and try again.

9. **Right-click anywhere in the drawing area and choose Enter from the cursor menu to indicate that you're finished selecting points.**

   The Boundary Hatch and Fill dialog box reappears.

10. **Click the Preview button to preview the hatch.**

    The Boundary Hatch and Fill dialog box (temporarily) disappears again, and AutoCAD shows you what the hatch will look like.

    ```
    Pick or press Esc to return to dialog or <Right-click to
         accept hatch>:
    ```

11. **Click anywhere in the drawing area to return to the Boundary Hatch and Fill dialog box.**

12. **Adjust any settings and preview again until you're satisfied with the hatch.**

13. **Click OK.**

    AutoCAD hatches the area inside the boundary. If you modify the boundary, the hatch automatically resizes to fill the resized area.

Occasionally, AutoCAD gets confused and doesn't resize a hatch after you resize the boundary. If that happens, erase and then re-create the hatch in the resized area.

Pushing the Boundary (of) Hatch

The remainder of this chapter shows you how to refine the techniques presented in the preceding section. I describe how to copy existing hatching, take advantage of the various options in the Boundary Hatch and Fill dialog box, and choose more complicated hatching boundaries.

Catch a hatch: Copying hatch properties

One slick way to hatch is by using the Inherit Properties button in the Boundary Hatch and Fill dialog box to copy hatch properties from an existing hatch object. Think of it as point and shoot hatching. If someone — such as you — added some hatching in the past that's just like what you want to use now, click the Inherit Properties button and pick the existing hatching.

Inherit Properties updates the hatch pattern settings in the Boundary Hatch and Fill dialog box to make them the same as the existing hatch pattern object that you picked. You can use the cloned hatch pattern specifications as is or modify them by making changes in the Boundary Hatch and Fill dialog box.

Consistency is a good thing in drafting, especially in computer-aided drafting, in which some or all your drawing may be used for a long time. Thus it's good to use the same hatch patterns, scales, and angles for the same purposes in all your drawings. Find out whether your project, office, company, or profession has hatching standards that apply to your work.

Hatch from scratch

You can use predefined, user-defined, or custom hatch patterns. Most of the time, you'll choose either predefined or user-defined hatch patterns, unless some generous soul gives you a custom pattern. The next four sections describe the hatch pattern type choices.

Pick a pattern, any pattern: Predefined hatch patterns

To use AutoCAD's *predefined* hatch patterns, select Predefined from the drop-down list box at the top of the Hatch tab in the Boundary Hatch and Fill dialog box. This selection sets the stage for choosing the hatch pattern.

You specify a predefined hatch pattern in one of two ways:

- If you know the name of the hatch pattern, select it from the Pattern drop-down list. The list is alphabetical, except that SOLID (that is, a solid fill) is at the very beginning.

- If you don't know the pattern's name, or you prefer the visual approach, click the Pattern button (the tiny button with the ellipsis [three dots] to the right of the Pattern prompt and pattern name) to display the Hatch Pattern Palette with pattern previews and names.

AutoCAD has about 80 predefined hatch patterns from which to choose. The list includes ANSI (American National Standards Institute) and ISO (International Standards Organization) standard hatch patterns. Figure 11-3 shows the Other Predefined hatch patterns, which cover everything from Earth to Escher to Stars. Hatch patterns whose names begins with AR- are intended for architectural and related industries.

Figure 11-3: Plenty of hatch patterns.

After you've selected a pattern, specify angle and scale, as I describe in the section "Getting it right: Hatch angle and scale," in this chapter.

Make it solid, man

Although you may not guess it, AutoCAD treats filling an area with a solid color as a type of hatching. Simply choose Solid from the top of the Pattern drop-down list.

Like any other object, a solid hatch takes on the current object color — or the current layer's color if you leave color set to ByLayer. Therefore, check whether the current object layer and color are set appropriately before you use the Solid hatching option (see Chapter 4 for details).

You can create the effect of a solid fill in AutoCAD in several other ways:

✔ If you want a filled-in circle or donut, use the DOnut command and specify an inside diameter of 0.

✔ If you want one or more line segments with either uniform or tapered widths, use the PLine command's Width option. (Chapter 5 discusses the DOnut and PLine commands.)

✔ If you want a pattern that starts out solid but then fades away (or transitions to a different color) in one or more directions, use the Gradient tab on the Boundary Hatch and Fill dialog box. This option creates a gradient fill. You can control the color(s), direction(s), and angle of the gradient.

Solid and gradient fills are a good way to mimic poché — an old hand-drafting technique in which you shade areas with a lighter colored pencil (usually red) to make those areas appear lightly shaded on blueline prints. The figure shows some examples of solid and gradient fills.

It's up to you: User-defined hatches

A *user-defined* hatch pattern makes a hatch pattern out of parallel lines. Use this option to create a simple pattern and specify the space between the lines in drawing units. For example, you can hatch a wall in a building plan with a user-defined pattern and specify that the hatch lines be three inches apart.

After you choose User Defined from the Type drop-down list in the Boundary Hatch and Fill dialog box, you specify the angle and spacing of the lines. You can select the Double check box to achieve a crosshatching effect (two perpendicular sets of hatching lines).

Getting it right: Hatch angle and scale

Predefined and custom hatch patterns require that you enter the angle and scale for AutoCAD to generate the hatching. You usually won't have any trouble deciding on an appropriate angle, but a suitable scale can be tricky.

The hatch scale usually should be a pattern-specific multiplier times the drawing scale factor, as described in Chapter 3. For example, the EARTH pattern (in the Other Predefined tab of the Hatch Pattern Palette; refer to Figure 11-3) looks pretty good in a full scale (1 = 1) drawing with a hatch scale of 0.75. If you're adding EARTH pattern hatching to a 1" = 1'–0" detail (drawing scale factor equals 12), try using a hatch scale of 0.75×12, or 9.0. This pattern-specific multiplier and drawing-scale-factor approach ensures that hatching looks consistent (that the spaces between the lines are the same) at all scales when you plot.

Assuming that you know your drawing's scale factor, the only complication is figuring out what the pattern-specific multiplier should be for a particular hatch pattern. In a more rational world, the pattern-specific multiplier would always be something sensible, like 1.0. Unfortunately, that's not the case for all hatch pattern definitions. Even worse, there's no way to predict before you use a hatch pattern for the first time what an appropriate pattern-specific multiplier might be. (Autodesk created the hatch patterns whose names begins with AR- — that is, the ones intended for architectural drawings — with a final hatch scale of 1.0 in mind, but in some cases you'll have to adjust up or down in order to achieve a suitable scale.) You have to use trial and error the first time, and then make a note of the hatch pattern and multiplier for future use.

The first time you use a hatch pattern definition, try 1.0 as the multiplier. Don't forget to multiply by the drawing scale factor. Preview the hatch and then adjust the hatch scale iteratively; preview after each change. After you settle upon a scale for the current drawing, calculate the corresponding multiplier (for future use); divide the hatch scale by the current drawing's scale factor.

User-defined patterns require that you enter an angle and spacing, not angle and scale. Spacing is expressed in the current drawing units.

Do fence me in: Defining hatch boundaries

After you specify the hatch pattern, angle, and scale you want to use, you define the boundary (or boundaries) into which you want to pour that hatch pattern in one of two ways:

- ✔ Picking points within the area(s) you want hatched
- ✔ Selecting objects that surround those areas

The actual operation involved in using either of these options is confusing to most people. You'll probably need a little practice before you get used to it.

The idea behind either definition option is simple when applied to simple areas — that is, closed areas with no additional objects inside them. To define the hatch boundary for a simple area, do one of these two things:

- ✔ Click the Pick Points button in the Boundary Hatch and Fill dialog box and then click a point *inside* the boundary.
- ✔ Click the Select Objects button and select one or more objects that form a fully closed boundary.

This simple hatching gets more complicated if you have one closed object inside another, as in Figure 11-4. The AutoCAD hatch preview and a bit of experimentation will clarify all these potentially puzzling permutations.

Pick one point between two areas

Pick inside a simple area

Pick points inside both areas

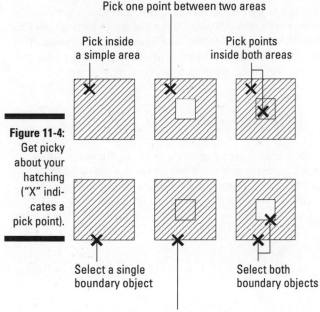

Figure 11-4: Get picky about your hatching ("X" indicates a pick point).

Select a single boundary object

Select both boundary objects

Select one boundary object with another nested inside

As I warn earlier in this chapter, boundaries must be *completely* closed before AutoCAD will hatch them. That's one of the reasons you should employ the precision techniques from this book whenever you draw or edit objects. If the lines surrounding your boundary don't either meet *exactly* or cross, AutoCAD scolds you with a `Valid hatch boundary not found` error message.

The `Valid hatch boundary not found` error message means you need to "repair" lines or other objects so they are a fully closed boundary. Sometimes you can use the Fillet command with a zero fillet radius to force two lines to meet exactly. Another possibility is to use grip editing to align one endpoint precisely with another. Chapter 6 discusses these two editing techniques.

If you don't want to go to the trouble of repairing your drawing in this way, you can use AutoCAD 2005's new Gap Tolerance setting, located on the Advanced tab of the Boundary Hatch and Fill dialog box, to tell AutoCAD to overlook small gaps when dealing with hatch boundaries.

Hatching that knows its place

In AutoCAD 2005, the Boundary Hatch and Fill dialog box includes a new Draw Order setting that controls where AutoCAD places the hatching with respect to the boundary in terms of object selection. (Refer to Figure 11-2.) The default setting, Send behind boundary, puts the hatching "underneath" its boundary for object selection purposes, and that's usually exactly what you want.

Have palette, will hatch

With Tool Palettes, described in Chapter 2, you can create click-and-drag hatch palettes. With a hatch palette, you click a tool (a swatch) and drag into an enclosed boundary to hatch the area. If your hatching needs are simple, you can create a Tool Palette for the patterns and scales you often use. See "hatches, adding to tool palettes" in AutoCAD's online help for more information.

Editing Hatch Objects

Editing an existing hatch pattern is simple after you're familiar with the Boundary Hatch and Fill dialog box. Follow these steps:

1. **Select the hatch object.**

2. **Right-click anywhere in the drawing area and choose Hatch Edit from the cursor menu.**

   AutoCAD opens the Hatch Edit dialog box and displays the hatch object's current settings.

3. **Make any desired changes, use the Preview button to look them over, and click OK to keep the changes.**

Alternatively, you can use the Properties palette (described in Chapter 6) to make most existing hatch pattern changes. The Properties palette is especially good for changing several hatches at once.

To make one hatch look like another, use the Match Properties button on the Standard toolbar.

The TRim command (described in Chapter 6) is now capable of trimming hatch patterns in most cases — although it removes associativity of the hatch pattern with the boundary.

Chapter 12

The Plot Thickens

Despite the increasing number of offices with a computer (or two) on every desk, many people still need to or want to work with printed drawings. Perhaps you thought that using AutoCAD means you don't have to rely on hard-copy versions of drawings, but can view them on-screen instead. Even if that's true, you may need to give hard-copy prints to your less savvy colleagues who don't have AutoCAD. You may want to make some quick prints to pore over during your bus ride home. You may find that checking drawings the old-fashioned way — with a hard-copy print and a red pencil — turns up errors that managed to remain hidden on the computer screen.

Whatever the reason, you'll want to print drawings at some point — probably sooner rather than later. Depending on where you are in a project, plotting is the pop quiz, midterm, or final exam of your drawing-making semester. This chapter helps you ace the test.

You Say Printing, I Say Plotting

Plotting originally meant creating hard-copy output on a device that was capable of printing on larger sheets, such as D size or E size, that measure several feet on a side. (See Chapter 3 for information about drafting paper sizes.) These plotters often used pens to draw, robot-fashion, on large sheets of vellum or Mylar. The sheets could then be run through *diazo blueline machines* — copying machines that create blueline prints — in order to create less-expensive copies. *Printing* meant creating hard-copy output on ordinary printers that used ordinary sized paper, such as A size (letter size, 8½ x 11 inches) or B size (tabloid or ledger size, 11 x 17 inches).

Nowadays, AutoCAD and most CAD users make no distinction between plotting and printing. AutoCAD veterans usually say "plotting," so if you want to be hip, you can do so, too.

Whatever you call it, plotting an AutoCAD drawing is considerably more complicated than printing a word processing document or a spreadsheet. CAD has a larger range of different plotters and printers, drawing types, and output procedures than other computer applications. AutoCAD tries to help you tame the vast jungle of plotting permutations, but you'll probably find that you have to take some time to get the lay of the land and clear a path to your desired hard-copy output.

The plotting system in AutoCAD 2005 is essentially the same as the one that Autodesk introduced in AutoCAD 2000, but with a reorganized, somewhat less imposing Plot dialog box. In addition, Autodesk has improved the page setups feature and added background plotting. I describe all these changes in this chapter.

Get with the system

One of the complications you face in your attempts to create hard copy is that AutoCAD has two distinct ways of communicating with your plotters and printers. Operating systems, and the programs that run in them, use a special piece of software called a *printer driver* to format data for printing and then send it to the printer or plotter. When you configure Windows to recognize a new printer connected to your computer or your network, you're actually installing the printer's driver. ("Bring the Rolls around front, James. And bring me a gin and tonic and a D-size plot while you're at it.") AutoCAD, like other Windows programs, works with the printers you've configured in Windows. AutoCAD calls these *system printers* because they're part of the Windows system.

But AutoCAD, unlike other Windows programs, can't leave well enough alone. Some output devices, especially some larger plotters, aren't controlled very efficiently by Windows system printer drivers. For that reason, AutoCAD comes with specialized *nonsystem drivers* (that is, drivers that are not installed as part of the Windows system) for plotters from companies such as Hewlett Packard, Xerox, and Océ. These drivers are kind of like nonunion workers. They ignore the tidy rules for communicating with Windows printers in order to get things done a bit more quickly and flexibly.

Using already-configured Windows system printer drivers usually is easiest, and they work well with many devices — especially devices that print on smaller paper, such as laser and inkjet printers. However, if you have a large plotter, you may be able to get faster plotting, better plot quality, or more plot features by installing a nonsystem driver. To find out more, choose Contents⇨Driver and Peripheral Guide⇨Use Plotters and Printers in the AutoCAD online help system.

The AutoCAD 2005 CD includes a Windows system printer driver for Hewlett-Packard DesignJet large format printers. This driver is optimized for CAD plotting. To install the driver, load your AutoCAD 2005 CD, click Install, and then click Hewlett Packard DesignJet Printer Drivers.

Configure it out

For now, you simply should make sure that AutoCAD recognizes the devices that you want to use for plotting. The following steps show you how:

1. **Launch AutoCAD and open an existing drawing or start a new, blank drawing.**

2. **Choose Tools⇨Options to open the Options dialog box, and click the Plot and Publish tab.**

3. **Click the drop-down arrow to view the list just below the Use As Default Output Device option, as shown in Figure 12-1.**

   The list includes two kinds of device configurations, designated by two tiny, difficult-to-distinguish icons to the left of the device names:

   • A little laser printer icon, with a sheet of white paper coming out the top, indicates a Windows system printer configuration.

   • A little plotter icon, with a piece of paper coming out the front, indicates a nonsystem (that is, AutoCAD-specific) configuration.

   The nonsystem configuration names always end in *pc3,* because they're stored in special AutoCAD Printer Configuration version 3 files. So, if you can't tell the difference between the icons, look for the *pc3* at the end of the name.

4. **Verify that the list includes the printers and plotters that you want to have available in AutoCAD.**

   If not, choose Start⇨Printers and Faxes (in Windows XP) or Start⇨ Settings⇨Printers (in Windows 2000), launch the Add Printer Wizard, and follow the instructions. If your printer isn't in the default Windows list, cancel the wizard and hunt down a driver disk that came with your printer, or, better yet, download the current driver from the printer manufacturer's Web site.

Nonsystem printers

System printers   List of devices

Figure 12-1:
System and
nonsystem
printer
configur-
ations.

5. **Choose the output device that you want to make the default for new drawings.**

6. **Click OK to close the dialog box and retain any change that you made in the previous step.**

You use the AutoCAD Plotter Manager Add-A-Plotter Wizard to create nonsystem driver configurations. (Choose File⇨Plotter Manager to display a window containing a shortcut to the wizard.) This wizard is similar to the Windows Add Printer Wizard; if you can handle adding an ordinary printer in Windows, you probably can handle adding a nonsystem plotter configuration to AutoCAD. When you complete the wizard steps, AutoCAD saves the information in a PC3 (Plot Configuration version 3) file.

A Simple Plot

Okay, so you believe me. You know that you're not going to master AutoCAD plotting in five minutes. That doesn't change the fact that your boss, employee, wife, husband, construction foreman, or 11-year-old son wants a quick check plot of your drawing.

Plotting success in 16 steps

Here's the quick, cut-to-the-chase procedure for plotting a simple drawing — a mere 16 steps! This procedure assumes that you plot in model space — that is, that the Model tab at the bottom of the drawing area shows the drawing in a way that you want to plot. (I cover plotting paper space layout tabs in the section "Plotting the Layout of the Land," later in this chapter.) This procedure doesn't deal with controlling plotted lineweights (see the "Plotting Lineweights and Colors" section later in this chapter for those details). It should, however, result in a piece of paper that bears some resemblance to what AutoCAD displays on your computer monitor.

Follow these steps to make a simple, not-to-scale, monochrome plot of a drawing:

1. **Open the drawing in AutoCAD.**

2. **Click the Model tab at the bottom of the drawing area to ensure that you're plotting the model space contents.**

   I explain model space and paper space in Chapter 3, and I explain how to plot paper space layouts later in this chapter.

3. **Zoom to the drawing's current extents (choose View⇨Zoom⇨Extents) so you can verify the area you're going to plot.**

   The extents of a drawing consist of a rectangular area just large enough to include all the objects in the drawing.

4. **To display the Plot dialog box, click the Plot button on the Standard toolbar.**

   The Plot dialog box appears, as shown in Figure 12-2.

5. **In the Printer/Plotter area, select a device from the Name list.**

6. **In the Paper Size area, select a paper size that's loaded in your printer or plotter.**

   Of course, you must make sure that the paper size is large enough to fit the drawing at the scale you want to plot it at. For example, if you want to plot a D-size drawing, but you have only a B-size printer, you're out of luck — unless you resort to multiple pieces of paper and lots of tape.

7. **In the Plot Area area (sponsored by the Department of Redundancy Department), choose Extents.**

   If you set limits properly, as I suggest in Chapter 3, then choose Limits instead in order to plot the drawing area that you defined. The Window option — that is, plot a window whose corners you pick — is useful when you want to plot just a portion of your drawing.

8. **In the Plot Offset area, choose Center the Plot.**

   Alternatively, you can specify offsets of zero or other amounts in order to position the plot at a specific location on the paper.

Figure 12-2:
The Plot
dialog box.

————More Options button

9. **In the Plot Scale area, either choose Fit to Paper or uncheck Fit to Paper and specify a scale (by choosing from the drop-down list or typing into the two text boxes).**

   For most real plotting, you'll plot to a specific scale, but feel free to choose Fit to Paper for now. If you do want to plot to a specific scale, see the "Instead of fit, scale it" section later in this chapter for guidance.

10. **Click the More Options button (at the bottom-right corner of the dialog box, next to the Help button.**

    The Plot dialog box reveals additional settings, as shown in Figure 12-3.

11. **In the Plot Style Table (Pen Assignments) area, choose Monochrome.ctb or Monochrome.stb.**

    AutoCAD may ask you whether to "Assign this plot style table to all layouts?" Answer Yes to make Monochrome.ctb (or Monochrome.stb) the default plot style table for the paper space layout tabs as well as the Model tab, or answer No to make the change apply only to the current tab.

    The "Plotting with style" section later in this chapter describes plot style tables.

12. **In the Plot Options area, make sure that Plot With Plot Styles is on and Save Changes to Layout is off, as shown in Figure 12-3.**

    Leaving Save Changes to Layout turned off tells AutoCAD to use any plot settings changes that you make only for this plot — AutoCAD will revert to the original plot settings the next time you plot the drawing.

Figure 12-3:
The
expanded
Plot dialog
box.

After you become confident with plotting, you may want to turn on this setting so that AutoCAD *does* save your plotting settings changes as the default. Alternatively, click the Apply to Layout button to make the current plot settings the default for future plotting of this tab (that is, the Model tab) in this drawing.

13. In the Drawing Orientation area, choose Portrait or Landscape.

The postage stamp-sized preview in the middle of the Plot dialog box should help you decide on the right orientation. If not, the full preview in the next step will tell you for sure.

14. Click the Preview button and check that the drawing displays on the paper at the correct orientation and size, as shown in Figure 12-4; then, right-click and choose Exit to return to the Plot dialog box.

15. If you found any problems in the preview, adjust the plot settings (for example, Plot Area, Plot Scale, or Drawing Orientation) and repeat the preview until the plot looks right.

16. Click OK to create the plot.

When AutoCAD finishes generating and sending the plot, it displays a "Plot and Publish Job Complete" balloon notification from the status bar. If you decide that you don't want to see these notifications, right-lick the Plot/Publish Details Report Available icon near the right end of the status bar and deselect Enable Balloon Notification.

There — 16 steps, as promised. If for some reason your plot didn't work, well, I warned you that AutoCAD plotting was complicated and temperamental! Read the rest of this chapter for all the details about the numerous other plotting options that can cause plotting to go awry. If you're in a big hurry, turn directly to the troubleshooting section, "Troubles with Plotting," at the end of the chapter.

Preview one, two

One of the keys to efficient plotting is liberal use of AutoCAD's partial and full preview features. (To maintain political fairness, I recommend conservative use of some other AutoCAD options elsewhere in the book.)

The postage stamp-sized partial preview in the middle of the Plot dialog box is a quick reality check to make sure your plot fits on the paper and is turned in the right direction. If the plot area at the current scale is too large for the paper, AutoCAD displays thick red warning lines along the side(s) of the sheet where the drawing will be truncated.

Press the Preview button to see a full preview in a separate window. You see exactly how your drawing lays out on the paper and how the various line-weights, colors, and other object plot properties will appear. You can zoom and pan around the preview by using the right-click menu. (Any zooming or panning that you do does not affect what area of the drawing gets plotted — zooming and panning is just a way to get a better look at different areas of the plot preview.)

Instead of fit, scale it

In most real plotting situations, you want to plot to a specific scale rather than let AutoCAD choose an oddball scale that just happens to maximize the drawing on the paper. And if you're going to plot the Model tab of a drawing to scale, you need to know its drawing scale factor. Chapter 3 describes setup concepts and Chapter 9 provides some tips for determining the scale factor of a drawing that someone else created.

If your drawing was created at a standard scale, such as 1:50 or ¼"=1'–0", then you simply choose the scale from the handy drop-down Scale list in the Plot dialog box. If your scale is not in the list, then type the ratio between plotted distance and AutoCAD drawing distance into the two text boxes below the Scale list, as shown in Figure 12-5. The easiest way to express the ratio usually is to type **1** (one) in the upper box and the drawing scale factor in the lower box. (See Chapter 3 for more information.)

Figure 12-5:
Lots of weighs to scale.

Fit

Choose a predefined scale

Type a ratio

Creating half-size plots for some purposes is common in some industries. To plot model space half-size, double the drawing scale factor. For example, a ⅛"=1'–0" drawing has a drawing scale factor of 96, which is equivalent to a plot scale of 1=96. To make a half-size model space plot of it, specify a plot scale of 1=192 (or choose ¹⁄₁₆"=1'–0" from the Scale drop-down list).

Even if you work with drawings that are created to be plotted at a specific scale, plotting with a Fit to Paper scale may be the most efficient way to make a reduced-size check plot. For example, drafters in your office might create drawings that get plotted on D size sheets (24 x 36 inch), whereas you have access to a laser printer with a B size (11 x 17 inch) paper tray. By plotting the D size drawings Scaled to Fit on B size paper, you end up with check plots that are slightly smaller than half size ($\frac{11}{24}$ size, to be exact). You won't be able to measure distances on the check plots with a scale, but you probably will be able to check them visually for overall correctness.

Plotting the Layout of the Land

In the previous section I show you how to plot the model space representation of your drawing by making sure that the Model tab is active when you open the Plot dialog box. However, paper space gives you many additional options for controlling the look of your output, without having to modify the underlying geometry or the way it looks to someone working on the DWG file. So in some drawings, you want to plot a paper space layout instead.

About paper space layouts and plotting

As Chapter 3 describes, you can use AutoCAD's paper space feature to compose one or more *layouts* for plotting your drawing in particular ways. Each layout lives on a separate tab, which you click at the bottom of the drawing area. In addition, AutoCAD saves plot settings (plot device, paper size, plot scale, and so on) separately for each of the tabs — that is, for each of layout tabs as well as the Model tab.

Whether to plot model space or a paper space layout in a drawing depends entirely on how the drawing was set up. If you or someone else went through a layout setup procedure similar to the one in Chapter 3, then you probably should plot the paper space layout. If not, then plot the Model tab.

Don't confuse the Model tab at the bottom of the drawing area with the MODEL/PAPER button on the status bar. The tabs control which view of the drawing (model space or a paper space layout) fills the drawing area. When a paper space layout fills the drawing area, the status bar button controls whether drawing and editing take place in paper space or in model space inside a viewport. When you plot a layout, it doesn't matter whether the MODEL/PAPER button says MODEL or PAPER — AutoCAD always plots the paper space layout (not just the contents of model space in the viewport).

The presence of a Layout1 tab next to the Model tab at the bottom of the drawing area doesn't necessarily mean that the drawing contains an already set up paper space layout. AutoCAD always displays a Layout1 tab when you open a drawing created in AutoCAD Release 14 or earlier, and displays a Layout1 and Layout2 tab when you open a drawing created in AutoCAD 2000 or later. Layout1 and Layout2 are simply AutoCAD's default names; the creator of the drawing may have renamed them to something more descriptive.

If you don't have any paper space drawings handy, you can use one of the AutoCAD sample drawings, such as the architectural floor plan drawing stored in \Program Files\AutoCAD 2005\Sample\8th floor plan.dwg.

The path to paper space layout plotting success

Plotting a paper space layout is pretty much like plotting model space, except that you need to find the appropriate layout first and make sure that its tab is selected before you open the Plot dialog box:

1. **Click the layout tabs at the bottom of the drawing area until you find a suitably set up layout.**

   If no one has set up the layout yet, AutoCAD creates a default layout. (If the Show Page Setup Manager for New Layouts setting on the Display tab of the Options dialog box is turned on, you'll see the Page Setup Manager dialog box first — just click the Close button.) The default layout probably won't be useful for real projects, but you use it to find out about the layout plotting procedure. Refer to Chapter 3 for instructions on creating a real layout.

2. **Click the Plot button on the Standard toolbar.**

   The Plot dialog box appears.

3. **Specify a Printer/Plotter Name and a Paper Size.**

4. **In the What to Plot list, choose Layout.**

5. **Specify the Plot Offset (such as zero in both the X and Y directions).**

6. **Specify a Plot Scale of 1:1.**

   One of the big advantages of layouts is that you don't need to know anything about drawing scale in order to plot the drawing — hence the name *paper* space. Figure 12-6 shows the proper settings for plotting a layout.

   To create a half-size plot of a layout, specify a plot scale of 1:2. In addition, turn on the Scale Lineweights setting in order to reduce lineweights proportionally. (I cover plotting lineweights later in this chapter.)

Figure 12-6: Settings for plotting a paper space layout.

Plot area = Layout

If you find that the layout is too big for your plotter's largest paper size at a plot scale of 1:1, you can change the What to Plot setting to Extents and then specify Fit to Paper for the Plot Scale. Alternatively, you can exit the Plot dialog box and fix the problem if you want to have a paper space layout that permanently reflects a new paper size. Use the Page Setup dialog box to modify the layout settings, or copy the layout and modify the new layout.

7. **Click the More Options button and change any additional plot options that you want to.**

   Refer to Steps 11 through 13 in the section, "Plotting success in 16 steps."

8. **Click the Preview button, check that the drawing displays on the paper at the correct orientation and size, right-click and choose Exit to return to the Plot dialog box.**

   If you found any problems in the preview, change your plot settings and Preview again until it looks right.

9. **Click OK to create the plot.**

Plotting Lineweights and Colors

In previous sections of this chapter I help you gain some plotting confidence. Those sections show you how to create scaled, monochrome plots with uniform lineweights in model space or paper space. Those skills may be all you need, but if you care about controlling plotted lineweights and colors, or adding special effects such as screening (plotting shades of gray), read on.

Plotting with style

Plot styles provide a way to override object properties with alternative plot properties. (See Chapter 4 for information about object properties.) The properties include plotted lineweight, plotted color, and screening (plotting shades of gray). Figure 12-7 shows the full range of options. They come in two exciting flavors:

 ✔ Color-dependent plot styles

 ✔ Named plot styles

Color-dependent plot styles are based on the standard way of plotting in earlier versions of AutoCAD (before AutoCAD 2000), whereas named plot styles provide a newer way.

Figure 12-7:
Editing a color-dependent plot style table.

It's remotely possible that you won't need to bother with plot styles. If the drawings you want to plot have layer and object properties (especially lineweight) that reflect how you want objects to plot, you can dispense with plot styles. But most people and most drawings use plot styles, so you should at least be familiar with them.

A couple of common reasons for using plot styles are to:

- **Map screen colors to plotted lineweights.** If this idea seems completely loony to you, try to suspend judgment until you've read the "Plotting through thick and thin" section, a bit later in this chapter.

- **Create *screened* lines on monochrome plots.** Lines that are screened display in various shades of gray, not black. Drafters sometimes use screened lines to de-emphasize secondary objects that otherwise would overwhelm the main objects in the drawing. Screening is expressed as a percentage, with 100% being completely black and 0% being invisible.

Using plot styles

If you want objects in your drawing to plot with properties that differ from their display properties, you need plot styles. For example, you can plot with different lineweights or colors from the ones you're using for display purposes. Or, as I mention in the preceding section, you may need to map display colors to plotted lineweights. AutoCAD groups plot styles into plot style tables, each of which is stored in a separate file.

Color-dependent plot style tables live in Color TaBle (CTB) files and they map the 255 AutoCAD display colors to 255 plot styles. AutoCAD automatically attaches the color-dependent plot styles to every object, based on — you guessed it — the object's color. (Are those AutoCAD programmers brilliant, or what?) Color-dependent plot style tables are especially handy for mimicking the old color-mapped-to-lineweight plotting approach of AutoCAD R14 and earlier releases; this remains the most common method in most companies.

Named plot style tables live in Style TaBle (STB) files. After you've created a named plot style table, you create one or more plot styles and give them any names you like. Then you can assign the named plot styles to layers or to individual objects. (See Chapter 4 for more information about object and layer properties.)

"Named" refers to the plot styles, not to the tables. Both color-dependent plot style *tables* and named plot style *tables* have names because both are stored in files and files have to have names. But color-dependent plot *styles* don't have names and named plot *styles* do have names.

To use a plot style table, and its included plot styles (whether they're color-dependent or named), you must attach it to model space or a paper space layout. The plot style table then affects plotting only for that tab. This approach lets you plot the same drawing in different ways by attaching different plot styles to different tabs.

You can attach a plot style to model space or a paper space layout by selecting its tab at the bottom of the drawing area, opening the Plot dialog box or Page Setup dialog box, and choosing the plot style table name in the Plot Style Table (Pen Assignments) area of the expanded Plot dialog box. See "Controlling plotted lineweights with screen colors," later in this chapter, for an example.

When you start a new drawing in the usual way — that is, by using a template drawing (see Chapter 3), the template drawing's plot style behavior determines whether you can choose CTB or STB files. (That's why most of AutoCAD's stock template drawings come in Color Dependent Plot Styles and Named Plot Styles versions.) If you want to change from color-dependent plot styles to named plot styles (or vice versa) in a particular drawing, use the CONVERTPSTYLES command.

The Plotting tab on the Options dialog box contains a setting called Default Plot Style Behavior For New Drawings, but it's practically useless. It doesn't change the current drawing and, despite its name, doesn't even affect new drawings that you start from a template drawing.

Creating plot styles

If you're really lucky, you won't need to use plot styles. If you're somewhat lucky, you'll need to use plot styles, but someone will provide the plot style table files for you. If that's the case, you must put the CTB or STB files in your Plot Styles folder in order for AutoCAD to recognize them. (To find the location of your Plot Styles folder, open the Options dialog box, choose the Files tab, and look for the Printer Support File Path⇨Plot Style Table Search Path setting.)

If you're not lucky at all, then you'll need to be smart — that is, you'll want to know how to create your own plot style table files. Here's how:

1. **Choose File⇨Plot Style Manager.**

   The Plot Styles folder opens in a separate window.

2. **Double-click the Add-A-Plot Style Table Wizard program shortcut.**

3. **Read the opening screen and then click Next.**

4. **Choose the Start From Scratch option, or one of the other three options if you want to start with settings from another file. Then click Next.**

   The remaining steps in this procedure assume that you chose Start From Scratch. If you chose another option, simply follow the wizard's prompts.

If the creator of a drawing provides you with an AutoCAD R14/AutoCAD LT 98 PC2 (version 2) or AutoCAD R12/AutoCAD LT 95 PCP (version 1) file, choose the Use A PCP Or PC2 File option. With this option, the wizard imports color-to-plotted-lineweight settings automatically.

5. **Choose whether you want to create a color-dependent plot style table (CTB file) or a named plot style table (STB file). Then click Next.**

   Choose Color-Dependent Plot Style Table in order to map screen colors to plotted lineweights. Choose Named Plot Style Table in order to leave screen colors alone (so that the colors plot as you see them on-screen) and to create named plot styles that you can apply to layers or objects.

6. **Type a name for the new CTB or STB file and then click Next.**

7. **Click the Plot Style Table Editor button.**

   The Plot Style Table Editor dialog box opens (refer to Figure 12-7).

8. **If you created a color-dependent plot style table, assign Lineweight, Screening, or other plot properties to each color that's used in the drawing. If you created a named plot style table, click the Add Style button and then assign plot properties to each of the named styles that you create.**

   To determine which colors are used in a drawing, switch to the AutoCAD window and open the Layer Properties Manager dialog box by clicking the Layers button located on the Object Properties toolbar.

   To change a setting for all colors or named styles, select all of them first by clicking the first color or named style, holding down the Shift key, scrolling to the end of the list, and then clicking the last color or named style. Any subsequent changes you make get applied to all the selected colors or named styles.

9. **Click the Save & Close button to close the Plot Style Table Editor dialog box. Then click Finish to complete the steps for the wizard.**

   The Plot Styles folder now displays your new CTB or STB file.

10. **Close the Plot Styles folder by clicking on the X in its title bar.**

Creating your first plot style table can be a harrowing experience, because you have so many options. Just remember that your most likely reason for creating one is to map screen colors to plotted lineweights (as I describe in greater detail in the next section). Also remember that you may be able to minimize your effort by getting a CTB file from the person who created the drawing that you want to plot.

In Chapter 4, I recommend that you limit yourself to the first 9 Standard AutoCAD Colors when defining layers, and not a patchwork of the 255 colors that AutoCAD makes available. If you follow my advice, your work to create a color-dependent plot style table will be much reduced, because you'll have to assign plot properties for only 9 colors, rather than worrying about 255 of them.

You can use \Program Files\AutoCAD 2005\Sample\Plot Screening and Fill Patterns.dwg for systematic testing of your CTB files. This drawing shows an array of color swatches for all 255 AutoCAD colors. Some of the other tabs (such as Grayscale and Screening 25%) also demonstrate how different CTB files attached to the same layout produce radically different results.

If you *really* get carried away and decide to take advantage of the 16 million-odd colors in AutoCAD's True Color capability, then you're not going to be controlling lineweights with color-dependent plot styles. CTB plot styles affect the lineweights only of objects that use the traditional 255 colors of the AutoCAD Color Index palette. If you want True Color, use object lineweights or named plot styles to control plotted lineweight.

Plotting through thick and thin

Long ago, manual drafters developed the practice of drawing lines of different thicknesses, or *lineweights,* in order to distinguish different kinds of objects. Manual drafters did it with different technical ink pen nib diameters or with different hardnesses of pencil lead and varying degrees of pressure on the pencil. Because a computer mouse usually doesn't come with different diameters of mouse balls or a pressure-sensitive button, AutoCAD and its developers had to figure out how to let users indicate lineweights on-screen and on a plot. They came up with two different ways to indicate lineweight:

- Mapping on-screen colors to plotted lineweights. I describe this common approach in Chapter 4.
- Displaying lineweights on-screen to match what the user can expect to see on the plot. This approach was introduced in AutoCAD 2000.

Controlling plotted lineweights with object lineweights

Plotting object lineweights is trivial, assuming that the person who created the drawing took the trouble to assign lineweights to layers or objects (see Chapter 4 for details). Just make sure that the Plot Object Lineweights setting in the expanded Plot dialog box is turned on. You may also want to turn off the Plot With Plot Styles setting, because plot styles can override the object lineweights with different plotted lineweights.

As long as you turn on the Plot Object Lineweights setting, you'll find that (those who hate cheap puns, read no further!) the plot thickens! It also thins, but that's not as funny.

If you *don't* want to plot the lineweights assigned to objects, you must turn off both the Plot Object Lineweights and Plot With Plot Styles settings in the Plot Options area of the Plot dialog box. Turning on Plot With Plot Styles turns on Plot Object Lineweights as well.

Plotting with plodders

Color-as-color and lineweight-as-lineweight seem like great ideas, but Autodesk knew when it added object lineweights back in 1999 that longtime users of AutoCAD weren't going to abandon the old colors-mapped-to-lineweights approach overnight. Thus, you can still control plotted lineweight by display color in AutoCAD.

AutoCAD veterans by and large have chosen to stick with their Old Way for now. They've done so for a variety of reasons, including inertia, plotting procedures and drawings built around the Old Way, third-party applications that don't fully support the newer methods, and the need to exchange drawings with clients and

subcontractors who haven't upgraded. In summary, the ripple effect of those who need to or want to continue using colors-mapped-to-lineweights is lasting a long time. Don't be surprised if you find yourself going with the flow for awhile.

The default setting in AutoCAD 2005 is to plot object lineweights, so that's the easiest method if you don't have to consider the historical practices or predilections of other people with whom you exchange drawings. Mapping screen colors to lineweights requires some initial work on your part, but after you've set up the mapping scheme, the additional effort is minimal.

Controlling plotted lineweights with screen colors

To map screen colors to plotted lineweights, you need a color-dependent plot style table (CTB file), as I describe in the section "Plotting with style," earlier in this chapter. If you're plotting a drawing created by someone else, that someone else may be able to supply you with the appropriate CTB file, or at least with a PCP or PC2 file from which you can create the CTB file quickly. At the very least, the creator of the drawing should be able to give you a printed chart showing which plotted lineweight to assign to each AutoCAD screen color. Use the instructions in the "Plotting with style" section to copy or create the required CTB file.

Unfortunately, no industry-wide standards exist for mapping screen colors to plotted lineweights. Different offices do it differently. That's why it's so useful to receive a CTB, PCP, or PC2 file with drawings that someone sends you.

After you have the appropriate CTB file stored in your Plot Styles folder, follow these steps to use it:

1. **Click the tab that you want to plot — the Model tab or the desired paper space layout tab.**

2. **Click the Plot button on the Standard toolbar.**

3. **In the Plot Style Table (Pen Assignments) area on the expanded Plot dialog box, select the CTB file from the Name list, as shown in Figure 12-8.**

   This action attaches the plot style table (CTB file) to the tab that you clicked in Step 1.

Figure 12-8:
Selecting a
plot style
table that
maps
screen
colors to
plotted
lineweights.

4. **Click the Apply to Layout button.**

   AutoCAD records the plot setting change with the current tab's configuration information. Assuming that you save the drawing, AutoCAD uses the CTB that you selected as the default plot style when you (or other people) plot that tab in the future.

5. **Continue with the plotting procedures described earlier in this chapter.**

If your drawing uses a named plot style table instead of a color-dependent plot style table, you follow the same procedure, except that you select an STB file instead of a CTB file in Step 3.

You can tell whether the current drawing was set up to use color-dependent plot styles or named plot styles by looking at the Properties toolbar. If the last drop-down list (Plot Style Control) is grayed out, the drawing can use color-dependent plot styles. If this list is not grayed out, the drawing can use named plot styles.

Plotting in color

Plotting the colors that you see on-screen requires no special tricks. In the absence of a plot style table (that is, if you set Plot Style Table (Pen Assignments) to None in the Plot dialog box), AutoCAD sends color information as it appears on-screen to the plotter. As long as your output device can plot in color, what you see should be what you get.

If you attach a plot style table to the tab that you're plotting (as described in the previous section), you can — if you really want to — map screen colors to different plotted colors. In most cases you don't want that kind of confusion. Instead, leave the Color property in the plot style table set to Use Object Color.

If your goal is *not* to plot color, make sure that you set the Color property for all plot styles to Black. If you try to plot colors on a monochrome device, you may find that objects appear in various shades of gray, like in a black and white newspaper photograph, with lighter colors mapped to lighter shades of gray and darker colors to darker shades of gray. This process of mapping colors to shades of gray is called *monochrome dithering,* and it usually is *not* what you want in a CAD drawing. To override it, use the Plot Style Table Editor, as described in the section "Creating plot styles," earlier in this chapter, to set the Color option for all colors to Black (the default setting is Use Object Color). If you don't already have a plot style table that you want to use, choose Monochrome.ctb (for color-based plot styles) or Monochrome.stb (for named plot styles), both of which come with AutoCAD.

When in doubt, send it out

Whether you plot to scale or not, with different lineweights or not, in color or not, consider using a service bureau for some of your plotting. In-house plotting on your office's output devices is great for small check plots on faster laser or inkjet printers. Large format plotting, on the other hand, can be slow and time consuming. If you need to plot lots of drawings, you may find yourself spending an afternoon loading paper, replenishing ink cartridges, and trimming sheets.

Good plotting service bureaus have big, fast, expensive plotters that you can only dream about owning. Also, *they're* responsible for babysitting those fancy devices, feeding them, and fixing them. As a bonus, service bureaus can make blueline prints from your plots, if you need to distribute hard-copy sets to other people.

The only downside is that you need to coordinate with a service bureau to make sure it gets what it needs from you and can deliver the kinds of plots you need. Some service bureaus plot directly from your DWG files, while others ask you to make PLT (plot) files. Some service bureaus specialize in color plotting, while others are more comfortable with monochrome plotting and making blueline copies.

When you're choosing a service bureau, look for one that traditionally has served drafters, architects, and engineers. These service bureaus tend to be more knowledgeable about AutoCAD, and they should have more plotting expertise than the desktop publishing, printing, and copying shops.

Whomever you choose, do some test plots well before the day when that important set of drawings is due. Talk to the plotting people and get a copy of their plotting instructions. Have the service bureau create some plots of a couple of your typical drawings and make sure they look the way you want them to.

If you do lots of plotting with a service bureau, look into whether you can charge it to your clients as an expense (just like bluelines or copying).

To see the full range of AutoCAD colors available on your plotter, or to see how a particular plot style table affects plotting, plot \Program Files\AutoCAD 2005\Sample\Plot Screening and Fill Patterns.dwg. The Screening 100% layout in this drawing contains color swatches for all 255 AutoCAD colors.

It's a (Page) Setup!

Page setups specify the plotter, paper size, and other plot settings that you use to plot a particular tab of a particular drawing. AutoCAD maintains separate page setups for model space and for each paper space model layout (that is, for each tab you see in the drawing area). When you click the Apply to Layout button in the Plot dialog box (or turn on the Save Changes to Layout setting and then click OK to plot), AutoCAD stores the current plot settings as the page setup for the current tab.

You also can give page setups names and save them. The advantage of doing so is that you can switch quickly between different plot settings and copy plot settings from one drawing tab to another. Named page setups are stored with each drawing, but you can copy them from another drawing into the current one with the Page Setup Manager dialog box (described later in this section).

If your plotting needs are simple, you don't need to do anything special with page setups. In the Plot dialog box, just click the Apply to Layout button or turn on the Save Changes to Layout setting to save any plotting changes with the tab you're plotting.

If you want to get fancier, you can create named page setups in order to plot the same layout (or the model tab) in different ways, or to copy plot settings from one tab to another or one drawing to another. Click the Add button in the Plot dialog box to create a named page setup from the current plot settings. After you create a named page setup, you can restore its plot settings by choosing it from the Page Setup Name list.

For even greater control, choose File➪Page Setup Manager to create, change, and copy page setups. In the Page Setup Manager dialog box, shown in Figure 12-9, you can create new page setups and modify existing ones. Click the Modify button to open the Page Setup dialog box, which is almost identical to the Plot dialog box. The primary difference is that you're changing plot settings rather than actually plotting. The Set Current button copies the page setup that you've selected n the Page Setups list to the current layout tab. With the Import button, you can copy a layout from another drawing or drawing template (DWT) file.

Page Setup Manager

Current layout: D-size layout

Page setups

Current page setup: <None>

D-size layout
Layout2
Half size

Set Current

New...

Modify...

Import...

Selected page setup details

Device name: 2 Plotter

Plotter: Hewlett-Packard HP-GL/2 Plotter

Plot size: 24.00 x 36.00 inches Landscape

Where: LPT1:

Description:

☐ Display when creating a new layout   Close   Help

Figure 12-9:
The Page
Setup
Manager
dialog box.

Continuing the Plot Dialog

In previous sections of this chapter, I cover most of the important options in the Plot dialog box. This section reveals a few more fine points that will make your plotting life easier. I don't cover every minute, obscure, useful-only-at-cocktail party-discussions detail. I do point out some occasionally useful options that will increase your vocabulary when you're communicating with the Plot dialog box.

Use the Plot dialog box's quick help to find out more about any part of the dialog box:

1. **Click the question mark next to the close button in the dialog box's title bar.**

2. **Point the cursor at the part of the dialog box that confuses you and click.**

3. **Click the Help button at the bottom of the dialog box if the pop-up help isn't enough.**

✓ **Printer/Plotter:** As I describe in the section "Configure it out," earlier in this chapter, you use the Name list to select the Windows system printer or nonsystem driver configuration that you want to use for plotting.

The Properties button opens the Plotter Configuration Editor dialog box, with which you can change media (type of paper) and other properties that are unique to the currently selected plotter or printer. In particular, you can define custom paper sizes.

As if AutoCAD's Plot dialog box settings weren't overwhelming enough, some plotter drivers hide important settings in the Plotter Configuration Editor dialog box, typically behind the Custom Properties button near the bottom of the dialog box. (For example, if you're using the HP enhanced Windows system driver mentioned earlier in this chapter, you can click the Custom Properties button and then the More Sizes button to specify which paper sizes are available to you on the Plot Settings tab of the main Plot dialog box.)

To make matters even more confusing, if you make any changes in the Plotter Configuration Editor dialog box, AutoCAD prompts you to save the changes to a separate PC3 file. You should choose `Save Changes to the Following File` (that is, create a new AutoCAD-specific configuration that includes the revised settings) and type a configuration name that you'll recognize later. When you want to plot with custom settings, remember to choose the AutoCAD-specific PC3 configuration near the end of the Plotter Configuration Name list, and not the Windows system printer configuration near the beginning of the list.

✔ **Plot to File:** If you need to plot to a file rather than directly to your plotter or network printer queue, turn on this option. When you click OK to plot, AutoCAD asks you for a plot file name and location.

This option is especially useful when you want to use the ePlot feature to publish a DWF file on a Web site. You also may need to create files to send to a plotting service bureau.

✔ **Plot Stamp On:** Use this option to turn on and off and configure the contents of a text string that AutoCAD adds automatically to the corner of each plot. The plot stamp can include useful information such as the drawing filename and plot date and time.

✔ **Plot Area:** Specify the area of the drawing to plot. Your choices include Display, Extents, and Window, regardless of whether you're plotting a paper space layout or the model space tab. If you defined named views in the drawing, AutoCAD adds a View option. The additional choice is Layout for a paper space layout tab or Limits for the model space tab.

- *Display* means the drawing as it's currently displayed in the drawing window (including any white space — or black space — around the drawing objects).

- *Extents* means the rectangular area containing all the objects in the drawing.

- *Limits* means the model space area that you specified (or should have specified) when you set up the drawing, See Chapter 3 for details.

- *Window* means a rectangular area that you specify.

- *View* means a named view, which you select from the drop-down list (Chapter 7 describes named views and how to create them).

Usually, you'll choose to plot Layout in paper space. For model space, the choice depends on whether the drawing was set up properly and what you want to plot. If you set limits properly, as I suggest in Chapter 3, then plot Limits in order to get the whole drawing area. If you're trying to plot a drawing in which the limits weren't set properly, try Extents instead. Use Window or View if you want to plot just a portion of model space.

✔ **Plot Offset:** A plot offset of X=0 and Y=0 positions the plot at the lower-left corner of the plottable area. If you want to move the plot from this default position on the paper, enter nonzero numbers or turn on the Center the Plot option. (The Center the Plot option is available only when you haven't selected Layout from the What to Plot list.)

✔ **Shaded Viewport Options:** If your drawing includes viewports showing shaded or rendered 3D models (see Chapter 8), use this area to control the plotted appearance.

✔ **Plot Options:** The Plot Object Lineweights option and the Plot with Plot Styles option control whether AutoCAD uses the features described in the "Plotting with style" and "Plotting through thick and thin" sections earlier in this chapter.

The Hide Paperspace Objects option controls whether AutoCAD hides objects that are behind other objects when a 3D model is displayed in a viewport. If your drawing is entirely 2D, then this option doesn't matter. If your drawing includes 3D objects, them turning on this setting is like applying the 3DOrbit command's Hidden option, described in Chapter 8, to the plot.

✔ **Plot Upside-Down:** Turn on this setting if you want to rotate the plot 180 degrees on the paper (a handy option for plotting in the southern hemisphere, or for avoiding having to cock your head at an uncomfortable angle as you watch plots come out of the plotter).

AutoCAD normally generates plots in the foreground — that is, the plotting process takes over the program for the entire time that the program is creating the plot. AutoCAD 2005 includes a new background plotting feature that returns control of the program to you more quickly. If you have a reasonably fast computer with adequate memory, turn on this feature in the Options dialog box: Choose Tools⇨Options, click the Plot and Publish tab, and turn on Plotting in the Background Processing Options area.

If you want to automate plotting for a batch of drawings, check out Chapter 15.

Troubles with Plotting

No matter how many times you read this chapter or how carefully you study the AutoCAD documentation, you'll occasionally run into plotting problems. You're especially likely to encounter problems when trying to plot other people's drawings, because you don't always know what plotting conventions they had in mind. (Plotting conventions aren't where spies meet; they're a standardized approach to plotting issues.) Table 12-1 describes some of the more common plotting problems and solutions.

Table 12-1	Plotting Problems and Solutions
Problem	*Possible Solution*
Nothing comes out of the plotter (system printer driver).	Check whether you can print to the device from other Windows applications. If not, it's not an AutoCAD problem. Try the Windows Print Troubleshooter (Start⇨Help⇨ Contents⇨Troubleshooting and Maintenance).
Nothing comes out of the plotter (nonsystem printer driver).	Choose File⇨Plotter Manager, double-click the plotter configuration, and check the settings.
Objects don't plot the way they appear on-screen.	Check for a plot style table with weird settings, or try plotting without a plot style table.
Objects appear "ghosted" or with washed-out colors.	In the plot style table, set Color to Black for all colors.
Scaled to Fit doesn't work right in paper space.	Change the plot area from Layout to Extents.
The HP enhanced Windows system driver that came on the AutoCAD 2005 CD, and the available paper sizes aren't right (for example, no architectural paper sizes).	On the Plot dialog box's Plot Device tab, click the Properties button, and then the Custom Properties button (near the bottom), and then the More Sizes button to specify the standard and custom paper sizes.
Something else is wrong.	Check the plot log: Click the Plot/Publish Details Report Available icon near the right end of the status bar and look for error messages.

Part IV
Share and Share Alike

In this part . . .

After you get the lines and text right, you may be justified in thinking that your work in AutoCAD is done. But AutoCAD enables you to do so much more! Blocks and external references help you manage data within drawings, between drawings, and across a network. AutoCAD 2005's new sheet sets feature bids fair to redefine how people organize drawings on larger, multisheet projects, so this section devotes a new chapter to it. If you plan to share drawings — whether among your own projects, with people in your office, or with folks in other companies, you need to think about consistency in presentation and drawing organization — in other words, CAD standards. The Internet is the biggest ongoing swap meet in human history, and AutoCAD offers some unique trading possibilities — and potential pitfalls — via e-mail and the Web. With the information in this part, you'll be teaching AutoCAD how to give and receive in no time.

Chapter 13

Playing Blocks and Rasteroids

Chapter 6 shows you how to copy objects within a drawing or even to another drawing. That's one way to use CAD to improve drafting efficiency. You can copy a DWG file and then modify it to create a similar drawing — an even better productivity-booster, as long as you're in the habit of making similar drawings. But all those are baby steps compared to the techniques that I cover in this chapter: treating drawings, parts of drawings, and raster images as reusable and updateable modules. If you want to make drafting production more efficient with CAD, then you want to know how to use blocks, xrefs, and raster files.

A *block* is a collection of objects grouped together to form a single object. You can *insert* this collection more than once in the same drawing, and when you do, all instances of the block remain identical, even after you change the *block definition*. Although a block lives within a specific drawing, you can transfer copies of it into other drawings. You can add fill-in-the-blank text fields called *attributes* to blocks.

An *external reference,* or *xref,* is like an industrial-strength block. An external reference is a pointer to a separate drawing outside the drawing you're working on. The referenced drawing appears on-screen and on plots as part of your drawing, but it continues to live as a separate document on your hard disk. If you edit the externally referenced drawing, the appearance of the drawing changes in all drawings that reference it.

A *raster* file (also called a *bitmap* file) stores a graphical image as a series of dots. Raster files are good for storing photographs, logos, and other images, whereas CAD *vector* files are good for storing geometrical objects such as lines and arcs, along with text and other annotations for describing the geometry. Sometimes it's handy to combine raster images with CAD vector files, and AutoCAD's IMage command makes the process straightforward.

Blocks, external references, and raster images enable you to reuse your work and the work of others, giving you the potential to save tremendous amounts of time — or to cause tremendous problems if you change a file on which other peoples' drawings depend. Use these features when you can to save time, but do so in an organized and careful way so as to avoid problems.

The way you use blocks and especially xrefs will depend a lot on the profession and office in which you work. Some disciplines and companies use these drawing organization features heavily and in a highly organized way, while others don't. Ask your colleagues what the local customs are and follow them.

Rocking with Blocks

First, a little more block theory and then you can rock right into those blocks.

To use a block in a drawing, you need two things: a block *definition* and one or more block *inserts*. AutoCAD doesn't always make the distinction between these two things very clear, but you need to understand the difference to avoid terminal confusion about blocks. (Maybe this syndrome should be called *blockheadedness?*)

A block definition lives in an invisible area of your drawing file called the *block table*. (It's one of those *symbol tables* that I describe in Chapter 4.) The block table is like a book of graphical recipes for making different kinds of blocks. Each block definition is like a recipe for making one kind of block. When you insert a block, as described later in this chapter, AutoCAD creates a special object called a *block insert*. The insert points to the recipe and tells AutoCAD, "Hey, draw me according to the instructions in this recipe!"

Although a block may look like a collection of objects stored together and given a name, it's really a graphical recipe (the block definition) plus one or more pointers to that recipe (one or more block inserts). Each time you insert a particular block, you create another pointer to the same recipe.

The advantages of blocks include:

- **Grouping objects together when they belong together logically.** You can draw a screw using lines and arcs, and then make a block definition out of all these objects. When you insert the screw block, AutoCAD treats it as a single object for purposes of copying, moving, and so on.

- **Saving time and reducing errors.** Inserting a block is, of course, much quicker than redrawing the same geometry again. And the less geometry you draw from scratch, the less opportunity there is to make a mistake.

- **Efficiency of storage when you reuse the same block repeatedly.** If you insert the same screw block 15 times in a drawing, AutoCAD stores the detailed block definition only once. The 15 block inserts that point to the block definition take up much less disk space than 15 copies of all the lines, polylines, and arcs.

- **The ability to edit all instances of a symbol in a drawing simply by modifying a single block definition.** This one is the biggie. If you decide that your design requires a different kind of screw, you simply redefine the screw's block definition. With this new recipe, AutoCAD then replaces all 15 screws automatically. That's a heck of a lot faster than erasing and recopying 15 screws!

Blocks *aren't* as great for drawing elements used in multiple drawings, however, especially in a situation where several people are working on and sharing parts of drawings with one another. That's because blocks, after they get into multiple drawings, stay in each drawing; a later modification to a block definition in one drawing does not automatically modify all the other drawings that use that block. If you use a block with your company's logo in a number of drawings and then you decide to change the logo, you must make the change within each drawing that uses the block.

External references enable you to modify multiple drawings from the original referenced drawing. You can find out more about external references in the section "Going External," later in this chapter.

If all you need to do is make some objects into a group so that you can more easily select them for copying, moving, and so on, use the AutoCAD *group* feature. Type **Group** and press Enter to open the Group Manager dialog box. Then select some objects, click the Create Group button, and type a name for the group. When you're editing drawings containing groups, press Ctrl+H to toggle "group-ness" on or off. If you've toggled "group-ness" on, picking any object in a group selects all objects in the group. If you've toggled it off, picking an object selects only that object, even if it happens to be a member of a group.

Creating block definitions

To create a block definition from objects in the current drawing, use the Block Definition dialog box. (The other way to create a block definition is by inserting another drawing file into your current drawing as a block, which I explain in the next section.) The following steps show you how to create a block definition using the Block Definition dialog box:

1. Click the Make Block button on the Draw toolbar.

The Block Definition dialog box appears (see Figure 13-1).

Figure 13-1:
The Block
Definition
dialog box.

Layers matter when you create the objects that makes up a block. Block geometry created on most layers retains the characteristics, such as color and linetype, of those layers. But if you create a block using geometry on Layer 0, that geometry has no characteristics, such as color and linetype of its own; chameleonlike, it takes on the features of the layer into which it's inserted.

2. Type the block definition's name in the Name text entry box.

If you type the name of an existing block definition, AutoCAD replaces that block definition with the new group of objects you select. This process is called *block redefinition*.

To see a list of the names of all the current blocks in your drawing, pull down the Name list.

3. **Specify the base point, also known as the insertion point, of the block, using either of the following methods:**

   • Enter the coordinates of the insertion point in the X, Y, and Z text boxes.

   • Click the Pick Point button and then select a point on the screen. (In this case, use an object snap or other precision technique, as described in Chapter 4, to grab a specific point on one of the block's objects.)

   The *base point* is the point on the block by which you insert it later, as I describe in the next section.

   Use an obvious and consistent point on the group of objects for the base point, such as the lower-left corner, so that you know what to expect when you insert the block.

4. **Click the Select Objects button and then select the objects that you want as part of the block.**

   AutoCAD uses the selected objects to create a block definition. Figure 13-2 shows the base point and group of selected objects during the process of creating a new block definition.

Base point

Figure 13-2:
Building a
block.

5. **Click a radio button to tell AutoCAD what to do with the objects used to define the block: Retain them in place, Convert them into a block instance, or Delete them.**

   The default choice, Convert To Block, is usually the best. See Step 9 for a description of what happens with each choice.

6. **Choose Create Icon From Block Geometry in the Preview Icon area.**

   Go ahead and create the icon; it will help you and others find the right block to use later.

7. **Specify the Insert units to which the block will be scaled in the Drag-and-Drop Units drop-down menu.**

   When you or someone else drags the block from one drawing into another via the DesignCenter palette (see Chapter 4) or Tool Palette (described later in this chapter), the units you specify here and the units of the drawing you're dragging into will control the default insertion scale factor.

8. **Enter the block Description.**

   Now is the time to think like a database manager and enter a useful description that will identify the block to yourself and others.

9. **Click OK to complete the block definition process.**

   If you typed the name of an existing block definition in Step 2, AutoCAD warns you that you'll redefine that block definition. Click Yes to redefine, which will update all instances of the block in the current drawing to match the changed block definition.

   AutoCAD stores the block definition in the current drawing's block table. If you chose the Convert To Block radio button (the default) in Step 5, Auto-CAD also creates a block insert pointing to the new block definition — the objects look the same on-screen, but now they're an instance of the block rather than existing as separate objects. If you chose the Retain radio button, the objects remain in place but aren't converted into a block insert — they stay individual objects with no connection to the new block definition. If you chose the Delete radio button, the objects disappear (but the block definition still gets created).

You can include in a block definition a special kind of variable text object called an *attribute definition*. When you insert a block that contains one or more attribute definitions, AutoCAD prompts you to fill in values for the text fields. Attributes are useful for variable title block information (sheet number, sheet title, and so on) and symbols that contain different codes or call-outs. I describe how to create and use attribute definitions later in this chapter.

BLOCK and WBLOCK

The Block command, which opens the Block Definition dialog box, is great for use within a drawing, but what if you want to use the block definition in multiple drawings? The easiest method is to use DesignCenter to copy a block definition from one drawing to another, as described in Chapter 4.

Another method involves the WBLOCK and Insert commands. I don't cover this method here, because it's less intuitive than using DesignCenter. But you may hear AutoCAD drafters talk about "wblocking" part of a drawing. So that you can keep these block-y names straight:

✔ The Block command creates a block definition from objects in the current drawing.

✔ The WBLOCK command creates a new DWG file from objects in the current drawing, or from a block definition in the current drawing.

Keep your common symbol drawings in one or more specific folders that you set aside just for that purpose. You may want use one of the following techniques to develop a *block library* of symbols that you use frequently:

✔ Create a separate DWG file for each symbol (using WBLOCK, or simply by drawing each one in a new drawing).

✔ Store a bunch of symbols as block definitions in one drawing and use DesignCenter to import block definitions from this drawing when you need them.

Inserting blocks

AutoCAD provides a number of ways to insert a block, but the most commonly used and most flexible is the Insert dialog box. Here's the procedure for inserting a block:

1. **Set an appropriate layer current, as described in Chapter 4.**

   It's a good idea to insert each block on a layer that has something to do with its geometry or purpose:

   • If all the objects in the block definition reside on one layer, then it's usually best to insert the block on that layer.

   • If the block geometry spans several layers, choose one of them to insert the block on.

If any of the block definition's geometry was created on layer 0, then that geometry will inherit the color, linetype, and other object properties of the layer that you insert the block on. It's like the chameleon changing color to match its surroundings or a politician changing his position to match the day's opinion polls.

2. Click the Insert Block button on the Draw toolbar.

The Insert dialog box appears, as shown in Figure 13-3.

Figure 13-3:
The Insert
dialog box.

3. Enter the block definition name or external filename by using one of the following methods:

- Use the Name drop-down list to select from a list of block definitions in the current drawing.

- Click the Browse button to select an external DWG file and have AutoCAD create a block definition from it.

You can use an external drawing to replace a block definition in your current drawing. If you click Browse and choose a file whose name matches the name of a block definition that's already in your drawing, AutoCAD warns you and then updates the block definition in your drawing with the current contents of the external file. This process is called *block redefinition*, and as described in Steps 2 and 9 in the preceding section, AutoCAD automatically updates all the block inserts that point to the block definition.

4. Enter the insertion point, scale, and rotation angle of the block.

You can either click the Specify On-Screen check box in each area, to specify the parameters on-screen at the command prompt, or type the values you want in the Insertion Point, Scale, and Rotation text boxes.

Check the Uniform Scale check box to constrain the X, Y, and Z scaling parameters to the same value (which in almost all cases you want).

5. **If you want AutoCAD to create a copy of the individual objects in the block instead of a block insert that points to the block definition, click the Explode check box.**

6. **Click OK.**

7. **If you checked Specify On-Screen for the insertion point, scale, or rotation angle, answer the prompts on the command line to specify these parameters.**

After you insert a block, all the objects displayed in the block insert behave as a single object. When you select any object in the block insert, AutoCAD highlights all the objects in it.

Another way to insert a block is to drag a DWG file's name from Windows Explorer and drop it anywhere in the current drawing window. AutoCAD then prompts you to choose an insertion point and optionally change the default scale factor and rotation angle. Similarly, you can drag a block definition's name from the Blocks section of the DesignCenter palette and drop it into the current drawing window. (Chapter 4 describes DesignCenter.)

AutoCAD provides one additional way of inserting blocks: the Tool Palette, which is described in Chapter 2. As is true of using Tool Palette for hatching (Chapter 11), you first must create and configure appropriate tools — that is, swatches. The easiest method is right-clicking a drawing in DesignCenter and choosing Create Tool Palette. A new page is added to the Tool Palette area containing all the block definitions from the drawing that you right-clicked. Simply click and drag a tool to insert its corresponding block into a drawing. As with hatching, you don't get the chance to specify a different insertion scale. You also can't use all of AutoCAD's precision tools to specify the insertion point precisely, so you may need to move the block into place after inserting it. I recommend that you first master the other block insertion methods described in this chapter — especially the Insert dialog box and DesignCenter palette. Then if you find yourself inserting the same blocks frequently, consider creating a Tool Palette containing them. See "tool palettes, adding drawings from" in the AutoCAD online help system for more information.

Be careful when inserting one drawing into another. If the host (or parent) drawing and the inserted (or child) drawing have different definitions for layers that share the same name, the objects in the child drawing takes on the layer characteristics of the parent drawing. For example, if you insert a drawing with lines on a layer called Walls that's blue and dashed into a drawing with a layer called Walls that's red and continuous, the inserted lines on the wall layer will turn red and continuous after they're inserted. The same rules apply to linetypes, text styles, dimension styles, and block definitions that are nested inside the drawing you're inserting.

If you need to modify a block definition after you've inserted one or more instances of it, use the REFEDIT command (Modify⇨Xref and Block Editing⇨ Edit Reference In-Place). Look up "REFEDIT" in the AutoCAD online help system.

Attributes: Fill-in-the-blank blocks

You may think of attributes as the good (or bad) qualities of your significant other, but in AutoCAD, attributes are fill-in-the-blank text fields that you can add to your blocks. When you create a block definition and then insert it several times in a drawing, all the ordinary geometry (lines, circles, regular text strings, and so on) in all the instances are exactly identical. Attributes provide a little more flexibility in the form of text strings that can be different in each block insert.

For example, suppose that you frequently designate parts in your drawings by labeling them with a distinct number or letter in a circle for each part. If you want to create a block for this symbol, you can't simply draw the number or letter as regular text using the mText or TEXT command. If you create a block definition with a regular text object (for example, the letter A), the text string will be the same in every instance of the block (always the letter A). That's not much help in distinguishing the parts!

Instead, you create an *attribute definition,* which acts as a placeholder for a text string that can vary each time you insert the block. You include the attribute definition when you create the block definition (as I demonstrate in the "Creating block definitions" section earlier in this chapter). Then each time you insert the block, AutoCAD prompts you to fill in an *attribute value* for each attribute definition.

The AutoCAD documentation and dialog boxes often use the term *attribute* to refer indiscriminately to an *attribute definition* or an *attribute value.* I attribute a lot of the confusion about attributes to this sloppiness. Just remember that an attribute definition is the text field or placeholder in the block definition, while an attribute value is the specific text string that you type when you insert the block.

If you've worked with databases, the correspondences in Table 13-1 between AutoCAD objects (blocks and attributes) and database terminology may help you understand the concept.

Table 13-1	Attribute and Database Comparison
AutoCAD	**Database**
block definition	database table structure
block insert	one record in the table
attribute definition	field name
attribute value	value of the field in one record

Attribute definitions

You use the Attribute Definition dialog box to create attribute definitions (clever, huh?). The procedure is similar to creating a text string, except that you must supply a little more information. Create attribute definitions with the following steps:

1. **Change to the layer on which you want to create the attribute definition.**

2. **Choose Draw⇨Block⇨Define Attributes to run the ATTDEF command.**

   The Attribute Definition dialog box appears, as shown in Figure 13-4.

   You rarely need to use any of the Mode settings (Invisible, Constant, Verify, or Preset). Just leave them unchecked. If you're curious about what the modes do, use the dialog box help to find out more.

Figure 13-4:
The
Attribute
Definition
dialog box.

3. **In the Attribute area, type the Tag (database field name), Prompt (user prompt), and Value (default value).**

   The Tag can't contain any spaces. The Prompt and Value fields may contain spaces.

Attribute values can include AutoCAD 2005's new automatically updating fields, such as date, filename, or system variable setting. Click the Insert Field button to the right of the Value text box to insert a field. See the "mText plays the field" section in Chapter 9 for more information.

4. **In the Text Options area, specify the Justification, Text Style, Height, and Rotation.**

The text properties for attribute definitions are the same as those for single-line text objects — see Chapter 9.

5. **Choose the Pick Point button and choose an insertion point for the attribute definition.**

An attribute definition's insertion point is like a text string's base point. Remember to use snap, object snap, or another precision tool if you want the eventual attribute values to be located at a precise point.

6. **Click OK to create the attribute definition.**

7. **Repeat Steps 1 through 6 for any additional attribute definitions.**

If you need to create a series of similar attribute definitions, create the first one using Steps 1 through 6. Then copy the first attribute definition and edit the copy with the Properties palette.

Block definition containing attribute definitions

After you create one or more attribute definitions — and any other geometry that you want to include in the block — you're ready to create a block definition that contains them. Follow the steps in the section, "Creating block definitions," earlier in this chapter.

At Step 4 in the section, "Creating block definitions," select any attribute definitions first before you select the other geometry. Select each attribute definition one-by-one (clicking on each attribute definition rather than selecting multiple attributes with a selection window), in the order that you want the attribute value prompts to appear in the Enter/Edit Attributes dialog box (see Figure 13-5). If you don't select the attributes one by one, your block and attributes will still work, but the order of the attribute prompts in the Enter/Edit Attributes dialog box may not be what you want.

You can use the Block Attribute Manager (choose Modify➪Object➪Attribute➪Block Attribute Manager) to reorder the attribute definitions in a block definition. You also can use this dialog box to edit other attribute definition settings, such as the prompt, text style, or layer. If you get tired of traversing four menu picks to get to this command, you can type the command name — BATTMAN (Block ATTribute MANager) — instead. I suppose it's only a matter of time before Autodesk adds a ROBIN (ReOrder Block INsert) command. . . .

Attributes are particularly useful for creating a title block. Use regular AutoCAD commands, including mText or TEXT, to draw the parts of the title block that will remain the same in all drawings. Then use ATTDEF to create an attribute for each text string in the drawing that might change on different sheets.

Insert a block containing attribute definitions

After you create a block definition that contains attribute definitions, you insert it just like any other block. Follow the steps in the section, "Inserting blocks," earlier in this chapter. At the end of the steps, AutoCAD should display the Enter Attributes dialog box, shown in Figure 13-5. The dialog box contains one row for each of the attribute definitions and has any default values filled in. You simply edit the values and then click OK.

Figure 13-5:
The Enter
Attributes
dialog box.

The ATTDIA (ATTribute DIALog box) system variable controls whether Auto-CAD prompts for attribute values in a dialog box (ATTDIA=1) or at the command line (ATTDIA=0). If you insert a block and see command line prompts for each attribute value, type a value and press Enter for each attribute value. When you return to the Command: prompt, type **ATTDIA**, press Enter, type **1**, and press Enter again. When you insert blocks with attributes in this drawing in the future, AutoCAD displays the Edit Attributes dialog box instead of prompting you at the command line.

Edit attribute values

After you insert a block that contains attributes, you can edit the individual attributes in that block insert with the EATTEDIT command (Enhanced ATTribute EDIT — nothing to do with eating). Choose Modify➪Object➪ Attribute➪Single and click on any object in the block insert. AutoCAD displays the Enhanced Attribute Editor dialog box with the current attribute values, as shown in Figure 13-6. The most common attribute editing operation is to edit the text value — that is, the text string that appears in the block insert. You also can change properties of the attributes, such as layer and text style.

Figure 13-6:
The
Enhanced
Attribute
Editor dialog
box.

Many people use attributes in the way I've described so far — as fill-in-the-blank text fields in blocks. But attributes also can serve as data extraction tools. For example, you can export attribute values, such as part numbers and quantities, to a text, spreadsheet, or database file for analysis or reporting. The Attribute Extraction wizard (Tools⇨Attribute Extraction) makes the process fairly straightforward. If you're hungry to find out more, look up "EATTEXT (Enhanced ATTribute EXTract) command" in the AutoCAD online help system.

Exploding blocks

The objects in each block insert act like a well-honed marching squadron: If you move or otherwise edit one object in the block insert, all objects move or change in the same way. Usually this cohesion is an advantage, but occasionally you need to break up the squadron in order to modify one object without affecting the others.

To *explode* a block insert into individual objects, click Explode (the firecracker button) on the Edit toolbar and then select the block insert. When you explode a block insert, AutoCAD replaces it with all the objects — lines, polylines, arcs, and so on — specified in the block definition. You then can edit the objects or perhaps use them to make more block definitions.

Don't make a habit of exploding blocks cavalierly, especially if you're working in someone else's drawing and aren't sure why the objects are organized as blocks. Most people use blocks for a reason, and if you go around exploding them left and right, you're likely to be treated the same way that anyone who blows up a lot of things gets treated.

Purging unused block definitions

Each block definition slightly increases the size of your DWG file, as do other named objects such as layers, text styles, and dimension styles. If you delete (or explode) all the block inserts that point to a particular block definition, then that block definition no longer serves any purpose.

You should run the PURge command periodically in each drawing and purge unused block definitions and other named objects. Choose File⇨ Drawing Utilities⇨Purge to display the Purge dialog box, as shown in the figure. Click the Purge All button in order to purge all unused named objects in the current drawing.

Purge

○ View items you can purge
○ View items you cannot purge

Items not used in drawing:

- All items
  - Blocks
    - BC4F
    - BC4S
    - Plank2x6
    - TA10
  - Dimension styles
  - Layers
  - Linetypes
  - Mline styles
  - Plot styles
  - Shapes
  - Table styles
  - Text styles
    - S-TEXL

☑ Confirm each item to be purged
☑ Purge nested items

Purge   Purge All   Close   Help

If you explode a block that contains attributes, the attribute *values* change back to attribute *definitions*. This usually isn't the sort of change that you want. If you really need to explode the block insert, you'll probably want to erase the attribute definitions and draw regular text strings in their place. If you've installed the AutoCAD Express Tools, you can perform this task automatically with the BURST command (Express⇨Blocks⇨Explode Attributes to Text).

Going External

In AutoCAD, an *xref,* or external reference, is a reference to another, *external* file — one outside the current drawing — that you can make act as though it's part of your drawing. Technically, a reference is simply a pointer from one file to another. The xref is the actual pointer, but many people call the combination of the pointer and the external file the xref.

Drawings that you include as xrefs in other drawings often are called *child* drawings. Drawings that contain pointers to the child drawings are called *parent* drawings. This family terminology gets a little weird when you realize that a child drawing can have lots of parent drawings that refer to it — apparently it's the commune version of family relations. If you find such relationships odd, you can, like the AutoCAD online help system, refer to the parent drawing as the *host* drawing. I prefer the terms *parent* and *child,* in part because they're easily extendable to describing more complex hierarchies, such as a parent drawing, which xrefs a child drawing, which in turn xrefs a grandchild drawing.

Xrefs have a big advantage over blocks: If you change a child drawing, AutoCAD automatically loads the change into all the parent drawings that reference the child drawing.

AutoCAD loads all xrefs into the parent drawing each time the parent drawing is opened. If the child drawing has been changed, AutoCAD automatically incorporates those changes into the parent drawing.

When you open a drawing containing xrefs, AutoCAD 2004 displays a little symbol (which looks like papers with a binder clip) on the right end of the status bar. This symbol alerts you to the fact that some of the things you see in the drawing are actually parts of other, xrefed drawings. If an xref changes while you have the parent drawing open (because you or someone else opens and saves the child drawing), the status bar xref symbol displays an `External Reference Files Have Changed` balloon notification. (If you want to change whether the notifications appear and how often AutoCAD checks for changes, look up XREFNOTIFY and XNOTIFYTIME in the online help.) You can use the Reload option in the Xref Manager dialog box to show the updated xrefs. See the "Managing xrefs" section later in this chapter for details.

Another advantage of xrefs over blocks is that their contents aren't stored in your drawing even once. The disk storage space taken up by the original drawing (that is, the xref) isn't duplicated, no matter how many parent drawings reference it. This characteristic makes xrefs much more efficient than blocks for larger drawings that are reused several times.

But you can always buy more hard disk space, so the storage issue isn't crucial. The key benefit of xrefs is that they enable you to organize your drawings in a modular way so that changes you make to a single drawing file automatically "ripple through" all the parent drawings to which it's xrefed. This benefit is even greater on larger projects involving multiple drafters, each of whose work may be incorporated in part or in whole in the work of others.

The automatic update feature of xrefs is a big advantage only if you're organized about how you use xrefs. Suppose that an architect creates a plan drawing showing a building's walls and other major features that are common to the architectural, structural, plumbing, and electrical plan drawings. The architect then tells the structural, plumbing, and electrical drafters to xref this background plan into their drawings, so that everyone is working from a consistent and reusable set of common plan elements. If the architect decides to revise the wall locations and updates the xrefed drawing, everyone will see the current wall configuration and be able to change their drawings. But if the architect absent-mindedly adds architecture-specific objects, such as toilets and furniture, to the xrefed drawing, or shifts all the objects with respect to 0,0, everyone else will have problems. If different people in your office share xrefs, create a protocol for who is allowed to modify which file when, and what communication needs to take place after a shared xref is modified.

Becoming attached to your xrefs

Attaching an external reference is similar to inserting a block, and almost as easy. Just use the following steps:

1. **Set an appropriate layer current, as described in Chapter 4.**

   I recommend that you insert xrefs on a separate layer from all other objects. Note that if you freeze the layer an xref is inserted on, the entire xref disappears. (This behavior can be either a handy trick or a nasty surprise.)

2. **Choose Insert⇨Xref Manager from the menu bar to start the XRef command.**

   The Xref Manager dialog box appears (see Figure 13-7).

   Don't choose Insert⇨External Reference. This menu choice jumps ahead to Step 4, which will be confusing at this point.

Figure 13-7: The Xref Manager dialog box.

3. **Click Attach.**

   The Select Reference File dialog box appears.

4. **Browse to find the file you want to attach, select it, and then click Open.**

   The External Reference dialog box appears.

5. **Specify the parameters for the xref in the dialog box.**

   Parameters include the insertion point, scaling factors, and rotation angle. You can set these parameters in the dialog box or specify them on-screen, just as you can do when inserting a block, as described earlier in this chapter.

   You can choose the Attachment or Overlay radio button to tell AutoCAD how to handle the xref. The choice matters only if you create a drawing that uses xrefs, and then your drawing is in turn used as an xref. Attachment is the default choice, and it means that the xrefed file will always be included with your drawing when someone else uses your drawing as an xref. Overlay, the other choice, means that you see the xrefed drawing, but someone who xrefs your drawing won't see the overlaid file. By choosing Overlay, you can xref in a map, for example, to your drawing of a house, but not have the map show up when someone else xrefs your house drawing. (That person can xref the map, if need be.) I recommend that you use the default Attachment reference type unless you have a specific reason to do otherwise.

   The Path Type drop-down list provides more flexibility in how the xref's path gets stored. See the "Forging an xref path" section later in this chapter for more information. For now, I recommend that you choose `Relative path` instead of the default `Full path`.

6. **Click OK.**

   The externally referenced file appears in your drawing.

Layer-palooza

When you attach or overlay an xref, AutoCAD adds new layers to your current drawing that correspond to the layers in the xrefed DWG file. The new layers are assigned names that combine the drawing name and layer name; for example, if you xref the drawing MYSCREW.DWG, which has the layer names GEOMETRY, TEXT, and so on, the xrefed layers will be named MYSCREW|GEOMETRY, MYSCREW|TEXT, and so on. By creating separate layers corresponding to each layer in the xrefed file, AutoCAD eliminates the potential problem I warned you about with blocks when layers have the same name but different color or linetype in the two drawings.

AutoCAD also creates new linetypes, text styles, dimension styles, and block definitions for each of these items in the xrefed file — for example, MYSCREW|DASHED, MYSCREW|NOTES, MYSCREW|A-DIMS, and MYSCREW|LOGO.

Creating and editing an external reference file

To create a file that you can use as an external reference, just create a drawing and save it (or use the WBLOCK command to create a new DWG from geometry in the current drawing). That's it. You then can create or open another drawing and create an external reference to the previous one. The xrefed drawing appears in your parent drawing as a single object, like a block insert. In other words, if you click any object in the xref, AutoCAD selects the entire xref. You can measure or object snap to the xrefed geometry, but you can't modify or delete individual objects in the xref — you open the xref drawing in order to edit its geometry.

AutoCAD 2004's XOPEN command (Modify⇨Xref and Block Editing⇨Open Reference) provides a quick way to open an xrefed drawing for editing. You just start the command and pick on any object in the xref. Alternatively, you can use the Open button in the Xref Manager dialog box to open one or more xrefs for editing. See the "Managing xrefs" section later in this chapter for more information.

An alternative to opening the xrefed file when you need to edit it is to use the REFEDIT command (Modify⇨Xref and Block Editing⇨Edit Reference In-Place). Look up "REFEDIT" in the AutoCAD online help system.

Forging an xref path

When you attach an xref, AutoCAD by default stores the xref's full path — that is, the drive letter and sequence of folders and subfolders in which the DWG file resides, along with the filename. This default behavior corresponds to the Full path setting in the Path Type drop-down list. (Figure 13-8 shows the three xref path options.) Full path works fine as long as you never move files on your hard disk or network and never send your DWG files to anyone else — which is to say, it almost never works fine!

At the other end of the path spectrum, the No path option causes AutoCAD not to store any path with the xref attachment — only the filename is stored. This is the easiest and best option if the parent and child drawings reside in the same folder.

If you prefer to organize the DWG files for a particular project in more then one folder, then you'll appreciate AutoCAD's Relative path option, shown in Figure 13-8. This option permits xrefing across more complex, hierarchical folder structures, but avoids many of the problems that Full path can cause.

For example, you may have a parent drawing H:\Project-X\Plans\First floor.dwg that xrefs H:\Project-X\Common\Column grid.dwg. If you choose `Relative path`, AutoCAD will store the xref path as ..\ Common\Column grid.dwg instead of H:\Project-X\Common\Column grid.dwg. Now if you decide to move the \Project-X folder and its subfolders to a different drive (or send them to someone else who doesn't have an H: drive), AutoCAD will still be able to find the xrefs.

Figure 13-8:
Chart your path when you attach an xref.

When you use `Relative path`, you'll see xref paths that include the special codes . and .. (single and double period). The single period means "this parent drawing's folder" and the double period means "the folder above this parent drawing's folder" (in other words, the folder of which the parent drawing's folder is a subfolder).

You can report on and change xref paths for a set of drawings with the AutoCAD Reference Manager. See Chapter 16 for more information.

If all these path options and periods have got you feeling punchy, you can keep your life simple by always keeping parent and child drawings in the same folder and using the `No path` option when you attach xrefs.

Managing xrefs

The Xref Manager dialog box includes many more options for managing xrefs after you attach them. Important dialog box options include:

✔ **List of external references:** You can change between a List and a Tree view of your drawing's external references just by clicking the appropriate button at the top of the dialog box. You also can resize the columns by dragging the column dividers or re-sort the list by clicking the column header names, just as in other Windows dialog boxes.

✔ **Detach:** Completely removes the selected reference to the external file from your drawing.

✔ **Reload:** Causes AutoCAD to reread the selected xrefed DWG file from the disk and update your drawing with its latest contents. This feature is handy when you share xrefs on a network and someone has just made changes to a drawing that you've xrefed.

✔ **Unload:** Makes the selected xref disappear from the on-screen display of your drawing and from any plots you do of it, but retains the pointer and attachment information. Use the Reload button to redisplay an unloaded xref.

✔ **Bind:** Brings the selected xref into your drawing and makes it a block. You might use this function, for example, to "roll up" a complex set of xrefs into a single archive drawing.

In many offices, binding xrefs without an acceptable reason for doing so is a crime as heinous as exploding blocks indiscriminately. In both cases, you're eliminating an important data management link. Find out what the policies are in your company. When in doubt, keep yourself out of a bind. And even when you do have a good reason to bind, you generally should do it on a copy of the parent drawing.

✔ **Open:** Opens one or more xref drawings in separate drawing windows after you close the Xref Manager dialog box. After you edit and save an xref drawing, return to the parent drawing and use the Reload option in the Xref Manager dialog box to show the changes.

None of these options (other than opening and editing the xref) affects the xrefed drawing itself; it continues to exist as a separate DWG file. If you need to delete or move the DWG file that the xref refers to, do it in Windows Explorer.

The fact that the xrefed drawing is a separate file is a potential source of problems when you send your drawing to someone else; that someone else needs *all* the files that your drawing depends on, or it will be useless to the receiving party. Make sure to include xrefed files in the package with your drawing. See Chapter 16 for a procedure.

AutoCAD (but not AutoCAD LT) includes an additional xref feature called *xref clipping*. You can use the XCLIP command to clip an externally referenced file so only part of it appears in the parent drawing. AutoCAD LT doesn't include the XCLIP command, but if you open a drawing containing an xref that was clipped in AutoCAD, the clipped view will be preserved.

Blocks, Xrefs, and Drawing Organization

Blocks and xrefs are useful for organizing sets of drawings to use and update repeated elements . It's not always clear, though, when to use blocks and when to use xrefs. Applications for xrefs include

- The parts of a title block that are the same on all sheets in a project.
- Reference elements that need to appear in multiple drawings (for example, wall outlines, site topography, column grids).
- Assemblies that are repeated in one or more drawings, especially if the assemblies are likely to change together (for example, repeated framing assemblies, bathroom layouts, modular furniture layouts).
- Pasting up several drawings (for example, details or a couple of plans) onto one plot sheet.
- Temporarily attaching a background drawing for reference or tracing.

On the other hand, blocks remain useful in simpler circumstances. Situations in which you might stick with a block are:

- Components that aren't likely to change.
- Small components.
- A simple assembly that's used repeatedly, but in only one drawing. (You can easily update a block in one drawing with the REDEFIT command.)
- When you want to include *attributes* (variable text fields) that you can fill in each time you insert a block. Blocks let you include attribute definitions; xrefs don't.

Everyone in a company or workgroup should aim for consistency in when and how they use blocks and xrefs. Check whether guidelines exist for using blocks and xrefs in your office. If so, follow them; if not, it would be a good idea to develop some guidelines. Chapter 15 discusses how to start such guidelines.

Mastering the Raster

AutoCAD includes another xreflike feature: the ability to attach *raster images* to drawings. This feature is useful for adding a raster logo to a drawing title block or placing a photographed map or scene behind a drawing. A raster, or *bitmapped,* image is one that's stored as a field of tiny points.

Most AutoCAD drawings are vector images. A *vector* image is an image defined by storing geometrical definitions of a bunch of objects. Typical objects include a line, defined by its two endpoints, and a circle, defined by its center point and radius. Vector-based images are typically smaller (in terms of the disk space they occupy) and more flexible than raster images, but also are less capable of displaying visually rich images such as photographs.

Raster images often come from digital cameras or other programs, such as Photoshop. Raster images also can come into the computer from some kind of scanner that imports a blueline print, photograph, or other image.

Whether you're doing your scanning yourself or having a service bureau do it for you, you need to know that AutoCAD handles most of the popular image file formats including the Windows BMP format, the popular Web graphics formats GIF and JPEG, the popular PCX and TIFF formats, as well as DIB, FLC, FLI, GP4, MIL, PNG, RLE, RST, and TGA.

Here are three scenarios to incorporate raster images in your drawing:

- ✔ **Small stuff:** You can add logos, special symbols, and other small images that you have in raster files.

- ✔ **Photographs and maps:** You can add photographs (such as a future building site) and maps (for example, showing the project location).

- ✔ **Vectorization:** To convert a raster image into a vector drawing by tracing lines in the raster image, you can attach the raster image in your drawing, trace the needed lines by using AutoCAD commands, then detach the raster image. (This procedure is okay for a simple raster image; add-on software is available, from Autodesk and others, to support automatic or semiautomatic vectorization of more complex images.)

Using raster images is much like using external references. The raster image isn't stored with your drawing file; a reference to the raster image file is established from within your drawing, like an xref. You can clip the image and control its size, brightness, contrast, fade, and transparency. These controls fine-tune the appearance of the raster image on-screen and on a plot.

When you attach raster images, you have to make sure that you send the raster files along when you send your drawing to someone else.

AutoCAD LT can open, view, and plot drawings containing attached raster images, but LT can't do the attaching. Raster masters require full AutoCAD.

Attaching an image

Follow these steps to bring a raster image into AutoCAD:

1. **Choose Insert⇨Image Manager from the menu bar or type** IMage **at the command line to start the IMage command.**

   The Image Manager dialog box appears (see Figure 13-9).

2. **Click the Attach button.**

   The Select Image File dialog box appears.

3. **Browse to find the file you want to attach, select it, then click Open.**

   The Image dialog box appears.

   Click the Details button in the Image dialog box to see more information about the resolution and image size of the image you're attaching.

4. **Specify the parameters for the attached image in the dialog box.**

   Parameters include the insertion point, scale factor, and rotation angle. You can set these parameters in the dialog box or specify them on-screen, similar to what you can do with blocks and external references, as described earlier in this chapter. Use the quick dialog box help (click the question mark in the dialog box's title bar and then click the area in the dialog box for which you want help) or click the dialog box's Help button to find out more about specific options.

   The AutoCAD 2005 IMage command includes the same Full path, Relative path, and No path options that debuted for xrefs in AutoCAD 2004. (See "Forging an xref path" earlier in this chapter.)

5. **Click OK.**

   The image appears in your drawing.

6. **If you need to ensure that the raster image floats behind other objects in the drawing, select the raster image, right-click, choose Draw Order, and then choose Send to Back.**

   The DRaworder command provides additional options for which objects appear on top of which other objects. If you need this kind of flexibility, look up "DRAWORDER command" in the AutoCAD online help system.

Managing images

You manage the images in your drawing with the Image Manager dialog box. It includes virtually the same options as the External References dialog box. You can view a list of image files that appear in the current drawing, detach (remove) image references, and unload and reload images when needed. You can't bind an image to your drawing; it always remains an external file.

You can clip images so that only part of the image is displayed in your drawing. Choose Modify⇨Clip⇨Image and follow the prompts to clip the image. You can have multiple overlapping or distinct pieces of any number of images in your drawing, and only the parts you need are loaded into memory when you have your drawing open.

Raster image files often are larger than DWG files of corresponding complexity; raster file size can affect performance within AutoCAD, because the raster file loads into memory when you are working on your drawing. Some workarounds speed up operations:

- Attach raster images late in the production process.
- Create a lower-resolution version of the raster file, just large enough to create the desired effect in your drawing.
- Use the Unload button in the Image Manager dialog box to temporarily disable an image without losing the attachment information.

In addition, raster files can increase the time that AutoCAD takes to generate plots (and the plot file sizes) dramatically. Before you settle on using large raster files in your AutoCAD drawing, do some testing on zooming, editing, and plotting.

Chapter 14

Sheet Sets without Regrets

● ●

● ●

A typical AutoCAD project can include dozens of drawings, scores of sheets, lots of layouts, copious cross-drawing references, and more than a few people working on those components at once. How do you create, manage, update, plot, and generally keep a handle on all that stuff without going crazy? The new sheets sets feature in AutoCAD 2005 is Autodesk's response to this challenge.

Without sheet sets, you must manage project drawings "manually" — that is, you have to make sure that all the project's drawings get created, get numbered and named correctly, and have up-to-date title block information. You also have to ensure that cross-sheet references are accurate (for example, when a plan includes references to details on other sheets). When the time comes to send drawings to clients or consultants, you must ensure that you include all the sheets and that all of them are up-to-date. For a large project with many drawings, these can be daunting tasks. It's easy to end up with missing sheets or sheets that contain obsolete title block or cross-reference information, especially when you add or renumber sheets later in a project.

Sheet sets comprise a new palette, a group of completely new commands, and a few updated existing features. Together these things make possible a new approach to managing all the drawings for a project. Sheet sets provide a single interface that lists all your sheets, their numbers, and their names. (AutoCAD stores this information, along with the relationships among the sheets, in a DST file.) You can add and renumber sheets easily. You can create cross-sheet references that update automatically after you renumber sheets, and you can create a sheet list on your title sheet that updates automatically after you change sheet numbers or titles. When you're ready to send or plot drawings, a sheet set enables AutoCAD to locate and gather all the required files.

Because the sheet sets approach is brand new, it remains to be seen how quickly (or whether) AutoCAD users adopt it. My prediction is that companies with well-managed CAD production staffs that work on larger projects requiring lots of sheets will find sheet sets compelling and move to adopt them quickly. Companies whose projects require only a few drawing sheets or whose AutoCAD users tend to do their own thing with little central organization probably will continue to deal with sheets as discreet, unconnected DWG files.

Sheet sets rely on other relatively sophisticated AutoCAD features, so make sure that you're familiar with the following before you delve into this chapter:

- ✔ Paper space layouts (Chapter 3)

- ✔ Named views (Chapter 7)

- ✔ Tables and text fields (Chapter 9)

- ✔ Blocks and attributes (Chapter 13)

- ✔ External references (Chapter 13)

Understanding external references and layouts is especially important because these features are central to the way that the Sheet Set Manager creates and organizes sheets.

Taming Sheet Sets

Your passport to the brave new world of sheet sets comes in the form of the Sheet Set Manager palette, shown in Figure 14-1. You use this palette for most sheet set operations. To toggle the palette on or off, click the Sheet Set Manager button (which looks like a roll of drawings) on the Standard toolbar or press Ctrl+4. If you choose to leave the palette on most of the time, you may want to turn on its auto-hide setting so that it gets out of the way automatically when you're not using it — refer to Chapter 2 for instructions.

The Sheet Set Manager palette's three tabs indicate the three major types of objects you use to create and manage sheet sets:

- ✔ **Resource Drawings** contain subcomponents such as individual plans, details, and elevations that you use to build your sheets. Resource drawings usually contain geometry and annotations in model space only. Resource drawings usually don't include title blocks or paper space layouts. You must add DWG files to the Resource Drawings tab before you can create Views and add them to Sheets.

- ✔ **Views** are areas of resource drawings that you place on a sheet. A sheet set view can be the entire resource drawing or just a portion of it that you've defined, using the AutoCAD named views feature. (Chapter 7 explains named views and shows how to create them.)

Figure 14-1:
The Sheet
Set
Manager
palette.

TIP

You don't *have* to use named views in order to take advantage of sheet sets, but you *may* use them to assemble different areas of a resource drawing onto one or more sheets. For example, if you draw a large plan that needs to be broken up onto several sheets in order to plot at a legible scale, you define a named view for each area of the plan and place each view on a separate sheet.

✔ **Sheets** are paper space layouts within drawing files. (Chapter 3 describes layouts and shows how to create them.) Each sheet corresponds to one sheet in the sheet set. With the sheet set methodology, AutoCAD attaches resource drawings as xrefs into sheet drawings and creates paper space viewports on a layout in order to show the desired area of the resource drawing — either a named view or the entire drawing. You use the Sheet Set Manager to tell AutoCAD which resource drawings and views to put on which sheets. AutoCAD then does the attach-xref-and-make-viewport procedure automatically.

AutoCAD stores the settings for all this stuff — the names of files and configuration data that control how the sheet set features work with those files — in a DST file. Each project has its own DST file, and multiple AutoCAD users can use one project's DST file at the same time.

Using an Existing Sheet Set

The quickest way to get started with sheet sets is to use one that someone else — such as a CAD manager in your office — has set up. You also can experiment with Autodesk's sheet set samples, located under C:\Program Files\AutoCAD Neo\Sample\Sheet Sets.

To open an existing sheet set configuration, do one of the following:

✔ Click the menu at the top of the Sheet Set Manager palette and choose Open. AutoCAD displays a file dialog box, in which you can navigate to the appropriate folder, select the sheet set data file, and click the Open button.

✔ In Windows Explorer, double-click on a DST file.

In either case, AutoCAD displays the sheet set information in the Sheet Set Manager palette, as shown in Figure 14-1. Click each of the three tabs to get an idea of how the particular sheet set that you opened is configured.

With a sheet set open, you're ready to perform tasks such as these:

✔ Double-click a name on any of the tabs to open the corresponding DWG file in AutoCAD. Double-clicking a sheet name on the Sheet List tab or a drawing name on the Resource Drawings tab opens that DWG file, while double-clicking a view name on the View List tab opens the DWG file and zooms to the view. Thus, you can use the Sheet Set Manager to navigate quickly among all the drawings for a project.

✔ Right-click the sheet set name or a sheet subset name on the Sheet List tab to create a new sheet, using the template drawing (DWT file) configured for the project or sheet subset. (The "Getting Your Sheets Together" section, later in this chapter, describes how to specify the DWT file for a sheet set or subset.)

✔ Right-click a resource drawing to place it — either the entire drawing or a named view within it — on a sheet drawing.

✔ Right-click a sheet or view to rename and renumber it. Names and numbers can be linked to labels on the sheets, so that when you change the names or numbers in the Sheet Set Manager, AutoCAD automatically updates them in all drawings where they appear. (See the next two paragraphs for more information.)

✔ Right-click the sheet set name to add a sheet list table (that is, an index of the drawings for the project) to the current drawing. AutoCAD uses the name and number data described in the preceding paragraph to create the sheet table list and keep it current.

✔ On the View List tab, right-click the sheet set name and choose Properties to specify label blocks and callout blocks. Then you can right-click view names to place these automatically updating blocks in drawings. Label blocks show the number and name of a part of a drawing (for example, a single detail or a plan). Callout blocks reference another part of the drawing set — usually on another sheet (for example, a pointer on a plan to an elevation or detail on a different sheet).

> ✔ Right-click sheets or subsets to publish (that is, plot) them, package them for electronic transmittal, or archive them for yourself. (Chapter 16 includes instructions for these tasks.)

The rest of this chapter provides details and procedures for many of these operations.

You don't have to use all the features described earlier in order to benefit from sheet sets. For example, you might use the Sheet Set Manager just to create a navigational list of your drawings, add a sheet index to the cover sheet of the drawing set, and batch plot all the sheets.

The Sheet Set Setup

If you don't have an obliging CAD manager to configure sheets sets for you, then you'll have to do it yourself. You use the Create Sheet Set wizard for this task. Follow these steps to create a new sheet set:

1. **Open the menu at the top of the Sheet Set Manager palette and choose New Sheet Set.**

   The Create Sheet Set wizard appears.

2. **Choose Create a Sheet Set Using Existing Drawings, and then click Next.**

   The Sheet Set Details page appears, as shown in Figure 14-2.

Figure 14-2:
Sheet Set
Details.

3. **Type a name and description for the sheet set, and choose a directory for the DST (sheet set configuration data) file.**

   By default, AutoCAD stores DST files that you create in your local My Documents\AutoCAD Sheet Sets folder. Unless you're the only person working on a project, you should instead put DST files in a commonly accessible place on your local network. You can store the DST files for all projects in a single network folder or simply keep each project's DST file in the same folder that holds the project's DWG files.

4. **Click the Sheet Set Properties button, review the other settings, and click OK.**

   You can change all this stuff later in the Sheet Set Manager palette, so don't worry too much about it now. Use the dialog box help (click the question mark and then click on a setting) to find out more about any of the settings.

5. **Click Next.**

   The Choose Layouts page appears. You can click the Browse button to add any drawing(s) that you've already created for the project to the sheet set, but it's just as easy to add them later in the Sheet Set Manager palette. (I show you how in the next section.)

6. **Click Next.**

   The wizard displays a summary of the settings that it saved to the new DST file.

7. **Click Finish.**

   AutoCAD closes the Create Sheet Set wizard and opens your new sheet set in the Sheet Set Manager palette.

The other way to create a new sheet set is to copy one from an existing DST file. If you choose Create a Sheet Set Using An Example Sheet Set in Step 2, then you can choose from half a dozen Autodesk samples or open a file dialog box and browse to other DST files. The Autodesk examples are fine for experimenting, but you will need to modify them in order to make them usable on real projects.

To change any of the sheet set properties (which you reviewed in Step 5 above), right-click the sheet set name on the Sheet List tab of the Sheet Set Manager palette and choose Properties.

Getting Your Sheets Together

A new sheet set without any sheets is a lonely thing indeed, so after you create a new sheet set, you'll need to populate the set with drawings. A common way to get started is to create a drawing with a suitable layout and title block in paper space and then *add* it to the set. The other method is to direct the Sheet Set Manager to *create* a new drawing, using the template and folder that's configured in the sheet set properties. I cover both methods here.

Adding existing sheets to a set

Use these steps to add an existing drawing to the sheet set for a project:

1. **Create and save at least one properly set up drawing, including a paper space layout. (See Chapter 3 for details.)**

   If you delete any unused layout tabs (right-click the tab and choose Delete), the sheet list will turn out cleaner and less confusing. When you're using sheet sets, it's usually best to set up and use just one layout per drawing file.

2. **Open the Sheet Set Manager palette.**

3. **(Optional) On the Sheet List tab of the Sheet Set Manager palette, right-click the sheet set name and choose New Subset. Type a subset name and click OK.**

   You can use sheets subsets to group your sheets into categories. See the "Sheet subsets" section after these steps for an explanation and examples.

   This isn't your only chance to assign a sheet to a subset. You can create the subset later and then drag the sheet into it.

4. **Right-click the sheet set name (or the subset name that you created in the previous step) and choose Import Layout as Sheet.**

   The Import Layouts as Sheets dialog box appears.

5. **Click the browse button (the one with an ellipsis on it).**

6. **Navigate to and select the drawing that you created in Step 1, and then click Open.**

   AutoCAD will report an error if you try to import a drawing that doesn't contain any configured layouts.

7. **Select one or more layouts to import into the Sheet List and click OK.**

   AutoCAD adds the layout(s) to the Sheet List, as shown in Figure 14-3. The sheet name is a combination of the DWG file name (S-sheet-plans-01 in this figure) and layout name (30x42).

8. **Right-click the newly imported sheet and choose Rename and Renumber.**

   The Rename and Renumber Sheet dialog box appears.

Figure 14-3:
An imported
sheet.

9. **Type a Sheet Number and Sheet Title in the text boxes, and then click OK.**

   If you later create a sheet list table — that is, a drawing sheet index — for your cover sheet, then AutoCAD will use what you type here to describe the sheet. (I demonstrate this procedure at the end of this chapter.) You usually should type the sheet number and title as they will appear in the title block. This information also helps you and others identify the sheet unambiguously in the Sheet List.

Sheet subsets

On the Sheet List tab, you can create sheet *subsets* to organize your sheets into types — for example, plan sheets, elevation sheets, and detail sheets. The advantages of using subsets are:

✔ On a project with lots of drawings, you can find drawings and understand what kinds of drawings make up the set more easily. This kind of organization also makes it easy to select a group of related files for plotting or transmitting to someone else.

✔ You can configure each subset to use a unique template drawing (for example, DWT file). Thus when you create new drawings with the Sheet Set Manager, as described in the next section, different kinds of drawings can start from different templates. For example, you might use one template to start plans and a different one to start details, based on different scales or other considerations.

✔ You can configure each subset to create new sheet drawings in different folders. For example, you might keep your plan sheets and detail sheets in two different folders.

To configure both of the second two options, right-click the subset name and choose Properties.

Don't confuse sheet *subsets* with sheet *selections*. You create the latter with the Sheet Selections button at the top of the Sheet List tab. A sheet selection is simply a grouping of sheets with a name attached to it. You can use sheet selections to grab a group of sheets quickly for transmitting, archiving, or publishing. (Chapter 16 describes these activities.) Sheet selections don't store any configuration information and don't affect the organization of the Sheet List. Sheet subsets do both of those things.

Creating new sheets for a set

Use the following steps to create a new sheet drawing, using the configuration settings for the sheet set:

1. **(Optional) On the Sheet List tab of the Sheet Set Manager palette, right-click the sheet set name and choose New Subset. Type a subset name and click OK.**

2. **Right-click the sheet set name or subset name and choose Properties.**

   The Sheet Set Properties dialog box appears.

3. **Verify or change the Sheet Creation properties, and then click OK.**

   Sheet Storage Location determines where the new sheet DWG file will get created, and Sheet Creation Template specifies the DWT file that it gets created from.

4. **Right-click the sheet set name or subset name and choose New Sheet.**

   The New Sheet dialog box appears, as shown in Figure 14-4.

Figure 14-4:
Creating a
new sheet.

New Sheet	
Number:	Sheet title:
S2.03	Roof Framing Plan
File name:	S-sheet-plans-03
Folder path:	H:\Drawings\SS Minnow
	OK Cancel Help

5. **Type a Sheet Number, Sheet Title, and File Name in the text boxes, and then click OK.**

   The previous procedure describes what the Sheet Number and Sheet Title are for. File Name determines the name of the DWG file that AutoCAD creates. AutoCAD generates the default file name by combining the sheet number and sheet title. You probably want to remove the sheet number from this automatically generated name, for the reasons described in the following Tip.

Don't type **.DWG** in the File Name box. AutoCAD always adds the file extension, so if you type .DWG, AutoCAD will create a file named Whatever.Dwg.Dwg.

If you anticipate ever having to renumber sheets on your project — and even if you don't anticipate it, it may happen! — you should name your sheet files based on their general contents rather than their (current) sheet numbers. For example, when you create an architectural floor plan that you anticipate will be sheet A-201, name the sheet file A-FP01.dwg (first floor plan in the series) instead of A-201.dwg. By giving sheet files names that are independent of their sheet numbers, you retain the flexibility to renumber sheets automatically later with just a few changes in the Sheet Set Manager.

Assembling sheet views from resource drawings

After you create a new sheet (or add an existing one that doesn't yet contain all the necessary drawing components), you use the Resource Drawing tab to compose views on the sheet. A view can be simply the entire drawing, or it can be a named view that you've created in the resource drawing. In all cases, the Sheet Set Manager attaches the resource drawing as an xref to the sheet drawing and creates a properly scaled viewport on the sheet drawing's layout. Each sheet can contain one view (for example, a large plan) or more than one (for example, several elevations or a dozen details).

To place an entire resource drawing on a sheet, follow these steps:

1. **On the Sheet List tab of the Sheet Set Manager palette, double-click the sheet to which you want to add the resource drawing.**

   AutoCAD opens the drawing for editing.

2. **Click the Resource Drawings tab.**

3. **If you haven't yet specified the folder that contains the resource drawing that you want to use, double-click Add New Location, browse to the directory, and click the Open button.**

You can add more than one folder to the Resource Drawings tab.

4. **Right-click the resource drawing that you want to add to the sheet, choose Place on Sheet, and move the cursor into the sheet drawing's layout.**

   AutoCAD attaches the resource drawing as an xref and creates a viewport for it. You position the viewport with the cursor.

5. **Right-click.**

   A scale menu appears, as shown in Figure 14-5.

6. **Choose the proper scale for the resource drawing.**

   AutoCAD rescales the viewport, and you continue to drag it with the cursor.

7. **Position the viewport where you want it and click.**

   AutoCAD places the viewport on the sheet.

   If you need to adjust the viewport later, select it and use grip editing, the Properties palette, or the Viewports toolbar to make changes.

8. **Click the View List tab on the Sheet Set Manager palette.**

Figure 14-5:
Adding a view to a sheet.

AutoCAD has added the resource drawing that you just used to the list of views for this sheet set.

9. **Right-click the new view name and choose Rename and Renumber.**

The Rename and Renumber Sheet dialog box appears, as shown in Figure 14-6.

10. **Type a View Number and View Title in the text boxes, and then click OK.**

As I describe earlier in this chapter, you can direct the Sheet Set Manager to use this information to create automatically updating labels. For example, if you place a detail on a sheet, AutoCAD feeds the information in this dialog box to a label block in the sheet drawing that shows the detail number and title. In addition, you can create callouts on other sheets that refer to this detail. If you later change the information in this dialog box, the Sheet Set Manager changes it in the detail label as well as in the callouts that reference the detail. (You create label and callout blocks in separate drawings, as described in Chapter 13. You then right-click the sheet set name or a view name and choose Properties to configure the sheet set or view to use these blocks.) Look up "callout blocks (for sheet views)" and "label blocks (for sheet views)" in the AutoCAD online help system for detailed instructions.

Figure 14-6:
Specifying a view's number and title.

After you specify callout and label blocks on the View List tab, use the view's right-click menu to place either kind of block.

On the View List tab, you can create view *categories* by right-clicking the sheet set name and choosing New View Category. Each view category can use different callout blocks — right-click the view category and choose Properties to configure callout blocks.

Placing a named view on a layout is just like placing an entire resource drawing, except that on the Resource Drawing tab you click the plus sign next to the drawing name to reveal its named views, right-click the desired view, and choose Place on Sheet. (If you haven't yet created the named view that you need, open the drawing by double-clicking it on the Resource Drawing tab, and choose View⇨Named Views to open the View dialog box. See the section titled "A View by Any Other Name. . ." in Chapter 7 for instructions on how to create named views.)

Making an Automatic Sheet List

After you create sheets and assemble views on them from resource drawings, you can take advantage of the additional sheet set features described in the "Using an Existing Sheet Set" section earlier in this chapter. For example, you can batch plot all the sheets for a project by right-clicking the sheet set name and choosing Publish⇨Publish to Plotter. (Chapter 16 describes the PUBLISH command.)

Before you publish your CAD *magnum opus*, however, you probably want to create an index. As long as you're diligent about filling in the sheet number and title properties, as I advise in the "Adding existing sheets to a set" and "Creating new sheets for a set" sections earlier in this chapter, the Sheet Set Manager will build a drawing index for you automatically. Even better, when you add, remove, renumber, or rename sheets, AutoCAD updates the index automatically. The Sheet Set Manager creates the drawing index, using AutoCAD 2005's new table object, for which reason it's called a *sheet list table*. (See Chapter 9 for information about tables.)

Use the following steps to create an automatic and automatically updateable sheet list table:

1. **On the Sheet List tab of the Sheet Set Manager palette, double-click the sheet to which you want to add the drawing index.**

   AutoCAD opens the drawing for editing.

2. **Right-click the sheet set name and choose Insert Sheet List Table.**

   The Insert Sheet List Table dialog box appears.

3. **If you're not happy with the fonts, text heights, colors, or text alignment of the table in the Table Style Settings area, click the ellipsis button to open the Table Style dialog box, create and configure a new style, and then click Close to return to the Insert Sheet List Table dialog box.**

   Chapter 9 shows how to create table styles.

   The default alignment for the data cells is Top Center. You may want to change it to Top Left (that is, align sheet numbers and titles left flush rather than centered).

4. **If you want to change the number of columns, which data appear in each column, and what the column headings and table title say, use the Table Data Settings area to do so.**

   Click the Add button to create an additional column. Drop-down lists in the Column Settings area show the types of data that you can include in the table. (Double-click the entry in the Data Type column to display the drop-down list.) Much of the additional, optional data come from the Drawing Properties dialog box, which I describe in Chapter 3. (The Sheet Number, Title, Description, and Plot data all come from the sheet set properties.)

5. **Click OK.**

   By default, AutoCAD displays a dialog box reminding you not to edit the sheet list table manually, because the Sheet Set Manager handles it automatically.

6. **Click OK.**

   AutoCAD creates the table, and you drag it with the cursor.

7. **Position the table where you want it and click.**

   AutoCAD places the table on the sheet. Each of the data cells is a field that gets its value from the sheet set properties (see Figure 14-7) or drawing properties.

After you make changes to the Sheet List, such as adding a sheet or editing a sheet title, select the table, right-click, and choose Update Sheet List Table. Now are computers great, or what?!

If you didn't quite get the sheet list table properties right on the first try, select the table, right-click, and choose Edit Sheet List Table Settings.

Figure 14-7:
An
automatic
sheet list
created
from a
sheet set.

Although sheet sets are too new to know for sure, they're poised to alter profoundly the way that people create and manage drawings in AutoCAD. Like all software innovations that increase the sophistication of a process and manage dependencies, sheet sets require some study, some configuration, and significant coordination on everyone's part. (One good resource is the group of sheet sets tutorials in Help⇨New Features Workshop.) In this case, those who expend the effort are likely to be well rewarded.

Chapter 15

CAD Standards Rule

• •

• •

*I*f you've ever worked with other people to create a multichapter, visually complex, frequently updated text document, then you probably understand the importance of coordinating how everyone works on the parts of the document. Even if you're someone who churns out documents from your one-person office or lonely cubicle, you probably try to ensure a reasonably consistent look and feel in similar documents. You employ consistent fonts, the same company logo, and the same paper size in most documents — or if you don't, you probably at least think that you should!

CAD exacts similar demands for reasonable consistency, only more so:

✔ Most companies would like to take pride in the clarity and consistency of their drawings. Sloppy drawings with randomly varying text heights and lineweights don't reflect well on you and make your drawings harder to read.

✔ CAD drawings that don't conform with some logically consistent scheme usually are harder to edit and to reuse by others who work on the project and by you when you work on other projects.

This stuff is important enough in CAD that it has a special name: *CAD standards*. Those people compulsive enough to fret about it all the time and sadistic enough to impose their fretting on others also have a special name: *CAD managers*. This chapter won't turn you into a CAD manager — a reassurance you're probably grateful for — but it does introduce the most important CAD standards issues. This chapter also suggests some ways to come up with your own simple CAD standards, in case you're going it alone and don't have the benefit of a ready-made company or project CAD standards document to guide you. The chapter ends with an overview of AutoCAD tools that can help you comply with and check conformity to CAD standards.

Why CAD Standards?

Throughout this book, I emphasize things like setting up your drawings properly, drawing objects on appropriate and consistent layers, and specifying suitable text fonts and heights. These practices amount to conforming to a CAD standard.

You need to do these things if you work with or exchange drawings with others. If you don't, several bad things will happen. You'll be pegged as a clueless newbie by experienced drafters, who understand the importance of CAD consistency. Even if your ego can handle the contempt, you'll make everyone's work slower and more difficult. And if the project has electronic drawing submittal requirements, you may find that your client rejects your DWG files and demands that you make them conform to the CAD standards in the contract.

Even if you work solo and don't have any particular requirements imposed from outside, your own work will go more smoothly and look better if you adhere to a reasonably consistent way of doing things in AutoCAD. You'll certainly find plotting easier and more predictable.

CAD standards originally grew out of a desire to achieve a graphical consistency on the plotted drawings that mirrored the graphical consistency on hand-drafted drawings. Before the days of CAD, most companies had manual drafting standards that specified standard lettering (text) sizes, dimension appearance, symbol shapes, and so on. Sometimes these standards were based on standard industry reference books, such as the *Architectural Graphic Standards*.

As CAD users became more sophisticated, they realized that CAD standards needed to incorporate more than just the look of the resulting plot. CAD drawings contain a lot more organizational depth than printed drawings — layers, screen colors, blocks, xrefs, text and dimension styles, and the like. If these things aren't subject to a modicum of standardization; then different people who work on the same drawings or projects are likely to end up stumbling over — or throwing things at — one another.

In short, the first job of CAD standards is to impose some graphical consistency on plotted output. CAD standards also encourage consistency in the way that people create, assign properties to, organize, and display objects in the CAD file.

The aesthetics of CAD

Manual drafting veterans frequently complain that CAD drawings don't look as good as the drawings that they used to create by hand. "Too 'flat,' too cartoonish, and inconsistent" are some of the refrains that you hear. These complaints are not just the whining of old-timers. Good manual drafters were justifiably proud of the appearance of their drawings. They focused on making the finished bluelines look sharp and read well.

When computers and CAD software got into the act, it became easy for CAD drafters to focus on the screen image and pay less attention to the plotted output. In the early days, CAD users struggled with a new way of making drawings and didn't have as much time to make them look good. By the time that CAD became commonplace, a new crop of CAD users had grown up without the benefit of discovering how to make good-looking drawings on paper.

There's no reason that CAD drawings can't look as good as manual drawings. It's a matter of understanding the look that you're after and caring enough to want to achieve it. If you see some especially clear and elegant printed drawings, find out who drew them and take that person out to lunch. You'll probably uncover some techniques that you can translate into making better CAD drawings. You may also gain new respect for the skills of those who made handsome and functional drawings with the simplest of tools.

Which CAD Standards?

If CAD standards are as important as I claim, you might expect that industries would've settled on a standardized way of doing things. No such luck. Although the manual drafting conventions in many professions have carried over to some degree into CAD, a lot of the things that need standardization have been left to the imagination of individual companies, departments, or people. For example, you'll find that different companies usually name layers differently and employ different schemes for mapping object screen color to plotted lineweight (see Chapter 12). In particularly disorganized companies, you'll find that different drafters use different layers and color-to-lineweight. And in the worst cases, the same drafter will do these things differently in different drawings!

As you can imagine, this proliferation of nonstandard standards makes sharing and reusing parts of CAD drawings a lot more difficult. You can at least minimize the pain within your own office by conforming to any existing CAD standards or, if there aren't any, by encouraging the development of some. (Later in this chapter, I give some suggestions for how to get started.)

Industry standards

Professional, trade, and governmental groups in some industries have made an attempt to promulgate CAD standards for the benefit of everyone in the industry. For example, the American Institute of Architects (AIA), together with several professional engineering associations, published a *CAD Layer Guidelines* document, which has become part of a so-called National CAD Standard that's now promulgated by the U.S. government's National Institute of Building Sciences, or NIBS (see www.nationalcad-standard.org). The International Organization for Standardization, or ISO (the acronym reflects the French ordering of the words), publishes ISO standards document 13567 (see www.iso.ch). This document, which comes in no fewer than three parts, attempts to provide a framework for CAD layer standards in the building design industries throughout the world.

These documents may be useful to you in your search for standards, but they aren't a panacea.

The majority of CAD-using companies has ignored officially promulgated CAD standards, because these companies developed their own standards and practices years ago and are loath to change. That doesn't mean that you can't use the officially promulgated standards, but they won't suddenly make you a part of some mythical CAD standards mainstream. Also, practical implementation of most official CAD standards in a specific company requires a generous amount of clarification, modification, and additional documentation. In other words, you don't just buy the document and then get to work; someone needs to tailor it to your company and projects. And finally, some of these officially promulgated CAD standards documents are shockingly expensive. Apparently these organizations haven't found out that the way to make something popular is to post it on the Web for free!

Even if you're lucky or perseverant enough to get a well-rounded set of CAD standards in your office, that may not be the end of it. CAD-savvy people from different companies who collaborate on projects often want to minimize the pain of inconsistency during drawing exchange. Although each company may have its own CAD standards house in order, there's no way that all those standards will be the same. Thus, one or more companies (often the lead consultant) may impose a set of *project-specific* CAD standards. Project-specific standards don't necessarily need to be as detailed as a full-blown company CAD standards document, but depending on the project and the person who created the project-specific CAD standards, they might be.

The result of this confusing muddle of industry practices, company CAD standards, and project-specific CAD standards is that you find yourself switching among different standards as you work on different projects. Before you start making drawings, find out whether any particular CAD standards apply. It's a lot easier to start off conforming with those standards than to fix nonconforming drawings later.

What Needs to Be Standardized?

If you are in a company or on a project without any CAD standards, put together at least a minimal set of guidelines. First, impose some consistency on *plotted appearance* and *use of layers*. If you make a few rules for yourself before you start, you'll end up with drawings that are more professional looking and easier to edit — and more likely to be useful on future projects.

A spreadsheet or word processing program is great for documenting your CAD standards decisions as they firm up. Many CAD standards components work best as tabular lists of layers, colors, and so on. (See Tables 15-1 and 15-2 in this chapter for examples.) Use the cells in a spreadsheet or the tables feature in a word processor to organize your CAD standards documentation.

Before you start, make sure that you're familiar with managing properties (Chapter 4) and plot styles (Chapter 12). You need a good understanding to make intelligent decisions about your plotting and layer standards. (If you want to make *unintelligent* decisions, don't worry about those chapters!)

Plotting

If you plan to use color-dependent plot styles (most people do), develop a color-to-lineweight plotting chart like Table 15-1. If you choose the more logical but lonelier named plot styles approach, make a similar chart, with plot style names instead of color in the first column. (See Chapter 12 for information about color-dependent and named plot styles.) After you complete a plotting chart, create a plot style table (CBT file for color-dependent plot styles or STB file for named plot styles), as in Chapter 12.

Table 15-1	Sample Color-to-Lineweight Plotting Chart
AutoCAD Color	*Plotted Lineweight*
1 (red)	0.15 mm
2 (yellow)	0.20 mm
3 (green)	0.25 mm
4 (cyan)	0.30 mm
5 (blue)	0.35 mm
6 (magenta)	0.40 mm

(continued)

Table 15-1 _(continued)_

AutoCAD Color	Plotted Lineweight
7 (white/black)	0.50 mm
8 (dark gray)	0.10 mm
9 (light gray)	0.70 mm

Your life will be easier — and your plotting chart will be shorter — if you limit yourself to a small portion of the 255 colors in the AutoCAD Color Index (ACI). The first nine colors work well for many people.

If your work requires _screened_ (shaded or faded-out) lines, extend the plotting chart to include a couple of additional AutoCAD colors. For each color, list the plotted lineweight and screen percentage ranging from 0% for invisible to 100% for solid black.

Layers

After you work out your plotting conventions, you're ready to develop a chart of layers. A chart of layers takes more thought and work, and you'll probably revise it more frequently than the plotting chart. Find a typical drawing from your office or industry and identify the things you'll draw — such as walls, text, dimensions, and hatching. Then decide how you'd like to parse those objects onto different layers (see Chapter 4). Here are some guidelines:

- ✔ **Objects that you want to plot with different lineweights go on different layers.** Assign each layer an appropriate color, based on how you want the objects to appear on the screen and on plots. If you're using object lineweights (Chapter 4) or named plot styles (Chapter 12), include a column for these settings in your chart. In all cases, let the objects inherit these properties from the layer.

- ✔ **Objects whose visibility you want to control separately go on different layers.** Turn off or freeze a layer in order to make the objects on that layer, and only the objects on that layer, disappear temporarily.

- ✔ **Objects that represent significantly different kinds of things in the real world go on different layers.** For example, doors should go on different layers from walls in an architectural floor plan.

As you make your layer decisions, you'll develop a layer chart that resembles Table 15-2. If you use named plot styles instead of color-dependent plot styles, add a Plot style column to the chart.

Table 15-2		Sample Layer Chart	
Layer Name	*Color*	*Linetype*	*Use*
Wall	5	Continuous	Walls
Wall-Belo	3	Dashed	Walls below (shown dashed)
Cols	6	Continuous	Columns
Door	4	Continuous	Doors
Text	3	Continuous	Regular note text
Text-Bold	7	Continuous	Large/bold text
Dims	2	Continuous	Dimensions
Patt	1	Continuous	Hatch patterns
Cntr	1	Center	Centerlines
Symb	2	Continuous	Annotational symbols
Nplt	8	Continuous	Non-plotting information

The layer chart in Table 15-2 is simpler than the layer systems used by experienced drafters in most companies. The layer names in the table are based on names in the *AIA CAD Layer Guidelines* document mentioned in the "Industry standards" sidebar. That document recommends adding a discipline-specific prefix to each layer name: A-Walls for walls drawn by the architectural team, S-Walls for walls drawn by the structural team, and so on.

Other stuff

The following settings and procedures deserve some consistency, too:

✔ **Text styles:** Decide on text fonts and heights and use them consistently. (See Chapter 9 for more information.)

Manual CAD drafting standards often specify a minimum text height of ⅛ inch or 3 mm, because hand-lettered text smaller than that becomes difficult to read, especially on half-size prints. Plotted ³⁄₃₂ inch or 2.5 mm CAD text is quite legible, but half-size plots with these smaller text heights can result in text that's on the margin of legibility. Text legibility on half-size — or smaller — plots depends on the plotter resolution, the lineweight assigned to the text, and the condition of your eyes. Test before you commit to using smaller text heights, or use ⅛ inch or 3 mm as a minimum.

✔ **Dimension styles:** Create a dimension style that reflects your preferred look and feel. (See Chapter 10.)

✔ **Hatch patterns:** Choose the hatch patterns that you need and decide on an appropriate scale and angle for each. (See Chapter 11.)

✔ **Drawing setup and organization:** Set up all the drawings on a project in the same way, and use sheet sets, blocks, and xrefs in a consistent fashion.

After you make standards, create a simple test drawing and make sure that the plotted results are what you want. You'll undoubtedly revise and extend your standards as you go, especially on your first few projects. In time, you'll find a set of standards that works for you.

Cool Standards Tools

Most of the hard CAD standards work happens outside of AutoCAD — thinking, deciding, documenting, revising, and so on. But ultimately you need to translate that work into your CAD practice, and AutoCAD includes some tools to make the job easier. Table 15-3 lists standards-related AutoCAD utilities.

Table 15-3		AutoCAD's CAD Standards Tools		
Utility Name	*Command Name*	*Menu Choice*	*Use*	*Cross-Reference*
DesignCenter	ADCenter	Tools⇨ Design-Center	Copy layers, dimension styles, and other named objects from other drawings	Chapter 4
Tool Palettes	ToolPalettes	Tools⇨Tool Palettes Window	Create symbol and hatch pattern libraries	Chapter 2 and "Tool Palettes" in the online help system
Layer Translator	LAYTRANS	Tools⇨CAD Standards⇨ Layer Translator	Translate from one set of layer names and properties to another	"LAYTRANS command, Layer Translator" in the online help system

Utility Name	Command Name	Menu Choice	Use	Cross-Reference
Configure Standards	STANDARDS	Tools⇨CAD Standards⇨ Configure	Assign particular standards requirements to the current drawing (and control what gets checked)	Figure 15-1 and "STANDARDS command, Configure Standards dialog box" in the online help system
Check Standards	CHECK-STANDARDS	Tools⇨CAD Standards⇨ Configure	Check the current drawing against the standards requirements that are assigned to it	Figure 15-2 and "CHECK-STANDARDS command, Check Standards dialog box" in the online help system
Batch Standards Checker	N/A	Start⇨(All) Programs⇨ Autodesk⇨ AutoCAD 2005⇨Batch Standards Checker	Checks multiple drawings against the standards requirements that are assigned to them or against a single standards requirement	"Batch Standards Checker" in the online help system

Figure 15-1:
Configuring
standards.
Check?

Figure 15-2:
Checking
standards.
Check!

AutoCAD standards checking tools require an AutoCAD Drawing Standards
(DWS) file. You create a DWS file from a drawing with all the allowed layers,
dimension styles, text styles, and linetypes; use File⇨Save As to save it as a
DWS (not DWG) file. The DWS file defines acceptable named objects for the
Check Standards and Batch Standards Checker utilities. See "standards files,
creating" in AutoCAD's online help system for information.

AutoCAD 2005 monitors CAD standards compliance when you've specified
standards for the current drawing. By default, a balloon notification appears
from the right end of the status bar. CAD managers can trade the balloon for
a message that offers to fix the mistake. To configure the notification level,
click the Settings button in the Configure Standards dialog box.

If your company does have CAD standards in place, someone may have created
custom tools to help you comply with those standards. For example, the CAD
manager may have put together template drawings with customized settings or
block libraries of standard symbols. CAD managers sometimes create custom
menu choices, scripts, or utility programs for the company's CAD standards.

Chapter 16

Drawing on the Internet

● ●

In This Chapter

▶ Understanding AutoCAD Internet features

▶ Exchanging drawing files via e-mail and FTP

▶ Using the Reference Manager to view and fix file dependencies

▶ Using the Drawing Web Format and ePlot

▶ Making multiple Web and paper plots with PUBLISH

▶ Viewing and plotting drawings without AutoCAD

▶ Protecting drawings with passwords and digital signatures

● ●

*U*nless you've been living under a rock for the past five years, you know that the Internet is causing major changes in the way that people work. (And even if you have been living under a rock, someone probably is offering broadband service to it by now!) Because of the Net, most of us communicate differently, exchange files more rapidly, and fill out express delivery forms less frequently.

AutoCAD users were among the online pioneers, well before the Internet burst onto the public scene. Despite this early adoption, the CAD world has been relatively slow to take the full-immersion Internet plunge. Exchanging drawings via e-mail and using the World Wide Web for CAD software research and support are pretty common nowadays. But it's still uncommon to find drawings incorporated into Web pages or Web-centric CAD applications. That's partly because CAD drafters have traditionally been somewhat insulated from the general computing community — they spend most of their time cranking out drawings and leave all that new-fangled Web design stuff to people who don't have real work to get done, thank you very much! Even the more forward-thinking CAD users tend to display a healthy, and often reasonable, skepticism about whether any particular innovation will help with the pressing job of getting drawings finished on deadline.

Many of the features described in this chapter have undergone frequent tinkering, revision, and refocusing in recent AutoCAD versions. AutoCAD 2005 adds new ETRANSMIT and PUBLISH capabilities to keep up with the new sheet sets feature, which is described in Chapter 14. The Standard toolbar includes a new Markup Set Manager for those who receive drawing markups from users of Autodesk DWF Composer. (DWF Composer is Autodesk's newest effort to draw more people into using the DWF format. The idea is that architects, engineers, and others who don't themselves use AutoCAD can mark up drawings by using DWF Composer and then transmit those markups to an AutoCAD drafter, who incorporates the changes into the DWG files.)

This chapter shows you how — and when — to use AutoCAD's Internet features. I also cover how the Internet features can connect with traditional CAD tasks, such as plotting. The emphasis of this chapter is on useful, no-nonsense ways of taking advantage of the Internet in your CAD work.

Your ticket to most of the features described in this chapter is an account with an Internet service provider (ISP). You probably already have Internet access through work or a private ISP account — or both; but if not, now is the time to get connected. Other CAD users will expect to be able to send drawings to you and receive them from you via e-mail. Software companies, including Autodesk, expect you to have Web access in order to download software updates and support information. Dial-up modem access to the Internet is acceptable, but if you're doing much drawing exchange or want to be able to download software updates without waiting all day, consider springing for broadband access, such as DSL (Digital Subscriber Line) or cable modem.

The Internet and AutoCAD: An Overview

As with all things Internet-y, AutoCAD 2005's Internet features are a hodge-podge of the genuinely useful, the interesting but still somewhat immature or difficult to use, and the downright foolish. I steer you toward features and techniques that are reliable and widely used today. I warn you about "stupid pet trick" features that may impress a 12-year-old computer geek but leave your project leader wondering what planet you come from. On the other hand, a few of today's questionable features are likely to become the reliable, commonplace ones of tomorrow. I give you enough context to see how everything works and where it may lead. Table 16-1 summarizes the AutoCAD 2005 Internet features and tells you where in this book to find more information.

Table 16-1	AutoCAD 2005 Internet Features		
Feature	*Description*	*Comments*	*Where You Can Find More Info*
ETRANSMIT command	Package DWG files for sending via e-mail or FTP or posting on the Web	Useful to most people	"Send it with eTransmit" in this chapter
Reference Manager	Report on and modify paths of referenced files	Useful for people who send drawings and use complex, multi-folder xref schemes	"Help from the Reference Manager" in this chapter
File navigation dialog box	Can save to and open from Web and FTP sites	Potentially useful for people who routinely work with files on Web or FTP sites	Chapter 2
DWF files	A lightweight drawing file format for posting drawings on the Web or sharing them with people who don't have AutoCAD	The recipient must have Autodesk Express Viewer installed; potentially useful for sharing drawings with people who don't have AutoCAD	"Drawing Web Format — Not Just for the Web" in this chapter
PUBLISH command	Create DWF files, plot (PLT) files, or paper plots in batches	Can help automate the traditional plotting procedure; if DWF files ever catch on, will streamline their creation	"Making DWFs (or Plots) with PUBLISH" in this chapter
Publish to Web	A wizard that builds and publishes a Web page containing drawings	Like most wizards, fairly easy to use, but limited; possibly useful as a quick-and-dirty Web publishing approach	"PUBLISHTOWEB command" in the AutoCAD online help system

(continued)

Table 16-1 (continued)

Feature	Description	Comments	Where You Can Find More Info
Insert hyperlink	Add hyperlinks to objects in drawings	Of questionable use, except in specialized applications	"Hand-y objects" in this chapter
Password protection	Requires a password in order to open a drawing	Useful for limiting access to sensitive DWG or DWF files	"The Drawing Protection Racket" in this chapter
Digital signatures	Provide electronic confirmation that someone has approved a particular version of a particular drawing	Requires an account with a digital certificate provider; new technology, so look before you leap — and talk to your attorney first	"The Drawing Protection Racket" in this chapter

Sending Strategies

E-mail and FTP (File Transfer Protocol) have largely replaced blueline prints, overnight delivery, floppies, and higher capacity disks as the standard means of exchanging drawings. Some companies even use specially designed Web-based services, such as Autodesk's Buzzsaw, as a repository for project drawings from all the companies working on a particular project. Whether you're exchanging drawings in order to reuse CAD objects or simply to make hard-copy plots of someone else's drawings, you need to be comfortable sending and receiving drawings electronically.

Sending and receiving DWG files doesn't differ much from sending and receiving other kinds of files, except for the following:

- ✔ **DWG files tend to be bigger than word processing documents and spreadsheets.** Consequently, you may need to invest in a faster Internet connection, as described earlier in this chapter.

- ✔ **You can easily forget to include all the dependent files.** I tell you in the next section how to make sure that you send all the necessary files — and how to pester the people who don't send you all their necessary files.

✔ **It's often not completely obvious how to plot what you receive.** Read Chapter 12 and the section, "Bad reception?" in this chapter to solve plotting puzzles.

Whenever you send DWG files together, follow the Golden Exchange Rule: "Send files unto others as you would have them sent unto you." That means sending all the dependent files along with the main DWG files, sending plotting support files (CTB or STB files — see Chapter 12), and including a description of what you're sending. And ask the recipient to try opening the drawings you send them right away, so you both have more time to respond if there's any problem.

Send it with ETRANSMIT

Many people naively assume that an AutoCAD drawing is always contained in a single DWG file, but that's often not the case. Each drawing file created in AutoCAD can contain references to other kinds of files, the most important of which are described in the following table. Thus, before you start exchanging drawings via e-mail or FTP, you need a procedure for assembling the drawings with all their dependent files.

Description	File Types	Consequences if Missing	Where the Use of These File Types is Explained
Custom font files	SHX, TTF	AutoCAD substitutes another font	Chapter 9
Other drawings (xrefs)	DWG	Stuff in the main drawing disappears	Chapter 13
Raster graphics files	JPG, PCX, TIF, and so on	Stuff in the drawing disappears	Chapter 13
Plot style tables	CTB, STB	Lineweights and other plotted effects won't look right	Chapter 12

As you can see from the table, the consequences of not including a custom font aren't that dire: The recipient still will see your text, but the font will be different. Of course, the new font may look odd or cause text spacing problems within the drawing. If, on the other hand, you forget to send xrefs or raster graphics that are attached to your main drawing, the objects contained on those attached files simply will be gone when the recipient opens your drawing. Not good!

Table 16-2 doesn't exhaust the types of files that your DWG files might refer to. Custom plotter settings (such as custom paper sizes) may reside in PC3 or PMP files. If you use the new sheet sets feature, a DST file contains information about the sheet structure. An FMP file controls some aspects of font mapping. (Like so much else in AutoCAD, the tools and rules for mapping missing fonts are flexible but somewhat complicated. Look up the "FONTALT" and "FONTMAP" system variables in the AutoCAD online help system for detailed information.)

Rapid eTransmit

Fortunately, the AutoCAD ETRANSMIT command pulls together all the files that your main DWG file depends on. Follow these steps to assemble a drawing with all its dependent files with ETRANSMIT.

1. **Open the drawing that you want to run ETRANSMIT on.**

   If the drawing is already open, save it. ETRANSMIT requires that any changes to the drawing be saved before you proceed.

2. **Choose File➪eTransmit.**

   The Create Transmittal dialog box appears, as shown in Figure 16-1.

Figure 16-1:
Rapid
eTransmit.

3. **On the Files Tree or Files Table tab, remove the check mark next to any file that you want ETRANMSIT *not* to copy with the main drawing.**

Unless you have assigned custom font mapping, you can omit the Acad.fmp file.

4. **Select a transmittal setup from the list.**

Transmittal setups are new in AutoCAD 2005. They contain settings that control how ETRANSMIT processes the drawings and creates the transmittal package. Click the Transmittal Setups button to create new or modify existing setups. The default Standard transmittal setup works fine for many purposes, except that you probably want to turn on the Include Fonts setting, as described in the next paragraph. In any case, you should view the settings (click the Modify button) just to see what options you can change if you need to later.

If you want AutoCAD to include SHX and TTF font files, including any custom fonts that you're using, you must turn on the Include Fonts setting in the transmittal setup. (Click Transmittal Setups, click Modify, and check the Include Fonts box.) Note, however, that many SHX and TTF files are custom fonts, which work like licensed software. Sending them to others is just like sharing your AutoCAD program CD with others. No, I don't mean that it's easy and fun; I mean that it's illegal and unethical. Before you send a custom font file to someone else, find out what the licensing restrictions are on the font and be prepared to work within them.

5. **Click the View Report button.**

You see a report listing the files that ETRANSMIT will copy, along with warnings about any files that it can't locate.

6. **Review the report and make sure that ETRANSMIT was able to find all the files.**

7. **Click OK.**

ETRANMSIT displays a file dialog box so that you can specify the name and location of the transmittal package (which is a ZIP file by default).

8. **Click Save.**

ETRANSMIT creates the transmittal package (which is a ZIP file by default).

Although AutoCAD 2005 automatically compresses its DWG files, zipping files manages to compress them even further (about 20 percent more, in my experience). More importantly, zipping creates a single, tidy package of all your DWG, raster image, plot style table, and font files. No one likes to receive an e-mail message carrying an endless cargo of attached files. Do everyone a favor: be hip and zip.

The only downside to zipping is that creating a zipped file and extracting files from it require a separate zip/unzip program. Several good shareware utilities are available, including WinZip (www.winzip.com).

Transmitting multiple drawings

In many cases, you'll want to send more than one drawing to a recipient. In this situation, you can open each drawing and run ETRANSMIT on each in turn. (In the transmittal setup, set Transmittal Package Type to `Folder (set of files)`, specify the Transmittal File Folder to copy the files to, and use Transmittal Options to control whether the files are copied to one or more than one folder.) When you've processed all the drawings, use a program like WinZip to package the files into a single zipped file before sending it.

AutoCAD 2005 provides a slicker way of transmitting multiple drawings, as long as you're using the new sheet sets feature (described in Chapter 14). In the Sheet Set Manager palette, just right-click the sheet set name and choose eTransmit. The Create Transmittal dialog box then will include an additional Sheets tab, as shown in Figure 16-2. This tab lists all drawings in the sheet set and includes them in the transmittal by default.

Figure 16-2: eTransmit faster with sheet sets.

AutoCAD 2005 includes a new ARCHIVE command, which functions identically to ETRANSMIT, but without the transmittal document and without saved setups. ARCHIVE works only with sheet sets. In the Sheet Set Manager palette, right-click the sheet set name and choose Archive. You use this command to save copies of a set of drawings at some milestone during a project — for example, at a design review or bid set submittal.

FTP for you and me

FTP, or *File Transfer Protocol,* is a simple but robust protocol for copying files over the Internet. A computer that's connected to the Internet can act as an FTP *server,* which means that part of its hard disk is accessible over the Internet. The person who configures the FTP server can place restrictions so that only people who enter a particular logon name and password can see and download files. FTP overcomes the file size limitations that often occur with e-mail.

Because of all these FTP benefits, it's increasingly common for people at larger companies to place drawing files on their company's FTP site and tell you to go get them. This approach relieves them of having to e-mail you the files, and relieves you of waiting for that 10MB e-mail download when you least expected it.

In most cases, the person making the files available to you via FTP will send you a Uniform Resource Locator (URL) that looks like a Web page address, except that it starts with FTP:// instead of HTTP://. If you open your Web browser and enter the FTP URL into the address field, the browser should connect to the FTP site, ask you for a location and name to use for the file when it gets copied to your system, and begin downloading the file. If the FTP site uses password protection, you'll have to enter a logon name and password first.

If you want fancier FTP download options, you can use an FTP utility program such as WS_FTP (www.ipswitch.com).

Even if you work for a small company, you may be able to post files on your ISP's FTP server in order to make them available to others. Check with your ISP to find out whether you can do it and, if so, what the procedures are.

FTP transfers are more prone to user confusion problems than are e-mail files, especially if the recipient hasn't used FTP before. For example, it's common for the person posting the files to forget to tell the recipient the logon name and password, or for the recipient not to have an FTP program — or to not know how to use it. Check with your recipient the first couple of times you use FTP to transfer files to make sure they got the files successfully — and don't be surprised if they ask you to use e-mail or overnight delivery instead.

Bad reception?

Other sections in this chapter focus on sending files to others. What happens when you're on the receiving end? Not everyone will be as conscientious as you are about following the Golden Exchange Rule. You'll receive drawings with missing dependent files and no information or support files for plotting.

When you receive an e-mail message or FTP download containing drawings (zipped, I hope!), copy the file to a new folder on your hard disk or a network disk and unzip the files.

Check at least a few of the drawings in the package to make sure that all the xrefs, fonts, and raster image files were included. You can perform this check by opening each main drawing in that folder. After you open each file, press the F2 key to view the command line window, and look for missing font and xref error messages of the following sort:

```
Substituting [simplex.shx] for [helv.shx].
Resolve Xref "GRID": C:\Here\There\Nowhere\grid.dwg
Can't find C:\Here\There\Nowhere\grid.dwg
```

A Substituting... message indicates AutoCAD couldn't find a font and is substituting a different font for it. A Can't find... message indicates that AutoCAD couldn't locate an xref. Any missing raster files appear as rectangular boxes with the names of the image files inside the rectangles. Alternatively, you can open the Xref Manager or Image Manager dialog box, which reveals any missing xref or raster image files. (See Chapter 13 for details.)

Write down each missing file and then tell the sender to get on the ball and send you the missing pieces. While you're at it, tell that person to buy this book and read this chapter!

Press the F2 key after opening *any* drawing that you didn't create so that you know right away if any fonts and xrefs are missing.

If you receive drawings with custom TrueType font files (files whose extensions are TTF), you must install those files before Windows and AutoCAD will recognize them. Choose Start➪Settings➪Control Panel. (In Windows XP, choose Start➪Control Panel and then click the Switch to Classic View link in order to see the Fonts applet.) Double-click the Fonts icon to open the Fonts window, and then choose File➪Install New Font.

Help from the Reference Manager

In Chapter 13, I warn you about the complications of xref paths and the potential perils of AutoCAD not being able to locate xrefs if you move project folders around or transfer drawings to or from someone else. A similar danger exists for raster image files (Chapter 13) and font files (Chapter 9). The ETRANSMIT command, described earlier in this chapter, does a good job of gathering together dependent xrefs, raster files, and font files, but it can't gather what AutoCAD can't locate.

AutoCAD's Reference Manager utility is a real lifesaver if you find yourself suffering from xref, raster image, or font path perils — whether they occur in your own company or when sending files to or receiving them from others.

Reference Manager is a separate utility program, not a command inside AutoCAD. Follow these steps to launch the utility:

1. **Choose Start⇨Programs⇨Autodesk⇨AutoCAD 2005⇨Reference Manager.**

   The Reference Manager program opens, as shown in Figure 16-3.

2. **Choose the Add Drawings button to add one or more DWG files to the drawings pane on the left.**

3. **Click the Export Report button to create a text report listing all the dependent files and their paths, or click the Edit Selected Paths button to modify paths.**

   Click the Help button in Reference Manager to find out more about the utility's capabilities.

Figure 16-3:
The Reference Manager.

Type	Status	File Name	Reference Name	Saved Path	Found Path	Host Drawing
A Font	✔ Resolved	txt	STANDARD		c:\program files\autoc...	H:\Drawings\SA-3.5\S-101.dwg
A Font	✔ Resolved	ARIBLK.TTF	Fancy		C:\WINDOWS\fonts	H:\Drawings\SA-3.5\S-101.dwg
A Font	✔ Resolved	txt	STANDARD		c:\program files\autoc...	H:\Drawings\SA-3.5\S-102.dwg
A Font	✔ Resolved	romans.shx	S-TEXT		c:\program files\autoc...	H:\Drawings\SA-3.5\S-102.dwg
A Font	✔ Resolved	txt	STANDARD		c:\program files\autoc...	H:\Drawings\SA-3.5\S-103.dwg
A Font	✔ Resolved	romans.shx	S-TEXT		c:\program files\autoc...	H:\Drawings\SA-3.5\S-103.dwg
A Font	✔ Resolved	txt	STANDARD		c:\program files\autoc...	H:\Drawings\SA-3.5\S-104.dwg
A Font	✔ Resolved	ARIBLK.TTF	Fancy		C:\WINDOWS\fonts	H:\Drawings\SA-3.5\S-104.dwg
Image	✔ Resolved	Foundation-repair.jpg	Foundation-repair		h:\drawings\sa-3.5	H:\Drawings\SA-3.5\S-101.dwg
Image	✔ Resolved	Iris.tif	Iris		h:\drawings\sa-3.5	H:\Drawings\SA-3.5\S-101.dwg
Image	✔ Resolved	Foundation-repair.jpg	Foundation-repair		h:\drawings\sa-3.5	H:\Drawings\SA-3.5\S-104.dwg
Image	✔ Resolved	Iris.tif	Iris		h:\drawings\sa-3.5	H:\Drawings\SA-3.5\S-104.dwg
Xref Attachment	! Not Found	DT-03.dwg	DT-03	H:\Projects...		H:\Drawings\SA-3.5\S-101.dwg
Xref Attachment	! Not Found	S-Detail-03.dwg	S-Detail-03			H:\Drawings\SA-3.5\S-104.dwg

Drawings added: 4 - Drawings broken: 2   References: 14 - Selected: 0

If you always keep parent and child DWG files in the same folder — the simplest approach to dealing with xref paths — then you probably won't need to use the Reference Manager.

Drawing Web Format — Not Just for the Web

In a previous section of this chapter, I explain how you can exchange drawings via e-mail and FTP. That's all the Internet connectivity that many AutoCAD users need, but if you're curious about connecting drawings to the Web or sharing drawings with people who don't have AutoCAD, this section is for you.

The AutoCAD Web features are built on two pieces of technology:

- ✔ A special lightweight drawing format called DWF that Autodesk originally developed especially for putting drawings on the Web.
- ✔ A free program from Autodesk called Autodesk Express Viewer that enables anyone to view and print DWF files without having AutoCAD.

All about DWF

The AutoCAD DWG format works well for storing drawing information on local and network disks, but the high precision and large number of object properties that AutoCAD uses make for comparatively large files.

To overcome this size problem and encourage people to publish drawings on the Web, Autodesk developed an alternative lightweight vector format for representing AutoCAD drawings: DWF (Design Web Format). A DWF file is a more compact representation of a DWG file. DWF uses less space — and less transfer time over the Web and e-mail — because it's less precise and doesn't have all the information that's in the DWG file.

DWF hasn't exactly taken the Web by storm; Autodesk has gradually recast it as a format for electronic plotting, or *ePlotting*, including for sharing drawings with people who don't have AutoCAD. In other words, Autodesk is pushing DWF as a CAD analogue to Adobe's PDF (Portable Document Format). Thus you can create DWF files from your drawings and send the DWFs to people who don't have AutoCAD. Your recipients can view and plot the DWF files after they download the free Autodesk Express Viewer program, which is available on Autodesk's Web site, www.autodesk.com.

ePlot, not replot

A DWF file captures a single, plotted view of your drawing, so, unlike a DWG file, it can provide a relatively unambiguous snapshot of what you want to see on paper. With a DWG file, on the other hand, you have to provide lots of information to other people — drawing view, scale, plot style settings, and so on — in order for them to get the same plotting results that you did.

Potential ePlotting scenarios include:

✔ Architects and other consultants on a building project periodically upload DWF files to the project Web site. Architects and engineers with some minimal CAD knowledge can review the drawings on-screen and create their own hard-copy plots, if necessary. Principals and clients who don't want anything to do with CAD, or even with computers, can have their secretaries or other employees create hard-copy plots for them to examine.

✔ When Internet-savvy people need hard-copy prints of your drawings, you e-mail a zipped file containing DWF files, along with the URL for Autodesk Express Viewer and simple instructions for creating plots from the DWF files. (Be ready to walk them through the process by phone the first time or two to reduce anxiety on everyone's part.)

✔ A CAD plotting service bureau encourages its customers to send DWF files instead of DWG files for plotting. The DWF files are much smaller and require less intervention on the part of the service bureau's employees.

The ePlot concept debuted in AutoCAD 2000 and hasn't yet caught on in a big way. Autodesk hopes to establish ePlot and the DWF format as a standard for CAD documents similar to what Adobe's PDF has become for word processing documents. It remains to be seen whether ePlotting will become a popular way to generate hard-copy output. In particular, many people outside of CAD-using companies don't have access to large-format plotters. They're limited to 8½-x-11-inch — or, at best, 11-x-17-inch — reduced-size check plots. Consequently, many people won't be able to plot your DWF files to scale, and may not even be able to plot them large enough to read everything.

Don't be afraid to try ePlotting with colleagues inside or outside your company, but don't become too dependent on it until you see whether the rest of the CAD world shares your enthusiasm. Otherwise, you risk becoming the only one who's willing to use your DWF files for plotting — in which case the next version of the feature will be called mePlot.

AutoCAD 2005 uses version 6 of the DWF format, which Autodesk introduced with AutoCAD 2004. (The DWF format changes at least as often as the DWG format, as Autodesk adds new features to AutoCAD and new Design Web Format capabilities.) The most important new feature in DWF 6 is multiple sheets in a single DWF file, as shown in Figure 16-4. It's like stapling together a set of drawings, except that you never have to worry about your stapler being empty.

Making DWFs with ePlot

As I describe in the previous section, AutoCAD treats DWF files like electronic plots, or ePlots. You create a DWF file from the current drawing just as if you were plotting it to a piece of paper, as I describe in Chapter 12. The only difference is that, in the Plot dialog box's Printer/Plotter area, you choose the plotter configuration named DWF6 ePlot.pc3, as shown in Figure 16-5. When you do so, AutoCAD automatically turns on the Plot To File setting. Then when you click OK to generate the ePlot, AutoCAD displays a file dialog box in which you specify a filename and location for the DWF file that gets created. The location can be a folder on a hard disk or a Web server.

Figure 16-4: One DWF file can include multiple sheets.

Figure 16-5:
"Look ma, no paper!" Plotting to a DWF file.

Pay particular attention to the Scale setting on the Plot Settings tab. If you're creating a DWF simply for viewing in a browser, you can plot Scaled To Fit. If you want to enable others to ePlot your DWF file to scale, as described earlier in this chapter, you need to choose the desired plot scale factor. Chapter 12 describes how to choose an appropriate plot scale factor.

Making DWFs (or Plots) with PUBLISH

The ePlot method of creating DWF files described in the previous section works fine for single drawings. But if you want to create DWF files for a lot of drawings or plot a bunch of drawings the good ol' fashioned way (on paper, that is), you can use the Publish dialog box, shown in Figure 16-6, to speed the process.

Figure 16-6:
Hot off the presses: AutoCAD Publish dialog box.

Although the Publish dialog box is wired to support DWF as well as regular (paper) plotting, for now, more people are likely to use it for paper plotting. (An alternative use is creating plot files to send to a plotting service bureau.) But if you do decide to go into large-scale DWF publishing, including multisheet DWF files, use the Publish Drawing Sheets dialog box, as in the following steps.

1. **Choose File⇨Publish.**

   The Publish dialog box appears (refer to Figure 16-6). The dialog box lists all tabs (Model and paper space layouts) of the current drawing for plotting. The Publish dialog box refers to each tab as a *sheet.*

2. **Use the buttons below the sheet list to preview any sheet, add sheets from other drawings, remove sheets from the to-be-plotted list, or rearrange the plotting order.**

   With the additional buttons, you can save and recall lists of sheets. See Step 4 for more information.

3. **After you specify the sheets that you want to plot, specify whether you want to plot them to an actual plotter or plot (PLT) file or to a DWF file.**

   You can select a specific plotter configuration for each sheet by choosing a Page Setup in the sheet list. See Chapter 12 for more information about page setups.

4. **Click the Publish Options button to display a dialog box containing additional settings.**

   Most of these options are of concern only if you're creating DWF files. The one exception is Default Output Directory, which also applies to creating plot (PLT) files.

5. **Click the Save Sheet List button to save the current drawings and settings list, if you anticipate having to publish the same group of drawings again.**

6. **Click the Publish button to start the process.**

AutoCAD 2005's new sheet sets feature (described in Chapter 14) includes a direct link to multisheet publishing. In the Sheet Set Manager palette, right-click the sheet set name and choose Publish. The submenu includes choices for publishing directly to a plotter or DWF file and for opening the Publish dialog box preloaded with all the sheet sets.

Don't confuse the PUBLISH command (File⇨Publish) with the PUBLISHTOWEB command (File⇨Publish to Web). The PUBLISH command creates sets of DWF files, plot files, or actual plots. The PUBLISHTOWEB Wizard creates a Web page containing images of your drawings. The results of this Wizard won't put any

Web designers or programmers out of work, but you can use it to create primitive Web page paste-ups of your drawings. See "PUBLISHTOWEB command" in the AutoCAD online help system if you'd like to give it a whirl.

Hand-y objects

No Web file format would be complete without hyperlinks, and DWF has those, too. You can attach a hyperlink to any drawing object in AutoCAD, not just to a text string. As you pass the cursor over an object with a hyperlink, the cursor changes from the ordinary pointer to a globe and two links of a chain (as in "World Wide Web" and "link," not "world-wide chain gang"). Right-click the object and select the Hyperlink option from the menu, which opens your browser and navigates to the URL that's attached to the object. If you create a DWF file that includes objects with hyperlinks, Autodesk Express Viewer embeds the links in the DWF file so that you can Ctrl+click to navigate to them.

Hyperlinks on objects are a clever trick, but they're of limited practical value in most DWG and DWF files:

 ✔ The drawing images are so small that it's difficult to distinguish the hyperlink on one object from the hyperlink on another object.

 ✔ Most people aren't used to associating hyperlinks with individual lines and other objects. The interface is likely to leave them perplexed.

If you'd like to experiment with hyperlinks in objects, look up "HYPERLINK command, about" in the online help system.

Autodesk Express Viewer

After you create DWF files, whether with ePlot or PUBLISH, you or the recipient of your DWF files can use Autodesk Express Viewer to view and print them. Autodesk Express Viewer, shown in Figure 16-4 earlier in this chapter, is a free viewer from Autodesk. You can download the current version from Autodesk's Web page, www.autodesk.com (click on Product and Solutions and then Autodesk Express Viewer).

When you install AutoCAD 2005, the setup program by default installs Autodesk Express Viewer as well. Choose Start➪Programs➪Autodesk➪Autodesk Express Viewer, or simply double-click on a DWF file in Windows Explorer, to launch it.

The Drawing Protection Racket

Whether you're sending DWG or DWF files, you may be concerned about their misuse (that is, by the wrong people or for the wrong purposes), abuse (for example, modification without your consent), or reuse (on other projects or by other people without due compensation to you).

The previous version, AutoCAD 2004, added two new features for securing your drawings when you send them to others:

> ✔ **Password protection** enables you to lock a DWG or DWF file so that only those who type the password that you've specified can open, insert, or xref it.
>
> Add password protection to drawings only when you really need it:
>
> • If you forget the password, then *you* no longer will be able to open the drawing. Neither AutoCAD nor Autodesk has any magical way to extract the password or unlock the drawing.
>
> • After you password protect a drawing, others can't insert the drawing as a block or attach it as an xref.

> If you're using a password, you probably should do it on a *copy* of the drawing that you send, and keep an *unprotected* version for yourself.
>
> ✔ **Digital signature** is a high-tech way to add an electronic marker to a DWG file that verifies that someone approved the drawing. AutoCAD's digital signature feature relies on fairly new technology by Microsoft. You must first get an account with a digital certificate provider, who serves to authenticate you and your computer. Of course, for this feature to be useful, you need to send drawings to someone who wants to receive digitally authenticated drawings from you (or vice versa) and who has the technological savvy to deal with digital certificates. For more information, see "digital signatures, learning more about" in the AutoCAD online help system.

To activate either of these options for the current drawing, choose File➪Save As to display the Save Drawing As dialog box, and then choose Tools➪Security Options to display the Security Options dialog box before you save the file. If you want to add a password to the current drawing, just type it in the text field on the password tab of the Security Options dialog box.

After you password protect and save a DWG file, anyone who tries to open, insert, or xref it will see a dialog box similar to the one shown in Figure 16-7.

Password

Enter password to open drawing:

H:\Drawings\Top secret baby.dwg

[▌▌▌▌▌]

[OK] [Cancel]

Figure 16-7:
Password,
please.

To password protect a DWF file, use the PUBLISH command and click the Publish Options button in the Publish dialog box.

Although electronic security features such as the ones described in this section can be useful as part of a strategy to protect your work from misuse, they're not a substitute for communicating clearly, preferably in the form of written contracts, what constitutes appropriate use of drawings that you send to or receive from others. http://markcad.com/autocad/elecdwg exchange.htm outlines the issues and suggests how to play well with your drawing exchange buddies.

Part V
The Part of Tens

The 5th Wave   By Rich Tennant

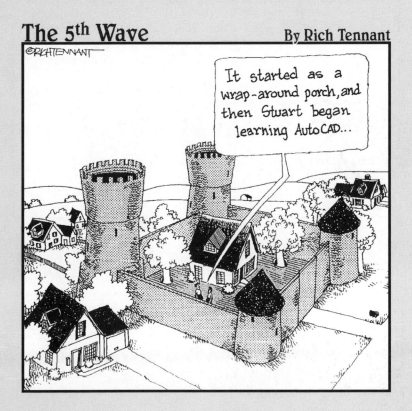

In this part . . .

Tens sounds a lot like *tense,* and tense is how AutoCAD may make you feel sometimes. But never fear — help is on the way! Checklists are always a big help in getting things right and fixing things that are wrong. And a Top Ten list is a good way to quickly spot the best — or the worst — of almost anything, AutoCAD included. This Part of Tens features lists that help you keep your drawings healthy and trade drawings with other people and programs.

Chapter 17

Ten Ways to Do No Harm

• •

*H*ippocrates of Greece is famous for many things, not least of which is the Hippocratic oath sworn by doctors. It begins "First, do no harm." This is not a bad approach to take when editing existing drawings with AutoCAD whether the drawings were created originally by you or by someone else. You can accidentally undo days or weeks of work by yourself and others in minutes. (Of course, you also can *purposefully* undo days or weeks of work by yourself and others in minutes, but I can't give much advice to stop you if you want to do that!)

Follow these guidelines to avoid doing harm to the hard work of others and the productive potential of yourself.

Be Precise

Throughout this book, I remind you that using precision techniques such as snap, object snaps, and typed coordinates is a fundamental part of good CAD practice. Don't try to use AutoCAD like an illustration program, in which you eyeball locations and distances. Use one of the many AutoCAD precision techniques *every* time you specify a point or distance.

Control Properties by Layer

As I describe in Chapter 4, AutoCAD gives you two different ways of controlling object properties such as color, linetype, and lineweight: by layer and by object. Unless you have a *really* good reason to assign properties by object — such as instructions from your company's CAD manager or the client for whom you're creating the drawing — use the by-layer method: Assign colors, linetypes, and lineweights to layers, and let objects inherit their properties from the layer on which they reside. Don't assign explicit color, linetype, or lineweight to objects.

Know Your Drawing Scale Factor

Chapter 3 describes the importance of choosing an appropriate drawing scale factor when you set up a drawing. Knowing the drawing scale factor of any drawing you're working on is equally important whether you set it up or not. You need this number in order to calculate lots of scale-dependent objects, such as text, dimensions, and hatching. Chapter 9 includes tips for figuring out the drawing scale factor of an existing drawing.

Know Your Space

Understand the difference between model space and paper space (described in Chapter 2) and know which space the different parts of the drawing you're looking at on-screen reside in. Above all, make sure that you draw objects in the appropriate space. When you're viewing a paper space layout, keep an eye on the status bar's MODEL/PAPER button so that you know which space the cursor currently is in. (Chapter 3 describes how to keep your model and paper space bearings.) When you plot, ensure that you've selected the right tab — either Model or one of the paper space layout tabs.

If Someone (Sheet) Set It, Don't Forget It

Sheet sets are brand new in AutoCAD 2005, and it remains to be seen how readily AutoCAD-using companies will take to them as a way of organizing drawing sets. If you create new drawings on a project that's organized with sheet sets, use the Sheet Set Manager palette to ensure that your drawing starts out as a full-fledged citizen of the set. If you find yourself working on a drawing that's part of a set, be sure that you understand how the sheet set as a whole is organized and how your drawing fits into it. Be aware that some information, such as title sheet data, sheet list, and pointer blocks, may be generated automatically for the sheet set, and avoid thwarting these automatic annotations by drawing separate text or symbols for the same purpose.

Explode with Care

The eXplode command makes it easy to explode polylines (Chapter 5), dimensions (Chapter 10), hatches (Chapter 11), and block inserts (Chapter 13) into their constituent objects. The only problem is that someone probably grouped those objects together for a reason. So until you understand that reason and know why it no longer applies, leave the dynamite alone.

Don't Cram Your Geometry

It's okay to cram for a geometry test, but don't cram geometry, dimensions, text, or anything (and everything) else into your drawings. A real temptation exists to put a lot of stuff into every square inch of your drawing, using AutoCAD's flexible panning and zooming capabilities to really work over all the available space. If you succumb to this temptation, you'll discover that editing is more difficult and adding more information may be impossible! In addition, the result probably will be harder to read. Instead of cramming stuff onto the sheet, use white (empty) space to surround areas of dense geometry. Put details on separate sheets. Attach a page of notes instead of putting a ton of text onto your drawing. Managing a reasonable number of drawings with less on each one is easier than having two or three densely packed sheets crammed with every bit of geometry and annotation needed for the project.

Freeze Instead of Erase

It's common to start with an existing drawing from another discipline when you want to add, say, an electrical system to a floor plan. But if you remove the landscaping around a building because you don't need it for the wiring, you may cause a great deal of rework when the landscaping information is needed again. And what if the person who did the landscaping work has, in the meantime, decided to leaf? (Sorry . . .) Unless you know that objects are no longer needed, use the AutoCAD Freeze or Off layer setting to make objects on those layers invisible without obliterating them. These settings are in the Layer Properties Manager dialog box, as described in Chapter 4.

Use CAD Standards

Become knowledgeable about CAD standards in your industry and company, and take advantage of any standardized resources and approaches that are available to you. (See Chapter 15 for suggestions.) By following standards consistently, you can apply your creativity, expertise, and energy to the interesting parts of the job at hand, not to arguing about which hatching patterns to use. And if you find that things are a mess in your company because no one else pays much attention to industry standards, well, knowing those standards makes you very employable as well.

Save and Back Up Drawings Regularly

As with all computer documents that you work on, get in the habit of saving your current AutoCAD drawing regularly. I recommend every 10 minutes or so. Each time you save, AutoCAD writes the current state of the drawing to the *drawingname*.DWG file, after renaming the previously saved version *drawingname*.BAK. Thus, you can always recover the next-to-last saved version of your drawing by renaming *drawingname*.BAK to *somethingelse*.DWG and opening it in AutoCAD.

AutoCAD also includes an automatic drawing save feature. It's useful as a secondary backup save, but you shouldn't rely on it exclusively. AutoCAD creates automatic save files with inscrutable names like `Drawing1_1_1_1478.SV$` and puts them in the folder specified by the Automatic Save File Location setting on the File tab of the Options dialog box. Save your drawing and save yourself the pain of lost work and the hassle of trying to locate the right automatic save file. If you find yourself in the unfortunate position of needing an automatic save file, move the SV$ files file from the automatic save folder to another folder. Rename the files from SV$ to DWG, open them in AutoCAD, and look for the one that corresponds to the drawing you're trying to recover. Note that AutoCAD deletes the SV$ file after you close the drawing, so it's usually useful only after a software or computer crash.

Backing up your data is prudent advice for any important work that you do on a computer, but it's doubly prudent for CAD drawings. A set of CAD drawings is a lot harder and more time consuming to re-create than most other computer documents. Unless you're willing to lose more than a day's worth of work, develop a plan of daily backups onto tape, CD-RW (CD ReWritable) discs, or another high-capacity medium.

Don't be lulled into complacency by the increasing reliability of hard disks. Although hard disk failure is increasingly rare, it still happens, and if it happens to you *sans backup,* you'll quickly understand the full force of the phrase "catastrophic failure." Also, backups aren't just protection against disk failure. Most of the time, backups help you recover from "pilot error" — accidentally erasing a file, messing up a drawing with ill-advised editing, and so on. Even if you're conscientious and never make mistakes, there's a good chance that someone else in your office who has access to your DWG files hasn't quite achieved your exalted level of perfection. Protect your work and minimize recriminations with regular backups.

Chapter 18

Ten Ways to Swap Drawing Data with Other People and Programs

. . . .

*A*t various times, you probably need to transfer information from one kind of document to another. You even may have taken the CAD plunge because you want to import AutoCAD drawing data into your word processing or other documents. If so, this chapter is for you. It covers exchanging AutoCAD drawing data with other programs — what works, what doesn't, and how to do it. I also tell you when to give up and reach for the scissors and glue.

This chapter frequently mentions vector and raster graphics file formats:

- ✔ A vector format stores graphics as collections of geometrical objects (such as lines, polygons, and text). Vector graphics are good for high geometrical precision and for stretching or squeezing images to different sizes. These two characteristics make vector formats good for CAD.

- ✔ A raster format stores graphics as a series of dots, or *pixels*. Raster graphics are good for depicting photographic detail and lots of colors.

Exchanging AutoCAD drawing data with other programs sometimes works great the first time you try it. Sometimes, you have to try a bunch of techniques or exchange formats to get all the data to transfer in an acceptable way. Occasionally, no practical exchange method exists for preserving formatting or other properties that are important to you. Where your exchange efforts fall in this spectrum depends on the kind of drawings you make, the other programs you work with, and the output devices or formats that you use. I provide recommendations in this chapter, but be prepared to experiment.

Table 18-1 lists exchange formats between common programs and AutoCAD.

Table 18-1	Swapping Between AutoCAD and Other Programs
Swap	**Recommended Formats**
AutoCAD to AutoCAD LT	DWG
AutoCAD 2004 to AutoCAD R14	R12 DXF
AutoCAD to another CAD program	DXF or DWG
AutoCAD to humans who don't have AutoCAD	PDF or DWF
AutoCAD to Word	WMF
Word to AutoCAD	RTF or TXT
AutoCAD to paint program	BMP
Paint program to AutoCAD	BMP or other raster format (use the AutoCAD IMAGE command)
AutoCAD to draw program	WMF
Draw program to AutoCAD	WMF
AutoCAD to the Web	DWF
Excel to AutoCAD	Windows clipboard, using Paste Special (see Chapter 9)
AutoCAD to Excel	CSV, using AutoCAD TABLEEXPORT command (see Chapter 9)

The remainder of this chapter gives you specific procedures for making most of the exchanges recommended in this table, as well as others.

DWG

DWG, AutoCAD's native file format, is the best format for exchanging drawings with other AutoCAD or LT users. Use the SAVE and SAVEAS commands to create DWG files and the OPEN command to open them.

AutoCAD LT can't *create* every kind of object that AutoCAD can — raster attachments and most 3D objects, for example — but it can successfully *read* and *save* DWG files that contain these objects.

Round-trip DWG fare

The most demanding — and elusive — kind of data exchange is called *round-trip transfer*. *Round-trip* means that you create and save a file in one program, edit and save it in another program, and then edit and save it in the first program again. A perfect round trip is one in which all the data survives and the users of both programs can happily edit whatever they want to. Unfortunately, the perfect round trip, like the perfect visit to your cousins, rarely happens.

In CAD, round-trip transfer becomes an issue when two people want to work on the same drawings with different CAD programs. AutoCAD and AutoCAD LT have excellent round-trip compatibility, as Chapter 1 explains. Expect a bumpier road if you're exchanging drawings with users of other CAD programs. Perform some test transfers before you assume that your drawings can get from here to there and back again unscathed.

AutoCAD 2005 can't save to the AutoCAD Release 14 DWG format. Apparently, the Autodesk bigwigs figure that the best way to persuade R14 users to upgrade is to make their lives as inconvenient and isolated as possible! If you need to send AutoCAD 2005 drawings to AutoCAD R14 users, save them in R12 DXF format instead of a DWG format. (See the "DXF" section for instructions.)

Autodesk does not document the native AutoCAD DWG file format, and recommends that all file exchanges between AutoCAD and other CAD programs take place via DXF files (see the next section). But several companies have reverse-engineered the DWG format, and it's now common for other CAD programs to read and sometimes write DWG files directly, with greater or lesser accuracy. Because the DWG format is complicated, isn't documented, and gets changed every couple of years, no one ever figures it out perfectly. Thus, exchanging DWG files with non-Autodesk programs always involves some compatibility risks.

When you send DWG files to other people — whether they use AutoCAD or a different CAD program — you need to make sure that their software can read the DWG file version that you're sending. See Chapter 1 for information about AutoCAD DWG file versions.

When you send DWG files to other people, remember to use the ETRANSMIT command to ensure that you send all the dependent files (fonts, xrefs, and raster images). See Chapter 16 for details.

DXF

DXF (Drawing eXchange Format) is the Autodesk-approved format for exchanging between different CAD programs. (Some other vector graphics applications, such as drawing and illustration programs, read and write DXF files, too.) DXF is a documented version of the DWG format. Because DXF more-or-less exactly mimics the DWG file's contents, it's (usually) a faithful representation of AutoCAD drawings.

How well DXF works for exchanging data depends largely on the other program that you're exchanging with. Some CAD and vector graphics programs do a good job of reading and writing DXF files, while others don't. In practice, geometry usually comes through well, but properties, formatting, and other nongeometrical information can be tricky. Test before you commit to a large-scale exchange, and always check the results.

To create DXF files, use the SAVEAS command (File⇨Save As) and choose one of the three DXF versions in the Files of Type drop-down list. To open a DXF file, do the same with the OPEN command (File⇨Open).

DWF

As Chapter 16 describes, DWF is Autodesk's special "lightweight" drawing format for posting drawings on the Web or sharing them with people who don't have AutoCAD. Those people can use Autodesk's free Express Viewer program to view and print DWF files (as well as DWG files). Chapter 16 describes how to create and use DWF files.

PDF

Adobe's PDF (Portable Document Format) is the most popular format for exchanging formatted text documents among users of different computers and operating systems. PDF also does graphics, as you probably know from having viewed PDF brochures on Web sites.

Autodesk has worked hard to make DWF the PDF for CAD drawing exchange, but DWF hasn't yet caught on in a big way. When AutoCAD users need to send drawings to people who don't have AutoCAD, many prefer to convert the drawings to PDF files. Most potential recipients are familiar with PDF and already have the free Adobe Reader installed on their computers, neither of which can be said of DWF.

The free Adobe Reader views and prints PDF files, but won't create them. In order to convert an AutoCAD drawing (or any other Windows document) into a PDF file, you'll need additional software. Adobe sells Acrobat Standard and Professional for this purpose — see www.adobe.com/acrobat/ for details and a trial version. Many other companies offer commercial and shareware PDF-creation programs. One such utility is Pdf995 (www.pdf995.com), which, despite its under-$10 price, does a good job of creating PDF files from AutoCAD drawings.

WMF

There are lots of different vector and raster graphics file formats, but Microsoft has been pretty successful at making its WMF and BMP formats the *lingua franca* — or should that be *lingua bill-a*? — for exchanging graphical information in Windows.

WMF (Windows MetaFile) is a vector format, so it does a decent job of representing AutoCAD objects such as lines, arcs, and text.

To create a WMF file showing some or all the objects in a drawing, use the EXPORT command (File⇨Export) and choose Metafile (*.wmf) in the Files of Type drop-down list. After you create a WMF file in AutoCAD, use the other program's file insertion command to place the image in a document.

AutoCAD puts objects in the WMF file with the colors and display lineweights that you see on the AutoCAD screen. To create a WMF file that looks like a *monochrome plot* — that is, with varying lineweights and all objects black — you need to set layer and object properties in AutoCAD so the objects look that way on-screen before you create the WMF file.

You can go the other direction, from a WMF file into AutoCAD, by using the WMFIN command (Insert⇨Windows Metafile).

BMP, JPEG, TIFF, and Other Raster Formats

BMP (BitMaP) is the standard Windows raster format. AutoCAD can create BMP files from drawing objects (via the EXPORT command) and place BMP files in drawings (via the IMage command). When you export AutoCAD drawing objects to a BMP file, all the objects get converted to dots. Turning a line into a bunch of dots isn't a swell idea if you want to change the line again. But it is useful if you need to copy a drawing into a company brochure.

One problem with BMP files is their big file size. Unlike some other raster formats, BMP doesn't offer compression. Because CAD drawings usually are fairly large in area, they can turn into monstrously large BMP files.

Creating a BMP file showing some or all the objects in a drawing is just like creating a WMF file: Use the EXPORT command (File⇨Export) but choose Bitmap (*.bmp) in the Files of Type drop-down list. After you create a BMP file in AutoCAD, you use the other program's File⇨Open to open it or the graphics file insertion command to place it in an existing document.

If you want to go the other direction, a BMP file into an AutoCAD drawing, use the IMage command, as described in Chapter 13.

Although BMP is a standard Windows format for exchanging raster data, it's certainly not the preferred format of many programs. Other common raster formats include PCX, JPEG, and TIFF (the latter two appears as JPG and TIF in Windows). Among their other advantages, these formats offer image compression, which can reduce the size of raster files dramatically.

If the program that you're trying to work with works best with other formats, or you want to avoid huge BMP files, you have a couple of options:

✔ Create an AutoCAD-friendly format (such as WMF or BMP) and translate it to another graphics format with a translation program such as HiJaak (www.imsisoft.com) or VuePrint (www.hamrick.com).

AutoCAD includes new JPGOUT, PNGOUT, and TIFOUT commands for creating JPG, PNG, and TIF files in the same way that you export WMF and BMP files. Type the command name, press Enter, specify a raster file name, and select the objects to be included in the image file. These commands use the current drawing area background color as the background color for the image. If you want your image background to be white, make sure that the AutoCAD drawing area color is white when you run the command. (Choose Tools⇨Options⇨Display⇨Colors to change display colors.)

✔ If you need to convert drawings to a raster format other than BMP or TIF, the second option is to use the AutoCAD Raster File Format driver. This driver enables you to "plot" to a file with one of nine raster formats, including PCX, JPEG, and TIFF. Before you can use the Raster File Format driver, you must create a new plotter configuration: Choose File⇨Plotter Manager and then run the Add-A-Plotter wizard. After you create the Raster File Format driver configuration, you use the Plot dialog box as described in Chapter 12 to generate "plots" to raster files.

To go the other direction, raster image file into an AutoCAD drawing, use the IMage command, as described in Chapter 13.

Windows Clipboard

If you need to transfer lots of WMF or BMP figures, you can do it a bit more quickly with the Windows Clipboard, which bypasses the creation of WMF and BMP files on disk. Instead, Windows uses your computer's memory to transfer the data. Choose Edit⇨Copy in the program from which you want to copy the data and Edit⇨Paste Special in the program to which you want to copy it. In the Paste Special dialog box, choose Picture to paste the image in WMF format or Bitmap to paste it in BMP format.

OLE

Microsoft Windows includes a data transfer feature, Object Linking and Embedding, or OLE. (In case you're wondering, that's "OLE" pronounced like the Spanish cheer, not like the Cockney way of saying *hole.*) Microsoft touts OLE as an all-purpose solution to the challenge of exchanging formatted data between any two Windows programs.

If you want to share data between two OLE-aware programs (and most Windows applications are OLE-aware), creating an embedded or linked document shouldn't be much more complicated than cut and paste. That's the theory.

Here's how it works. In OLE lingo, the program that you're taking the data from is the *source*. The program that receives the data is called the *container*. For example, if you want to place some word processing text from Microsoft Word into an AutoCAD drawing, Word is the source, and AutoCAD is the container.

In Word, you select the text that you want to put in the AutoCAD drawing and choose Edit⇨Copy to copy them to the Windows Clipboard. Then, you switch to AutoCAD and choose Edit⇨Paste Special. The Paste Special choice displays a dialog box containing the choices Paste and Paste Link. The Paste option creates a copy of the object from the source document and *embeds* the copied object into the container document. The Paste Link option *links* the new object in the container document to its source document so any changes to the source document are automatically reflected in the container document. In other words, if you link word processing text to an AutoCAD drawing, changes that you make later in the Word document get propagated to the AutoCAD drawing automatically. If you embed the same spreadsheet object in an AutoCAD drawing, changes that you later make to the text in Word aren't reflected in the AutoCAD drawing.

Should you shout, "OLE!"?

Unfortunately, OLE is afflicted with several practical problems.

✔ Compound OLE documents can slow performance — a lot. If you plan to use OLE, you should have a fast computer with lots of memory — or lots of time on your hands.

✔ Supporting OLE well is a difficult programming job, and many applications, including AutoCAD, suffer from OLE design limitations and bugs. (For example, when you link or embed a word processing document, only the first page appears in AutoCAD.)

✔ Previous versions of AutoCAD exhibited more OLE problems than AutoCAD 2005. In particular, plotted OLE output often underwent creative but undesirable transformations. If you exchange drawings with users of earlier versions, what they see on the screen and plot may not match what you created.

AutoCAD 2005 includes a bevy of OLE improvements, which address some of the limitations:

✔ You can control text size more easily, via the MOLESCALE system variable and OLESCALE command.

✔ Editing of OLE objects with commands such as Move and CoPy is more consistent with editing of native AutoCAD objects.

✔ You can control the quality of plotted OLE objects with a setting on the Plot and Publish tab of the Options dialog box.

Even with the OLE improvements in AutoCAD 2005, you should consider carefully and test extensively before embedding or linking documents into drawings. If you want to play it safe, use the alternative methods described in this chapter, and save OLÉ for your next trip to Spain.

That's how it's *supposed* to work. In practice, the container application sometimes doesn't display or print all the linked or embedded data correctly. See the "Should you shout, 'OLE!'?" sidebar for details.

Screen Capture

If your goal is to show the entire AutoCAD program window, not just the drawing contained in it, create a *screen capture*. Most of the figures in this book are screen captures. You might use similar figures to put together a training manual or to show your mom all the cool software you use.

Windows includes a no-frills screen capture capability that is okay for an occasional screen capture. It works like this:

1. **Capture the whole screen or active window with one of these steps:**

    • Press the Print Screen key to capture the entire Windows screen, including the desktop and taskbar.

    • Hold down the Alt key and press the Print Screen key to capture just the active program window (for example, AutoCAD).

    Windows copies a bitmap image to the Windows Clipboard.

2. **Paste the bitmap image into another program. You have two options:**

    • Paste into a paint program (such as the Paint program in Windows). Use that program to save a raster image as a BMP file format.

    • Paste the bitmap image directly into a document (such as a Word document or an AutoCAD drawing) without creating another file.

If you do lots of captures, a screen capture utility program makes the job faster and gives you more options. You can control the area of the screen that gets captured, save to different raster file formats with different monochrome, grayscale, and color options, and print screen captures. One good screen capture utility program is FullShot by Inbit, Inc. (www.inbit.com).

When you create screen captures, pay attention to resolution and colors:

✔ High screen resolutions (for example, above 1280 x 1024) can make your captures unreadable when they get compressed onto an 8½-x-11-inch sheet of paper and printed on a low-resolution printer.

✔ Some colors don't print in monochrome, and a black AutoCAD drawing area is overwhelmingly dark. For most of the screen captures in this book I used 1024 x 768 resolution, a white AutoCAD drawing area, and dark colors — mostly black — for all the objects in the drawing.

TXT and RTF

TXT (Text, also called ASCII for American Standard Code for Information Interchange) is the simplest format for storing letters and numbers. TXT files store only basic text, without such formatting as boldface or special paragraph characteristics. RTF (Rich Text Format) is a format developed by Microsoft for exchanging word processing documents (text plus formatting).

Select Import Text from the Multiline Text Editor window's right-click menu to import an TXT or RTF file. AutoCAD imports plain text from TXT and RTF files. When you import an RTF file, AutoCAD even brings along most of the text formatting and alignment. Chapter 9 covers the Multiline Text Editor window.

Because no sane person would use AutoCAD as a word processor, AutoCAD doesn't provide any special tools for exporting text. You can select AutoCAD text, copy it to the Windows Clipboard, then paste it into another program.

Index

Notes

Notes

Notes

FOR DUMMIES®

The easy way to get more done and have more fun

FOR DUMMIES®

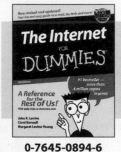

FOR DUMMIES®

Helping you expand your horizons and realize your potential

INTERNET

0-7645-0894-6

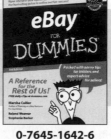

0-7645-1659-0

0-7645-1642-6

DIGITAL MEDIA

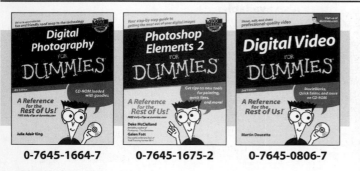

0-7645-1664-7   **0-7645-1675-2**   **0-7645-0806-7**

GRAPHICS

0-7645-0817-2

0-7645-1651-5

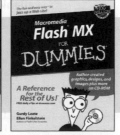

0-7645-0895-4

FOR DUMMIES®

The advice and explanations you need to succeed

SELF-HELP, SPIRITUALITY & RELIGION

Sex FOR DUMMIES
0-7645-5302-X

Parenting FOR DUMMIES
0-7645-5418-2

Religion FOR DUMMIES
0-7645-5264-3

Also available:

The Bible For Dummies
(0-7645-5296-1)

Buddhism For Dummies
(0-7645-5359-3)

Christian Prayer For Dummies
(0-7645-5500-6)

Dating For Dummies
(0-7645-5072-1)

Judaism For Dummies
(0-7645-5299-6)

Potty Training For Dummies
(0-7645-5417-4)

Pregnancy For Dummies
(0-7645-5074-8)

Rekindling Romance For Dummies
(0-7645-5303-8)

Spirituality For Dummies
(0-7645-5298-8)

Weddings For Dummies
(0-7645-5055-1)

PETS

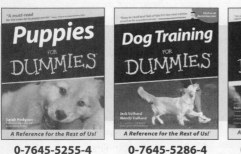

Puppies FOR DUMMIES
0-7645-5255-4

Dog Training FOR DUMMIES
0-7645-5286-4

Cats FOR DUMMIES
0-7645-5275-9

Also available:

Labrador Retrievers For Dummies
(0-7645-5281-3)

Aquariums For Dummies
(0-7645-5156-6)

Birds For Dummies
(0-7645-5139-6)

Dogs For Dummies
(0-7645-5274-0)

Ferrets For Dummies
(0-7645-5259-7)

German Shepherds For Dummies
(0-7645-5280-5)

Golden Retrievers For Dummies
(0-7645-5267-8)

Horses For Dummies
(0-7645-5138-8)

Jack Russell Terriers For Dummies
(0-7645-5268-6)

Puppies Raising & Training Diary For Dummies
(0-7645-0876-8)

EDUCATION & TEST PREPARATION

Spanish FOR DUMMIES
0-7645-5194-9

Algebra FOR DUMMIES
0-7645-5325-9

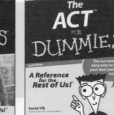

The ACT FOR DUMMIES
0-7645-5210-4

Also available:

Chemistry For Dummies
(0-7645-5430-1)

English Grammar For Dummies
(0-7645-5322-4)

French For Dummies
(0-7645-5193-0)

The GMAT For Dummies
(0-7645-5251-1)

Inglés Para Dummies
(0-7645-5427-1)

Italian For Dummies
(0-7645-5196-5)

Research Papers For Dummies
(0-7645-5426-3)

The SAT I For Dummies
(0-7645-5472-7)

U.S. History For Dummies
(0-7645-5249-X)

World History For Dummies
(0-7645-5242-2)

FOR DUMMIES®

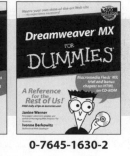

We take the mystery out of complicated subjects